FAILURES

OF

IMAGINATION

FAILURES
OF
IMAGINATION

*The Deadliest Threats to Our Homeland
—and How to Thwart Them*

U.S. CONGRESSMAN MICHAEL McCAUL

Chairman, Homeland Security Committee
U.S. House of Representatives

CROWN FORUM

NEW YORK

Copyright © 2016 by Michael McCaul

All rights reserved.
Published in the United States by Crown Forum, an imprint of the Crown
Publishing Group, a division of Penguin Random House LLC, New York.
www.crownpublishing.com

Crown Forum with colophon is a registered trademark of Penguin Random
House LLC.

Photos on pages 6 and 252 courtesy of the author.

Library of Congress Cataloging-in-Publication Data is available upon request.

ISBN 978-1-101-90541-8
eBook ISBN 978-1-101-90542-5

Printed in the United States of America

Jacket design: M80 Design
Jacket photography: Shutterstock

10 9 8 7 6 5 4 3 2 1

First Edition

To my wife, Linda Mays McCaul, who tracked Soviet submarines
during the Cold War, and ended up tracking me at the Air & Space Museum
in Washington, DC. Every day, I'm glad you did.

And to our children—Caroline, Jewell, and the triplets Lauren,
Michael, and Avery—in the hope that our generation will be
able to leave a safer world for yours.

CONTENTS

7: Final Approach:

Terror in the Skies of Los Angeles on Oscar Night   189

8: North Atlantic Storm:

Russia Launches a New Cold War   215

INTRODUCTION

In the weeks before the Allied landing at Normandy, thousands of young men flew dangerous missions over occupied Europe to prepare the way for the historic American-led invasion. These were desperate hours. The Nazi war machine was on the march, and for the pilots as well as their commanders, victory was uncertain.

The Allies' B-17s—often called "Flying Fortresses"—were remembered by some of those pilots as little more than tin cans with wings. They were vulnerable to attacks from the Luftwaffe in the air and Nazi antiaircraft artillery stationed on the ground. On some of those missions, as many as one out of every three planes was gunned down.

When he first climbed into his B-17, my father was a twenty-year-old bombardier navigator in the Army Air Corps. He flew thirty-five missions over the European theater, many of them harrowing. Thankfully, he was among those blessed to find their way back home to their families after World War II was over.

For many decades before the Second World War, Americans like my dad had lived under the comfortable and false assumption that we were protected from turmoil and terror by the vast oceans along our coastlines. On December 7, 1941, we learned we were wrong. And, unfortunately, not for the last time.

The two deadliest attacks perpetrated against Americans on our own soil—the bombing of Pearl Harbor and the terrorist airliner hijackings of September 11, 2001—came as complete surprises to the intelligence community. They shouldn't have been.

In hindsight, there was nothing improbable in 1941 about Japanese fighter-bombers descending from the skies over the most vulnerable American port in the Pacific. Similarly, there was nothing improbable in 2001 about civilian airliners being turned into cruise missiles targeting America's symbols of financial, military, and political power. Indeed, less than a decade earlier, terrorists had bombed the very same World Trade Center with the intention of toppling both towers.

As the 9/11 Commission put it in their oft-referenced report on the attacks: "The most important failure was one of imagination." Admiral Bobby Inman, a veteran of the intelligence community who served in senior positions at the CIA, DIA, and NSA, said that 9/11 was "grounded in a failure of the imagination," the kind in which "you don't know what you are looking for; you don't know where to look."[1] We didn't see the enemy coming. Because we didn't want to.

Expanding the limits of our imagination is the purpose of this book. The goal is not to frighten people and certainly not to entertain. Instead, it is to envision possible scenarios through which terrorists, foreign nations, and their allies could inflict great damage on our homeland. In other words, we can't afford to live under comfortable and false assumptions any longer. We need to imagine the worst in order to prevent it.

Today, the free world faces numerous dangers, many of them brought to us by the same sort of radical Islamists who once allied themselves with Hitler. These enemies of civilization seek the death and destruction of the American way of life, and they view no citizen of our nation as an innocent bystander. They seek the world's most lethal weapons and will gladly kill any man, woman, or child in their line of sight.

There are other dangers that await us in this new century, too, from lone-wolf terrorists seeking to sow chaos to amoral cyber-mercenaries to nations seeking to undermine America's global leadership and maybe even the very foundations of our democracy itself.

Make no mistake about it: the United States of America is still very much a target. Operations against us, using diverse methods, are discussed around the world—and here at home—every single day. Our vulnerabilities are being probed, our fortitude tested. Foreign citizens, even our fellow Americans, are being recruited to wage acts of horror and violence on our homeland. Some of these attacks have been thwarted in their planning stages; others were stopped when they were far closer to being carried out. Other plots are forming even now, waiting for just the right moment. And we are not ready for them.

Fourteen years since the September 11 attacks, the United States is not any safer. In fact, we are less safe, even as the threats against our people multiply. That is why this book is needed so urgently.

Before my election to Congress, I was a federal prosecutor. I served as the chief of counterterrorism and national security in the U.S. Attorney's Office for the Western District of Texas, where I led the Joint Terrorism Task Force (JTTF) and got a firsthand look at the threats against our citizens. Now, as chairman of the U.S. House of Representatives' Committee on Homeland Security, I see every day the interconnected threats that span the world and link together America's web of enemies.

I've also met the dedicated men and women working around the country and around the world to stave off these threats. One exercise in which the intelligence community frequently engages is setting up so-called Red Teams, informal groups of people tasked with the job of thinking like our enemies, probing our own weaknesses, and gaming out future scenarios in which American security might be put at risk.

This book is a series of Red Team exercises in which ordinary Americans can be observers. They have been developed in consultation with experts in a number of fields and reflect the latest unclassified intelligence assessments. There are, of course, any number of different potential terror scenarios to choose from, but for the purposes of this book, our list includes:

➤ A "decapitation strike" on America's political leadership at the U.S. Capitol

- ➤ Detonation of a "dirty bomb" smuggled into Texas across the Rio Grande

- ➤ A foreign agent connected to China tampering with an American presidential election

- ➤ A shooting rampage at the Mall of America the day after Thanksgiving

- ➤ A devastating and debilitating attack on the East Coast's power grid as part of a wide-ranging cyber strike

- ➤ Radicalized "black widows" releasing a deadly strain of smallpox at Disney World

- ➤ A jetliner explosion over downtown Los Angeles—on Oscar night

- ➤ Russia invading the Baltic states, neutralizing the NATO Alliance, and threatening the American coastline

Each of these scenarios is shown through the eyes of those who would see it play out on the ground. You will see the perspectives of the attackers and their victims. And you will experience, in real time, the launching of a major assault on the United States.

From there, we will move to an analysis that delves deeper into the possible avenues for planning and executing such an attack, including hints from real-world events that should be taken into account and flaws that could be exploited. Finally, we will discuss the future in the form of recommendations and strategies to prevent these kinds of attacks from happening.

When counterterrorism work consumes so much of your life, it's easy to become complacent and assume that others are aware of these issues as well. The truth is, most people aren't—even if they should be. That's why I wrote this book. I have intended it to be accessible to every American: policy makers, intelligence officials, our military servicemen and -women, and to any member of the public who wants to understand the ever-growing—and ever-changing—nature of the dangers to our country.

At the very least, we should expect our own government to be honest with us. Too often the Obama administration has down-played the threats we face as a nation. The president has spread a false narrative based on distorted intelligence for cynical political purposes. The American people deserve to know the truth—and that is what this book is all about.

This material is based on open-source information. Indeed, there is nothing in these pages that terrorists have not already actively considered. The chapters in this book serve as warning signs to policy makers so we can better protect the American people.

I also wrote this book for another, simpler reason. My wife and I have five children. They are growing up in a post-9/11 world, a world whose parameters we, their elders, are still working to define. The world is already a far more complicated place than it was for my generation. Or for my father's. But it is sobering to consider that, despite all of the advances in weaponry and tech-nology, some things remain the same.

My dad's mission—the mission that millions of other young Americans joined after the attack on Pearl Harbor—was to help roll back the threat posed by a radical ideology. To literally save the free world as they knew it from Nazism and fascism. Unfortu-nately, victory against Hitler did not lead to universal peace. What followed in those years was another long struggle against another form of violent extremism—communism—that tested another generation of Americans, many of whom fought and died in places like Korea and Vietnam until the Cold War was won.

Now, in the dawn of a new century, yet another generation has been handed a similarly daunting test. I for one believe that we can rise to the challenge just as Americans did before.

In April 2015, I visited Normandy, the site of unfathomable courage and carnage so many decades ago. Thinking of my dad and the millions of young people like him who, in John F. Kennedy's words, "paid any price" and bore any burden to assure freedom's survival, I placed a wreath at the monument to the Americans who perished for this sacred cause. I still remember the scene of white crosses that dotted the landscape and the somber tune of taps that echoed in our ears.

The end of World War II and the defeat of Hitler's forces marked the eradication of fascism from the face of the earth. This was accomplished because people all over the world recognized the threat, stood up, and fought against it under the leadership of men like Winston Churchill and Franklin D. Roosevelt who understood that appeasement had no place in foreign policy and that strength led to peace. Decades later, President Kennedy and President Reagan stood firm against the next totalitarian foe to threaten the free world: communism. In that struggle, too, the West emerged victorious. Now we face no less of a threat from Islamist extremism and other increasingly dangerous elements around the world.

Those who joined the fight against the Nazis and the communists were often frightened, occasionally uncertain, but always courageous and ever confident in America's ultimate victory. This spirit was what gave the Greatest Generation its name, faced down Soviet missiles in Cuba, and demanded that the wall come down in Berlin. But I've also seen that determination and optimism from those defending our nation today. There's no mistaking that the men and women serving on the front lines have the fortitude and grit to overcome our enemies. But where is our Churchill? Our Kennedy? Our Reagan? Who will step up as the leader of the free world to meet the challenges to our way of life?

As Texas hero Sam Houston told his men before the attack at San Jacinto in 1836: "We view ourselves on the eve of battle." Unlike the soldiers that day, we don't know exactly when the next battle will come or even whom we will be fighting against. But if and when that battle is joined, we cannot be caught unprepared. Consider this book an exercise in preparedness—a small piece of an effort to make sure that our imaginations never fail us again.

1
Unfinished Business
A Decapitation Strike at the U.S. Capitol

BELTSVILLE, MARYLAND
THURSDAY, SEPTEMBER 10, 2026
10:44 P.M.

"Are you awake?"

The glow from the incoming text message emerged from the gloom, as if the bearded young man sitting so reverently still had summoned it from somewhere in the depths of his meditations. He liked to think in the dark: it held fewer worldly distractions. But worldly distractions, he had been taught, were permitted when they served a higher purpose, and the mobile phone from which this simple message now shone would help him serve the highest purpose of all.

"I am," he typed back.

The reply came in a matter of seconds: "We finally finished all cooking for the party tomorrow."

"That is good. Our Father will be so pleased."

Rashid Rahmani turned off his mobile phone and set it on the table in front of him. He closed his eyes, overwhelmed, but not with fatigue. Sleep was the last thing on his mind. He felt, instead, a growing tension as the palpable force of his destiny pulled him forward. There would be no sleep tonight and therefore, he realized, likely never again.

The intrusion of this fact into Rashid's mind elicited hardly any reaction at all. It was as it would be. His journey had taken him thousands of miles over several years, and tomorrow it would end.

It had begun, he thought amusedly to himself, in his father's garage in Raqqa, Syria, where he had been desultorily working as a mechanic. Since leaving school he'd spent most of his days working under cars with his father, a hard man who hardly let Rashid have any life outside the garage. The chaos brought on by Syria's civil war had at least shaken things up, but when fighting in Raqqa had forced his father to close the garage, Rashid found himself even more bored than he'd been fixing cars.

When the soldiers of the Islamic State arrived in the city, Rashid took notice. As they paraded through the streets in their gleaming new trucks, he saw something more than just more men with guns: he saw adventurers, a brotherhood of holy warriors who offered an escape from the ruins of the war and the lackluster life he'd led before it. What's more, he saw a winning team.

He left home without a word and was welcomed into the forces of the caliphate with open arms. He made friends quickly among his fellow recruits, and attracted the notice of his superiors due to his natural skill with an AK-47 on the rifle range. His rise through the ranks was accelerated when he volunteered to help with some English translation work; the language had been his best subject in school, and he was finally putting it to some use. It wasn't long before one of the caliph's top lieutenants took Rashid aside and told him he'd been selected for a special assignment.

After that, the planning began in earnest. A few years went by in a whirlwind of e-mails, texts, and furtive, coded cell phone calls. There were the first tense exchanges with their new brothers from Al Qaeda, once a rival organization that had been awakened to the wisdom of partnering with ISIS to carry the jihad into the next generation. Their pledge of *bayat*, an oath of allegiance to ISIS, had smoothed over many difficulties, but there was still the matter of arranging travel to Canada so Rashid and his fellow operatives—men from both groups—could slip over the border into the United States. Then there was the anxious journey south toward Washington, sleepless nights in safe houses and

motel rooms paid for with cash. Once they had all settled in relative anonymity in the D.C. area, it was time to gather materials
and reconnoiter the targets—slowly, gradually, so as not to arouse
suspicion.

Finally, everything was in place for the "party" they had
planned. Tomorrow, all their caution would pay off. It would at
last be time for action.

EAST FRONT
UNITED STATES CAPITOL
WASHINGTON, D.C.
FRIDAY, SEPTEMBER 11, 2026
10:17 A.M.

Staff Sergeant Herman Alvarez shifted the weight of his
trombone on his knee. He was sitting in the now-familiar concert formation with the rest of the United States Marine Band,
"The President's Own." He was in a line with his fellow trom-
bonists: the trumpets were to the left, and the French horns to
the right. As far as he could remember, he thought, it had always
been like this, going back to his days in elementary school band in
East L.A.

And since those days, his mind had had a tendency to wander
before every performance. Maybe it was because he spent weeks
practicing, focusing narrowly on measures and notes until he
knew he'd conquered every piece. Once he got onstage, though, it
was no use worrying anymore. He trusted in his training and let
instinct take over.

That method hadn't failed him yet. It had landed him a full
scholarship to study music at Oberlin—a world away from East
L.A.—before he joined the Corps, and that training had helped
him nail the audition for "The President's Own." He was prepared
to let his mind wander a bit, then focus completely on the music
once the colonel tapped his baton to begin the program.

But Herman's mind didn't wander today. He had only been a
toddler on September 11, 2001, but he was well aware that he'd
grown up in "post-9/11 America." And even though his military

service was confined to playing the trombone, he knew his unit represented all of his brother and sister Marines when they played. Herman never forgot that, especially when they played on this date.

This was Herman's third 9/11 ceremony at the Capitol, but because it was the twenty-fifth anniversary of the attacks, it was by far the most significant. For the last several years, senators and members of the House of Representatives had gathered on the Capitol steps to sing "God Bless America," as they had done spontaneously at a press conference held in that spot the night that followed that terrible morning.

Every year they sang, the party leadership made speeches, and then they went back to arguing as always. But for a moment they stood united. Herman and his bandmates were there to play just the one song, "God Bless America," to accompany Congress's singing. But as Herman adjusted his instrument once more, he knew it would be the proudest moment of his year.

UPPER SENATE PARK
CONSTITUTION AVENUE NW AND DELAWARE AVENUE SE
WASHINGTON, D.C.
FRIDAY, SEPTEMBER 11, 2026
10:26 A.M.

Rashid allowed himself to admit it: they'd been extraordinarily lucky. Almost immediately he cursed his vanity. It was not luck, of course, but providence.

Their van was parked along the southern edge of Upper Senate Park between the Russell Senate Office Building and the Senate wing of the Capitol itself. Despite the many reconnaissance drives he'd taken along this very stretch, it never ceased to amaze him how close they'd been able to come without any interference. Men and women in nice suits with shiny gold pins on their lapels and aides in tow made the members of Congress easily identifiable. One reason they may have escaped detection was probably due to Muhammad's inspired idea to stencil CAPITOL CLEAN-SWEEP INC. in block letters along the sides of both vans, complete with a legitimate but inactive Maryland phone number along with the forged temporary parking permit they'd laminated at home and waved casually at the Capitol Police.

Rashid looked over at Muhammad, who sat next to him in the driver's seat, the sweat just starting to materialize above his brow. "It's finally happening," Rashid said to his companion.

Muhammad said nothing, only gave a short nod. He was a brother in *jihad* straight from the killing fields of Iraq, and except for his idea to disguise the vans, he was far better at using the AK-47 that lay at his feet than using his mind or his mouth. Waqar, crouched in the back of the van, was the same. Between the two of them, they had about twenty words of English. But they wouldn't have to do any talking today, or ever again.

A text popped up on Rashid's phone: "The acrobats are on the way."

He reached down to pick up his laptop and opened it. Taking advantage of the city's universal Wi-Fi, he quickly headed to a live video-streaming Web site ISIS had used often in the past. There was the link, right on the homepage. He clicked it, and a few seconds of buffering later he saw shaky but clear footage of a green field: a park a short distance away.

The footage was being filmed by a drone, a basic backyard unmanned aerial vehicle that had been assembled from a do-it-yourself kit. This was one of the larger models, because it had a payload to carry: several pounds of explosives tightly bound together and attached to the drone's underbelly.

As Rashid watched, the machine cleared the treetops of the park. Guided by his colleague Marwan, a drone expert from Mosul who was calmly sitting on a bench in the park, the machine spun around and headed with purpose in a new direction—toward Rashid and the Capitol.

Satisfied that the plan was now set in motion, Rashid checked another video camera—his own. He, Muhammad, Waqar, and the other three men in a similar van parked near the House office buildings on the other side of the complex all wore body cameras affixed to their bulletproof vests. He checked those links as well, and when he saw they were working properly, the cameras of all six men operating with clear views of what was in front of them, he e-mailed the live-stream page out to his list of media contacts and posted it to social media—his final message. Then he closed the laptop.

Now all he had to do was watch. It would be another three or four minutes before the drone arrived and crashed into the Capitol dome, sending the crowds assembled for the ceremony below into total panic. That was when he and his men would emerge, AK-47s at the ready, and begin their true mission. They wore body armor, to stay standing as long as possible, but no masks; they wanted the world to see their faces. More than that, they wanted the world to see what they saw, through their eyes, through the cameras strapped to their chests: mayhem delivered live over the Internet onto the computer and television screens of millions.

EAST FRONT
UNITED STATES CAPITOL
WASHINGTON, D.C.
FRIDAY, SEPTEMBER 11, 2026
10:32 A.M.

Reverend Jenkins had just begun his invocation, and the Speaker of the House squinted in the sunlight as she stood behind the House chaplain and listened. Margaret Bowerman was in the first of several rows of congressmen and senators, all arrayed on the steps leading up to the House Chamber. She felt guilty about not being able to concentrate fully on his prayer, but she was silently saying her own, asking God to help give wing to her words as she prepared to speak next.

After just eight months in the Speaker's chair, Margaret knew she was preparing to give one of the most significant speeches of her career. She and her team had been working on it for weeks. As she paid tribute to the victims of the worst terror attack in the nation's history, she would remind everyone listening at home and abroad that she—and the country—had not forgotten the horror of twenty-five years before. She would renew America's solemn vow, in the name of our own fallen and countless other victims around the world, to stamp out the menace of terrorism wherever it flourished.

This was personal for the new Speaker. She had been in her senior year at Annapolis on 9/11, and it had made her prouder than ever to start her naval service afterward. Today she was unveiling her majority party's foreign policy agenda: an ambitious plan to fight terror that she only hoped would be matched by a drive to actually get the plan through the Appropriations Committee. But that was a worry for another day.

Now Margaret tried to clear her mind as Reverend Jenkins began to wind down. She looked up and noticed that the sky was crystal clear—not a cloud in sight, just like that day in 2001. Then a movement lower down in her field of vision caught her eye. It was Lieutenant Henderson of the Capitol Police, head of her security detail, who was positioned at the bottom of the steps off to the side.

His head had dropped quickly to look at his phone, which was unusual. Still more unusual was when he turned to the woman next to him, Sergeant Valdez—the lone female member of her detail—and showed her something on the screen. Normally, both of them were impossible to distract. They both craned their necks to look skyward.

The strange buzzing sound intruded just as Reverend Jenkins uttered his final "Amen." As Margaret prepared to step to the podium, gasps erupted from the crowd below. She and her colleagues all turned around just in time to see a small object traveling at great speed crash into the side of the Capitol dome, launching a brilliant ball of orange fire and gray smoke into the bright blue sky.

Grit and debris rained down. Margaret watched as, seemingly in slow motion, a chunk of cast iron the size of a small car fell away from the charred dome. It broke off other pieces of the Capitol's façade as it crashed downward, landing with a dull, flat crunch on the East Front plaza, a few feet from the Marine Band's clarinet section. There was a split second of silence, of collective disbelief, and then pandemonium.

Senators, congressmen, reporters, and tourists fled, running in every possible direction. Members tripped over themselves and each other as they struggled to get down the Capitol steps. Some—Reverend Jenkins among them—attempted to hold hands as they ran, praying audibly. A few TV crews abandoned their cameras, while others kept rolling, determined to record whatever this was that they were witnessing. Political feuds had ceased to matter entirely. There was only one concern now: survival.

This was evident even to the Speaker of the House, who instinctively recalled her training at Annapolis, staying low while moving off the steps. Soon Lieutenant Henderson and Sergeant Valdez reached her and towered over her, forming a shield with their bodies as she crouched down. "Madam Speaker," Henderson said, in a voice that was surprisingly calm, "we need to move *now*." The final syllable was emphatic. Bowerman looked up and saw on Henderson's and Valdez's faces a look of fear unlike anything she'd seen since her ship took incoming in the Strait of Hormuz. She nodded her head, and the trio rose.

GLOBAL NEWS NETWORK STUDIOS
WASHINGTON, D.C.
FRIDAY, SEPTEMBER 11, 2026
10:35 A.M.

In all his years as a GNN anchor, Jim Bridgeman had never seen anything quite like this. But he had a feeling he would be spending the rest of the day talking about it. He had been sitting at his anchor desk on set with less than half an hour to showtime, e-mailing back and forth with the producers of his late-morning political news show, when the first alerts came in from the Capitol. His lunch, a protein bar, sat half-eaten on the table in front of him.

On his tablet, the GNN live feed was shaky. He saw people running, saw what looked like some smoke coming from the Capitol dome, but hadn't been able to get any confirmation on anything at all. He could feel the tension rising in the studio as GNN staffers dashed around his set. The last few minutes had been spent on his mobile phone, attempting to scroll through an overloaded Twitter feed and e-mail his producers, scrapping their preexisting plans for the show—a taped 9/11 retrospective—to focus on the breaking news.

Jim switched back to Twitter and saw he had a personal notification. He checked and found it came from an account he didn't recognize. It caught his eye immediately, however: the account name was in Arabic and the picture showed a masked figure. The tweet read, in English:

> @JimBridgeman, we're livestreaming what's going on at the Capitol.
> It isn't over.

There was a link to a popular live-streaming Web site embedded.

Jim looked at the phone in his hands, then back at the chaos unfolding on the screen of his tablet. He had to think quickly. If he helped spread this, maybe someone would be able to help identify the source. After all, it was news. He had to get it out. That was his job.

With a few taps, he retweeted the live-stream link to his more than four hundred thousand followers.

EAST FRONT
UNITED STATES CAPITOL
WASHINGTON, D.C.
FRIDAY, SEPTEMBER 11, 2026
10:37 A.M.

As Speaker Bowerman and her security detail moved across the plaza toward the entrance to the secure facility in the underground Capitol Visitor Center, she turned to look behind her. All she could hear was shouting. The Capitol dome was smoldering, and at least a third of it was missing. Twisted steel girders protruded from the marble at unnatural angles. She saw a Marine Band member, a trombonist, throw his instrument to the ground in order to help a fallen comrade to his feet. From the corner of her eye, the Speaker spotted the Senate's oldest serving member, ninety-two-year-old Lloyd Abernathy of Nevada, who had been in a wheelchair since a fall last winter, being carried away by two staff members. Capitol Police officers struggled to keep order, shouting for everyone to head to their rally points.

As Margaret and her bodyguards moved through the panicked crowds, she felt all the energy in her body and mind suspend itself for a moment. In that moment she realized that her country and her life were being irrevocably changed—again. They'd come back. Twenty-five years later, they'd come back.

A screeching of tires drew her attention toward Constitution Avenue, where she saw a white van lurch from the street onto the curb. The doors opened and three hooded men charged forward. They wore body armor and carried AK-47s, and they were screaming as they took aim at the crowd.

After-Action Report to the President on the
Terrorist Attack of 9/11/2026

September 12, 2026

LOCATION: Undisclosed

KILLED: 27, including 5 United States Senators and 16 Members of the
House of Representatives

WOUNDED: 68, including nine Senators and 17 House Members currently
unable to return to legislative business. (Latest report on the Speaker of
the House is that she remains in serious condition at George Washington
University Hospital.)

AFTERMATH: A significant portion of the eastern face of the Capitol Dome
has been destroyed. Engineers are evaluating further structural damage. A controlled demolition of additional portions of the dome may be
necessary.

The Capitol complex has been closed and sealed off. Federal law enforcement and the military are conducting a thorough search for additional
suspicious materials.

Transportation in Washington, D.C., has been mostly suspended. All flights
are grounded, passenger and cargo trains halted, and ground transportation has been funneled through checkpoints on major arteries only. The
Washington Beltway is turned into a "ring of steel," a blockade through
which goods and people can only transit after searches.

Surviving Members of Congress have been removed to a secure location,
but legislative business has been suspended.

Governors in several states have mobilized National Guard units and
have deployed tactical units of state and local law enforcement agencies.
Coordination of response strategy with state capitals continues to prove
difficult.

Secretary of the Treasury recommends that trading on Wall Street remain
suspended after an immediate 24 percent drop in stock prices.

SUMMARY: Intelligence indicates that this was an attack perpetrated against the United States Capitol complex by operatives of the Islamic State—or ISIS—and Al Qaeda, who have entered into a formal alliance. The assault teams were composed of seasoned veterans from the campaigns of terror in the Middle East—where ISIS's caliphate continues to expand and brutalize citizens trapped in its territory with relative impunity.

The date had been chosen for obvious significance. Like the original 9/11 planners, those who mapped out this attack made sure to choose a date that fell when Congress was going to be in session.

Planning for the operation was carried out seamlessly between ISIS and Al Qaeda's joint command center in Iraq and elements in the United States, with the radicalized American converts acting as stateside coordinators. Thanks to increased cyber-warfare capabilities and sophistication among the terrorists, they were able to plan the operation without the traffic being flagged by intelligence agencies.

With the help of friendly operatives in radical Islamist enclaves in the northern United States, ISIS and Al Qaeda operatives were able to slip into the country undetected via the Canadian border. They then made their way to the Washington, D.C., area where they conducted reconnaissance and made final preparations for their attack.

The individuals who made the journey from the Islamic State, through Turkey, to Canada and eventually to the U.S. included: skilled small-arms experts who knew how to fire controlled, accurate bursts of AK-47 fire in a short period of time; an explosives expert who was able to pack the most possible firepower into the smallest, lightest possible package; and a drone pilot, who had originally honed his skill with a joystick by playing video games.

The final team that deployed into the field consisted of seven members. Six of these were divided into smaller teams of three, and traveled in fraudulent service vans to opposite sides of the Capitol complex—one to the House side and one to the Senate side. They were able to pass the barricades by presenting a forged temporary parking permit commonly issued to workers called in for jobs at the Capitol and various office buildings. Several test runs had assured the operators that this document would not be carefully scrutinized.

The men in the vans wore body armor and carried AK-47 assault rifles along with several 30-round magazines per person. Once they were in position, they trained their eyes on the Capitol dome and waited for the signal to move.

The seventh man, the drone pilot, took up position in a public park located close to the Capitol but outside the areas subject to additional law enforcement attention. From the bed of his pickup truck he removed a large but lightweight drone, a consumer model purchased on the Internet.

Using a laptop, he logged on to a well-known website used for live-streaming videos, and checked to make sure the live stream for the camera he'd affixed to the drone was working. He presumably checked the shoebox-sized package of explosives taped to the drone's undercarriage.

Using a remote control, he switched on the machine, and using the video for guidance he steered it toward the Capitol. This flight pattern had been rehearsed many times over different fields in rural Maryland and Virginia. He had never used the same location for two test flights, so as to avoid attracting attention from locals.

It was anticipated that the drone would travel too low to be picked up by radar, but even if it was detected, the flight itself would only last a few minutes. There would be little or no time for law enforcement or the military to react.

The drone crashed into the Capitol dome, and the bomb detonated on impact. This caused significant damage to the dome exterior, and caused panic among the elected officials and others gathered for the 9/11 commemoration ceremony at the East Front of the Capitol.

The drone attack was only the first wave. The terrorists were able to anticipate the reaction of their targets. They simply waited for panic to set in before making their move. When the men in the vans saw the fireball from the drone explosion and the crowd erupt into chaos, they gunned their vans and drove as far as they could up the curb before hitting barriers. At that point the men jumped out of the vans and charged into the fleeing crowd, firing their weapons at whoever crossed their path but taking special care to look for individuals in suits wearing gold Member of Congress pins. Their secondary targets were police officers and members of the military. The fire coming into the crowd from both sides was devastating: as the terrorists had predicted, Members instinctively fled toward their respective office buildings. Instead they ran into the three-man shooter teams positioned between the Capitol Plaza and the offices, and many were cut down.

Thanks to the extensive police presence, all of the terrorists were eventually neutralized. Some, however, were able to evade police for some time by taking cover behind vehicles, trees, and other natural barriers. The last of the terrorists killed engaged officers in a standoff at the top of the Senate steps for several minutes. The gunmen were obviously highly trained, and were likely drawn from the ranks of ISIS' and Al Qaeda's most skilled fighters.

The death toll was grave. In addition to the elected officials killed, others killed included police officers, audience members, journalists covering the event, and members of the Marine Band. Some bodies have yet to be identified, and a number of individuals believed to have attended the ceremony remain unaccounted for.

At the moment, the United States does not have a functioning legislature. All business was suspended while Congress was moved to a secure facility. Governors have been advised to appoint new Senators to vacant seats and schedule special House elections as quickly as possible. Constitutional law experts are being consulted to ensure faithful adherence to Constitutional principles in the face of this unprecedented attack.

Before these events were covered by mainstream news outlets, word spread over social media in a particularly horrific way. ISIS and Al Qaeda-linked Twitter and Facebook accounts posted links to watch the videos of the attack streaming live via services such as Periscope and Meerkat. They appear to have a sophisticated knowledge of influential American and international media personalities, and in many cases sent them these links directly over social media. Enough were re-tweeted to send the live-stream link viral almost immediately, even before these individuals' networks covered the story. Viewers could see the video taken by the drone as it sped toward the Capitol, and even more gruesome video feeds from body cameras worn by the shooters. Viewers all around the world were able to see the attack take place in real time before the links were taken down. By that point the videos had already been captured and redistributed. Already, Jordanian intelligence has identified at least one new ISIS recruiting video which features footage believed to depict this attack.

Efforts remain under way in Washington and the surrounding areas to determine if any elements of this plot remain. The drone operator has thus far eluded capture, and presumably intends to make his way back to the Middle East.

★★★

Could It Really Happen?

You've just read the details of a fictional attack, but—like all the scenarios you will read—the strategy and tactics involved have a strong basis in fact. The elements involved, as you will see, are all too familiar.

Unfinished Business: The U.S. Capitol

On September 11, 2001, United Airlines Flight 93, the fourth plane hijacked by Al Qaeda terrorists, crashed in a field in Pennsylvania. The hijackers' plans were thwarted by a courageous group of passengers and crew including Todd Beamer, a software salesman from New Jersey, who was heard saying "Let's roll" over an open phone line just before they stormed the cockpit. Their heroic actions won the first victory in the war on terror and no doubt saved many other American lives.

We will never know for certain whether Flight 93 was headed for the Capitol or the White House, though in my estimation the Capitol was the target. As the 9/11 Commission reported, when planners first gathered to discuss targets in 1999, "all of them wanted to hit the Capitol."[1]

Terrorists take great pains to achieve the element of surprise against their victims, but their actions can sometimes be more predictable than they might like to think. Al Qaeda, for instance, has a well-established tendency to take their unfinished business very seriously. If they miss an opportunity to take out a target, if they fail in the execution, or if they pull off the attack but are not able to do significant enough damage to achieve their goals, that target will remain on their hit list. The evidence suggests they will attack again.

They showed this tendency even before 9/11. The October 2000 bombing of the destroyer USS *Cole* came about because Al Qaeda terrorists in Yemen bungled their first attempt to damage an American warship in the port of Aden. In January they managed to launch a small boat loaded with explosives with the intent of attacking another destroyer, USS *The Sullivans*, which was docked in Aden at the time. However, they had misjudged the weight of the explosives and the overloaded boat sank.[2] They missed their target but found another when the USS *Cole* arrived in October. Using the same method of operation and having learned from their mistakes, they were able to launch a successful suicide-boat attack against the *Cole* that cost the lives of seventeen American sailors and wounded dozens more.[3]

Similarly, after 9/11, Al Qaeda targeted but was not initially able to kill American diplomatic personnel in Jordan. They eventually assassinated Laurence Foley, an administrator for the United States Agency for International Development, in 2002—but, according to the Jordanian government, Foley "was not their main target." When the gunmen were captured and confessed, Jordanian officials learned that Al Qaeda had an unidentified "main target" in Jordan but "must have thought that Mr. Foley was an easier target at the time."[4] But killing American diplomats was the goal, and once again a loose end was tied up.

A more complicated example is the relationship between the 1993 World Trade Center bombing and the attacks of September 11, 2001. While the involvement of Osama bin Laden and Al Qaeda proper has not been conclusively proven, there were distinct connections. Ramzi Yousef, who planted the bomb that killed six people and wounded more than a thousand, was a nephew of Khalid Shaikh Mohammed and had received money from his uncle before the 1993 attack.[5] KSM, of course, would go on to work closely with bin Laden to plan the 9/11 assault. Furthermore, Ramzi Yousef was known to have stayed in a home in Pakistan owned by bin Laden himself.[6] When the 1993 bombing killed only six people—which a responding FBI agent described as "a miracle," according to the 9/11 Commission—Yousef was disappointed. Apparently, he had hoped to kill closer to 250,000.[7]

It is not difficult to imagine that Ramzi Yousef's failure to inflict mass casualties at the World Trade Center—the "unfinished business" of 1993—featured in the thinking of his uncle, Khalid Shaikh Mohammed, the mastermind of 9/11. The World Trade Center was always on the list of targets discussed, going back to the earliest planning meetings in 1999.[8] Also on that list: the United States Capitol.

Political Sophistication

The temptation of many Americans is to view terrorists as bloodthirsty maniacs with little education in or understanding of our way of life. That can be a dangerous mistake.

During the planning of the 9/11 attacks, Osama bin Laden appears to have expressed a specific desire to hit the White House and the president. He likely assumed that American power was concentrated around the single individual in charge of the executive branch of the government.

But lead hijacker Mohamed Atta, who was to be the operational commander in the field, leaned instead toward a strike on the U.S. Capitol. Atta seemed to have sensed the power of the legislative branch of the American government—and believed that crippling Congress so it was no longer able to hold sessions would be a devastating blow to the United States. He also understood that the Capitol was perhaps the most vivid symbol of American democracy. Indeed, in a sign of how politically sophisticated terrorists can be, it was Atta who specifically pegged a date range for the attacks "after the first week in September," because he knew Congress would be in session after their August recess.[9]

An Al Qaeda–ISIS Alliance

Al Qaeda may harbor a strong desire to go after the Capitol again, but for a major operation like that, they might need help. The Islamic State would make an ideal partner. This cooperation could be born out of a general alliance between the two groups, an eventuality that is hardly out of the realm of possibility.

ISIS and Al Qaeda have had a complicated relationship. ISIS

initially grew out of Al Qaeda's Iraqi affiliate but first made a name for itself in Syria's civil war, where it fought against not only Bashar al-Assad's forces but against other rebel groups, including the Al Qaeda–sponsored Nusra Front. As ISIS captured more and more territory and shocked the world with horrific acts played out on video for all to see, the conventional wisdom was that Al Qaeda's stock was falling[10], that it was being pushed out by the younger, brasher terror group on the scene.

But Al Qaeda should not be counted out. Their leader, Ayman al-Zawahiri, is still at large and is certainly a seasoned veteran of the global jihad. Other top-tier Al Qaeda operatives congregate as part of the Khorasan Group, a very small, elite unit of such concern to the United States that our military launched a series of strikes targeting them specifically in 2014. And Al Qaeda is apparently still capable of taking advantage of a crisis. Secretary of Defense Ashton B. Carter admitted in April 2015 that, thanks to the ongoing civil war in Yemen, Al Qaeda in the Arabian Peninsula, or AQAP, is "making direct gains on the ground there."[11]

In the fall of 2014, the Associated Press reported that Al Qaeda and ISIS may already have engaged in some limited cooperation in Syria.[12] High-level meetings at least took place, which indicates the potential for closer collaboration. It would be difficult to predict whether any eventual partnership would be on equal terms; this would depend on each group's fortunes. The two groups remain engaged in a deadly competition for dominance, with ISIS currently leading the race for leadership in the global jihad. They may end up merging in the years to come.

One option for Al Qaeda, especially if it finds itself weakened—by, say, the death of al-Zawahiri—would be for them to pledge their allegiance to ISIS by swearing an oath of *bayat*. This was what Boko Haram, a Nigerian terrorist group with a fearsome reputation of its own, did in March of 2015.[13] Their leader, Abubakar Shekau, released an audio tape on which he swore his group's "allegiance to the Caliph of the Muslims," ISIS leader Abu Bakr al-Baghdadi.[14] A few days later, ISIS formally accepted Boko Haram's fealty.[15]

While the extent of coordination between these groups in different parts of the world remains to be seen, it is significant that Boko Haram has offered itself to the service of ISIS's growing caliphate. Boko Haram referred to the ISIS head as "Caliph of the Muslims," their true religious leader, and CNN reported that ISIS's acceptance message expressed their view that "the caliphate . . . has expanded to western Africa."[16]

It's likely too early to say for certain, but we may be looking at signs of increased coalescence among Islamist extremist forces around the world. Pragmatic minds in Al Qaeda's leadership may well see the wisdom in getting the disparate elements of the global jihad to join forces. This would create a far more lethal, like-minded jihadist army with access to money and weaponry and dedicated to the single mission of attacking the United States, undermining Americans' way of life, and creating chaos and casualties wherever possible.

Infiltration Through Canada

When Americans talk about "the border," they almost always mean the 1,993-mile line separating the southern United States from northern Mexico. As we will see later in this book, the situation on our southern border is certainly disturbing. But we cannot forget about our northern border between Canada and the top of the continental United States, which is almost exactly twice as long: 3,987 miles. There are 1,538 additional miles of border between eastern Alaska and the Canadian provinces of British Columbia and the Yukon Territory.[17] Simply put, that's a lot of room for something to go wrong.

Our enemies are likely aware of the fact that the southern border gets more attention among the media and politicians than the northern, which is precisely why they might use this avenue to smuggle operatives into the United States. While we work very closely with the Canadians to keep our border safe, the vast and often barren expanses of the area present a particular challenge. A Fox News investigation in 2014 offers a snapshot of some of the difficulties in just one area:

Along the 545-mile border between Montana and Alberta, for example, there are six official, manned ports of entry. But FoxNews.com found dozens more unofficial and undefended crossings. A stretch of road that runs parallel to the border just outside of Sweetgrass, Mont., includes six roads that cross between the countries with nothing but an occasional sign notifying travelers of the border.[18]

One incident in August of 2014 that generated elevated concern was the apprehension of Jean Léonard Teganya near a Canadian border crossing in Maine. According to news reports, someone called in about a "'suspicious person' walking near the border" who turned out to be a fugitive Rwandan war criminal. When Teganya was arrested, however, he had already managed to get across the border from Canada into the United States.[19] Had someone not happened to notice him, he could be living secretly in the United States to this day. If an international fugitive can get that close, there's no reason why a dedicated terrorist cannot succeed.

Drones and Video

Both Al Qaeda and ISIS have shown themselves to be adept at using technology in the commission of their acts of terror. ISIS in particular has shown proficiency in the use of drones. *The Daily Beast* identified an ISIS video from 2014 called "Clanging of the Swords, Part 4" that clearly made use of drone-filmed footage. They also reported that our military has destroyed at least one ISIS drone—in Iraq in March 2015—that had been used for "conducting surveillance."[20]

ISIS likely only has access to civilian drone models, but that hardly matters. Any drone can easily become weaponized. Christopher Harmer of the Institute for the Study of War, among others, has speculated that it is "just a matter of time before they jury-rig surveillance drones into flying IEDs. Basically, they could turn them into little kamikaze drones."[21] A "little kamikaze drone" with a moderate payload is all that's needed to inflict damage and spread further panic.

There is precedent for using small, remotely piloted aircraft to attack high-value targets. In September of 2011, the FBI arrested twenty-six-year-old Rezwan Ferdaus, who had been planning to crash model airplanes packed with explosives into the Capitol and the Pentagon.[22] Ferdaus, an American citizen from Ashland, Massachusetts, became radicalized by pro-jihad videos he found on the Internet.[23] Working with supposed coconspirators who were in fact undercover FBI informants, Ferdaus developed a plan that involved purchasing a model of an F-86 Sabre jet at 1/10 scale for $6,500 that he could then fill with explosives. He even took a reconnaissance trip to Washington, D.C., to scout sites from which to launch the model plane. Ferdaus was arrested after he had amassed all of his materials, and was sentenced to seventeen years in prison.[24]

The possibility of small manned aerial vehicles cannot be discounted. This was made clear by Florida postal worker Doug Hughes and his gyrocopter, which he landed at the Capitol in April 2015 as part of a protest over campaign financing. In subsequent investigations, it was discovered that Hughes and his craft had in fact shown up on radar but had not registered as a large enough object to cause concern.[25] An unmanned drone would be even smaller than Hughes's aircraft.

Hughes also decided to post a live stream of the flight on a Web site. A camera mounted on a remotely piloted drone would be able to broadcast a similar stream, enabling terrorists to allow people around the world to watch with horror—or, for some, excitement—as the Capitol dome gets closer and closer before the drone explodes. Live streams from GoPro-style body cameras worn by active shooters would provide a ground-level and live view of the carnage and broadcast their wearers' martyrdom. Watching the murder of dozens of people in real time on the Internet has fortunately not come to pass, but the merger of social media with terrorist sociopaths will surely be something we will witness in the not-so-distant future.

The footage could then be downloaded and edited into one of the sharply produced propaganda videos for which ISIS is known. A report in the UK's *Daily Telegraph* noted that ISIS members are uploading videos "daily," and a British intelligence official commented that "the 'production values' were high."[26]

One individual who often features in these slick ISIS productions is Mohammed Emwazi—also known as "Jihadi John"—an ISIS fighter from London who has been filmed delivering sinister messages and subsequently executing hostages. For Emwazi, participating in gruesome video shoots is apparently a family affair. His younger sister, just nineteen in 2015 when her brother's identity was revealed, reportedly made a film as a student called *The Killer's Footsteps*. The British press reported that her film featured "a dead schoolgirl, bloodied footsteps and a hooded maniac brandishing a knife."[27] It also supposedly contains a positive message against bullying, but the similarities to the ISIS videos are hard to ignore.

Active Shooters

In this scenario, the drone strike is only one component of the attack. It is a prelude designed not only to damage a prominent building but also to touch off panic and remove all semblance of order from the situation. Into this chaos charge active shooter teams, which can inflict serious casualties before being stopped.

Active shooters also featured in Rezwan Ferdaus's plot against the Capitol and the Pentagon, to be used in conjunction with explosive model airplanes. According to the Department of Justice, "Ferdaus indicated that his ground assault plan would involve the use of six people, armed with automatic firearms and divided into two teams" who would "keep firing to create chaos and take out everyone."[28] The plan is simple, but could very well be deadly. Ferdaus may have taken inspiration from other jihadist attacks both at home and abroad that have made use of active shooter teams:

MUMBAI ATTACKS. On November 26, 2008, ten operatives from Pakistani Islamist extremist group Lashkar-e-Taiba attacked seven locations in the Indian city of Mumbai using small arms and grenades. Targets included a train station, hotels, a hospital, and a Jewish community center. The operatives arrived by boat and subsequently divided into separate teams to proceed to targets. Hostages were taken in some locations, many of whom were killed. In a number of instances, the attackers simply fired "indiscriminately into crowds." It was three days before the last terrorists holed up in the Taj Mahal Palace hotel were killed. The total death toll was 164.[29]

FORT HOOD SHOOTING. On November 5, 2009, United States Army psychiatrist Major Nidal Malik Hasan walked into Building 42003 at Fort Hood in Texas and began firing on soldiers who had reported for pre- and post-deployment medical checkups. Eyewitnesses reported that Hasan shouted *"Allahu Akbar"* before he began shooting.[30] He fired a total of 146 rounds from an FN Herstal 5.7 semiautomatic pistol, for which he carried multiple high-capacity magazines, before he was brought down by a civilian police officer. One witness reported that Hasan "sprayed bullets at soldiers in a fanlike motion, before taking aim at individual soldiers."[31] Hasan, who was born in Virginia, had expressed rage over American involvement in the Middle East and was known to have corresponded with radical cleric Anwar al-Awlaki. He killed thirteen and wounded more than thirty.[32]

CHARLIE HEBDO **ATTACK.** At about 11:30 on the morning of January 7, 2015, two masked men speaking perfect French and carrying automatic weapons along with a grenade or rocket launcher approached the offices of *Charlie Hebdo* magazine in Paris. They forced an employee to let them in and began "killing people as they saw them."[33] Eyewitnesses reported that the men announced they were affiliated with "Al Qaeda in the Yemen," or Al Qaeda in the Arabian Peninsula.[34] They said they were there to take revenge in the name of the prophet Muhammad, who had been depicted in a satirical cartoon on the magazine's cover. They hunted down certain staff members by name, beginning with the editor, who was killed along with a bodyguard assigned to him by the police due to previous death threats.[35] All told, twelve people were killed, including a Muslim police officer who was first wounded and then shot in the head by the attackers as they fled. The gunmen, brothers Saïd and Chérif Kouachi, were killed two days later in a standoff with police.[36]

CHATTANOOGA MILITARY SHOOTINGS. Shortly before 11:00 a.m. on July 15, 2015, Muhammad Youssef Abdulazeez began a shooting rampage that targeted two military sites in Chattanooga that eventually left five U.S. servicemen dead. Abdulazeez was twenty-four, had a history of depression along with alcohol and drug problems, and had been arrested for drunk driving three months prior. It was later discovered that Abdulazeez had sought solace from his troubles in radical interpretations of Islam at least as far back as 2013, when he searched for "guidance" on committing acts of jihadist violence.[37] He was found to possess videos and CDs of sermons by Anwar al-Awlaki—an American-born Al Qaeda cleric and recruiter killed in 2011[38]—and had written in his diary about "becoming a martyr."[39] Driving a rented silver Ford Mustang convertible, Abdulazeez first pulled up to a military recruiting center and fired several volleys at the building before speeding away. No one was killed at this location. He then drove to a U.S. Naval and Marine Reserve center approximately seven miles away, crashed his car through the gate, and entered the building carrying a rifle and a handgun along with extra ammunition. In an assault that lasted between three and five minutes, he killed four people on the premises and fatally wounded another before being killed by a police officer.[40]

All of these attacks can be studied as examples of a single active shooter or a small group of active shooters causing a great deal of damage. In addition to the deaths, each of these attacks was given significant media coverage and contributed to a climate of fear, the terrorists' ultimate goal.

What Can We Do to Stop This?

Understanding this potential threat will help us combat it. The most important thing to remember is Lenin's simple statement that "the purpose of terrorism is to terrorize." A few dozen people killed doesn't compare with the thousands killed on a day like 9/11, but terrorism isn't about those killed. It's about the spectacle and the reaction after the attack. An attack like this would, through the act itself and the media generated afterward, spread fear among the public. In addition, especially by perpetrating an attack against a high-profile government target as our scenario envisions, terrorists would also seek to undermine the credibility of the government to protect American citizens.

To keep our people safe from attacks at home, we need to take a firm stance on terror around the world. Through executive inaction on the part of the Obama administration, the jihadist threat has been allowed to proliferate and our nation has been left more vulnerable.

In January 2014, President Obama referred to ISIS as a "JV team." Within a year the group had been responsible for fifteen successful terror attacks outside of Syria.[41] But why would President Obama seek to downplay the threat? Because that would better fit the narrative that he has been pushing since his reelection campaign in 2012: the idea that under his leadership the threat of terrorism "has diminished." The reality is somewhat different: studies have shown that the number of jihadist groups around the world actually increased by nearly 60 percent between 2010 and 2013.[42]

The continued refusal to recognize the threat of radical Islamist terrorism has been a systemic failure of the Obama administration and has informed our country's foreign policy in several detrimental ways. This President, for instance, prefers to look at fighting terror as a matter of routine law enforcement rather than a war focused on defeating enemies. He made cuts to our military in the face of threats around the world, preferring to adopt a strategy of "leading from behind."

The rise of terrorist "safe havens" proves that this failed strategy only leads to a place of greater danger. ISIS is the prime example. In a remarkably short amount of time, they have erased the Syria-Iraq border and grown to dominate millions in an area about the size of Belgium. They maintain an army in the tens of thousands and a propaganda arm that has inspired terrorism around the world.[43]

We need a concrete strategy to go after ISIS, and we needed it yesterday. There is no time for vacillation and indecision. Every moment we waste without a strategy is a moment in which ISIS grows stronger. President Obama has let the group sow mayhem across the Middle East and become a magnet for disaffected Muslim youth. Not only that, his failure to act has created a leadership vacuum being filled by Vladimir Putin, who has been building up Russia's military presence in Syria to provide support to the embattled Assad regime and to increase Russian influence in the region.

ISIS and other jihadist groups will only grow into even greater threats to the homeland unless the United States acts to stop them. The following ideas could form the basis of a strategy to combat these groups and prevent a scenario like the one we discussed in this chapter:

> **Define the threat.** It's time to call our enemies what they are: "violent Islamist extremists." We are fighting people who follow a warped and twisted interpretation of a religion. They can be found fighting under many different banners in many different countries, but they share the goal of undermining Western democracy and the United States especially. Nor should we make the mistake of underestimating them. The formation of ISIS was announced by Abu Bakr al-Baghdadi in April 2013.[44] Astoundingly, the very next month, President Obama announced that the Global War on Terror was over and that American efforts would be refocused on fighting "specific networks of violent extremists."[45] ISIS, apparently, remained off the radar, since on January 7, 2014, President Obama responded to an interview question about the group—which

had just taken over Fallujah, scene of a bloody battle between U.S. Marines and insurgents ten years before—by saying: "If a JV team puts on Lakers uniforms, that doesn't make them Kobe Bryant."[46] By that June, the "JV team" had captured enough territory and resources to formally declare the establishment of their own caliphate. Downplaying the ISIS threat has been a hallmark of this administration and a downright dangerous failure. The next president must articulate an understanding of the ISIS threat and a concrete plan to defeat them abroad so we are not forced to fight them at home.

▸ **Take the fight to the enemy with a U.S.-led coalition.** ISIS is carving out its own terrorist state and building up an infrastructure that can be used to contribute to attacks on America and our allies. That's why we must work with Turkey, Jordan, the Gulf States, and other allies in the Middle East to create a coalition, firmly led by the United States, to undo the terrorists' gains. Sunni Arab nations in the region must band together to fight the Sunni extremists perverting their own faith, and America should lead the fight. However, we must choose our allies carefully. The Obama administration placed too much faith in former Iraqi prime minister Nouri al-Maliki, whose political malfeasance led to the near collapse of the Iraqi government and the systemic inability of that country to protect itself against ISIS. The Iraqi National Army has proved to be a national embarrassment: its soldiers simply threw down their weapons and ran as ISIS advanced on Mosul in June 2014. Nearly a year later, I met with al-Maliki's successor, Haider al-Abadi, in Baghdad to discuss the ISIS threat; about a week after that visit, ISIS took over the Iraqi city of Ramadi. The problem is systemic in Iraq, and it will not be solved, as the Obama administration seems to think, by relying on Iran-backed Shiite militias. This only inflames local Sunnis and drives some to support, or at least not actively oppose, ISIS. Meanwhile, with Iranian-backed forces at large in Iraq, we run the risk of creating a power vacuum that Iran can very easily fill. This would only further destabilize the region. One group in Iraq that has reliably stood strong against ISIS are the Kurdish Peshmerga forces, and these deserve the direct support of the United States. A formidable Peshmerga contingent, directly armed, trained, and equipped by the United States, would form a valuable part of our on-the-ground coalition. But this coalition cannot be forced to fight with one hand behind its back. This administration has imposed stringent rules of engagement for air strikes against ISIS, and both our own military commanders and foreign allies have told me it makes it difficult to accomplish their mission. When aircraft are returning from sorties with 75 percent of their missiles left un-fired, it's time to change the rules. Furthermore, the task of defeating ISIS should not be left to an air campaign alone. For this coalition to be truly effective, a substantive ground force made up of indigenous troops from Iraq and allied nations, with American special forces embedded, will likely prove necessary. General Ray Odierno suggested the embedding strategy in August 2015, shortly before stepping down as the Army chief of staff. In addition, U.S. forward air controllers on the ground could be used—potentially on a temporary basis until the indigenous forces' capabilities are brought up to speed—to make the air campaign more lethal to the terrorists. Any commitment of U.S. troops for combat roles, however limited, would need to be considered extremely carefully. But repeatedly ruling out this possibility—as President Obama has done—only serves to embolden our enemies.[47]

➤ **Establish a clear sense of mission.** Our anti-ISIS coalition needs to be clear about its objectives and have a plan for before, during, and after the military action. The territory in Iraq and Syria controlled by ISIS cannot be allowed to descend back into lawlessness once ISIS is defeated. This administration has already made that mistake. In their mad rush to remove troops from Iraq to fulfill a campaign promise, they failed to enact a status-of-forces agreement, and a power vacuum was created that allowed ISIS to flourish.[48] Iraq was simply not a priority: Hillary Clinton made only one visit to Baghdad during her tenure as secretary of state. This policy failure clearly shows that the zeal to adhere to a campaign narrative cannot outweigh strategic realities.

> **Remove Bashar al-Assad to help stabilize the region.** Bashar al-Assad remaining in power only contributes to his country's suffering and ensures that it will remain a safe haven for ISIS and other terrorist groups. In addition, he is a close ally of Iran and welcomes their support for his war efforts. Our coalition must include vetted opposition forces in Syria who can force Assad to abandon his fight and step down. The U.S.-led coalition can then help Syria rebuild its infrastructure and promote economic development while clearing out the nests of jihadists who have made their home there.[49]

> **Cut off terrorists' flow of capital.** Radical Islamist groups depend on money, expertise, and manpower in order to operate. Working with our allies, we can do a lot more to cut off these various streams. For instance, terrorists should not be able to fill their coffers by ransoming captives or by selling oil drilled in territory they have seized. The foreign fighters and experts who travel to join them must also be tracked and interdicted.[50]

> **Confront threats early.** We must take a lesson from the rise of ISIS. Never again can a terror group be allowed to spread across so much territory so quickly, especially because of American underestimation of their capabilities. With much of the Middle East in turmoil, we must identify areas at risk of becoming terrorist safe havens and work quickly to prevent that from happening.[51]

> **Offer an alternative.** In addition to fighting threats as they appear, we should work to keep new problems from developing by showing people around the world that the radical Islamists aren't the ones with the answer. By embracing a foreign policy that doesn't apologize for America's presence in the world but instead celebrates our values of freedom, liberty, and dignity

for all, we can help stop the seeds of terror from being sown in others' hearts and minds.[52]

➤ **Strengthen our northern border.** We must take the border with Canada as seriously as the one we share with Mexico. We need tighter coordination with the Canadian government to use manned or unmanned means to monitor long stretches of exposed border where crossing is possible.

➤ **Tighten security protocols at the Capitol.** The Capitol complex is still very much an open area. Anyone can walk right up to the building. The Capitol Police are extremely dedicated and the public should not have the seat of their democracy hidden behind a fortress, but we must find a way to balance the realities of keeping the legislative branch secure. We can begin by enhancing our radar capabilities so that small objects—like drones and gyrocopters—flying near the Capitol can be more easily detected.

No one individual has all the answers, but one thing is certain: our foreign policy needs a dramatic reevaluation. Without that, terrorism on a massive scale may visit our shores sooner and more dramatically than we care to imagine. But with the right goals and mind-set, and by not being afraid to take the fight to the enemy, we can be proactive in our own defense.

2

The Venezuelan Connection

Hezbollah Goes Radioactive on Our Southern Border

QUDS FORCE NATIONAL HEADQUARTERS
AHVAZ, IRAN
FEBRUARY 2, 2027

"It's on the plane?" whispered Ahmad.

"Yes," said Behzad, much more softly than he usually spoke. "Everything went according to plan in Isfahan. No problems. It leaves Tehran tonight."

They were the only two men in Behzad's office. But they never knew who was listening. It was hard to keep a secret in Iran. It was especially difficult to do so at the Quds Force National Headquarters, where everyone around them was trained to hear things not meant to be heard and see things not meant to be seen.

"Is it as much as we were promised?" asked Ahmad.

"Even more," said Behzad. "Our friend in Isfahan is a believer."

"Soon they will all be believers," said Ahmad, allowing himself to crack the slightest of smiles.

Ahmad had known Behzad since they were boys. Both born in 1979, the year of Iran's great revolution, they had grown up only minutes from each other's homes in Tehran. Their parents ate dinner together at least once a week, and the two boys, neither of whom had siblings, saw each other a lot more often than that. Every weekday at school. Most weekends on the soccer field. And many nights sleeping over at one or the other's house.

As boys get older, make new friends, and pursue their careers, they often drift away from the acquaintances of their childhoods.

Not so for Ahmad and Behzad. The shorter, slighter Ahmad followed his friend Behzad to college, and then the army, and finally into the Quds Force of the Iranian Revolutionary Guard Corps. Ahmad knew that Iran's most elite fighting unit, the one responsible for overseas terrorist operations against the enemies of Islam, had been hesitant to let him join them. But he also knew that Behzad, strongly recruited by the Quds Force, had made clear that it was a two-for-one deal: if they wouldn't take Ahmad, they wouldn't get Behzad.

Now, some two decades later, the two friends were middle-aged men with graying hair and close-cropped beards. And Ahmad, quiet by nature, felt unusually chatty. But he tried to contain his thoughts and his excitement. Loose lips were a liability, and today—the day he and Behzad had been preparing for since Ahmad first mentioned his idea nearly a decade earlier—was no time for taking any more risks on top of the monumental ones they had already taken.

Ahmad's smile would have been even broader if today were the end of their operation rather than the beginning—if today were the day of the first fatalities of the Red Death, which would precede the arrival in Mecca of the Mahdi, the "hidden Imam" and redeemer of the faithful, who would rid the world of infidels, apostates, and all other forms of evil polluting Allah's creation.

"Death to America," said Behzad.

"Death to America," his old friend replied.

"God is great," said Behzad.

"God is great," said Ahmad.

Now they were both smiling.

35,000 FEET ABOVE THE ATLANTIC OCEAN
FEBRUARY 3, 2027

Captain Miguel Chavez had flown this route many times. Tehran to Damascus. Damascus to Caracas. The three hours to Damascus weren't so bad. But the sixteen hours to Venezuela's capital were exhausting. Thank goodness, he thought, for his copilot.

A father of two teenage boys—who had little time for family, schoolwork, or basic manners, all of which bored them—and an unfaithful husband of an aging wife whose former good looks had been the only reason he had impulsively married her, Captain Chavez had only one true friend: his copilot. They had been flying this route for nearly a decade, and they had their routine down pat. The first four hours out of Damascus, Chavez napped. Then he took over for four hours while his copilot napped. Then four more hours of sleeping, four more hours awake, and by 3:00 a.m. Venezuela standard time, he was touching down in his hometown.

For four days after that, he would be free to do whatever he wanted, with whomever he wanted. For at least one of those nights, usually the last one, he'd have dinner with his wife and, if they bothered to show up, his kids. The other nights he'd sleep in the bed of his mistress in Barrio Bolívar. Or the mistress in San Bernardino. Or the one in Santa Teresa. And then, on the fifth day, he'd be back in the air, heading to Tehran by way of Damascus, leaving behind three soulless mistresses, two surly kids, and one nagging wife.

The job with Conviasa, Venezuela's state-run airline, was a cushy one. It paid quite well, especially considering that he was only required to fly twice a week. And he never had to deal with cranky passengers, because even though the plane looked like a passenger plane, it carried nothing but cargo. There were only three rules, somewhat unspoken but always understood, that might have deterred a different man from volunteering for the route. First, never ask questions about the cargo. Second, never reveal the route. And third, never leave the job.

Chavez was not naïve. He figured most of the cargo in the flight to Tehran carried drugs. He guessed most of the cargo on the return flight to Caracas—the flight he was piloting tonight—carried guns. It wouldn't have surprised him if most of the flights also carried more cash than he would ever see in his entire lifetime.

What would have surprised Chavez, however, were the contents of a small box, not much bigger than a backpack, tucked quietly into a corner of the plane yesterday by a man whose name he would never know and whose face he would never see.

Chavez never imagined that he was personally transporting a small quantity of spent nuclear fuel. But, then again, he wasn't the imagining type. The less imagining he did, the easier it was to sleep at night.

MARGARITA ISLAND, VENEZUELA
FEBRUARY 4, 2027

"How much is he charging?" asked Saeed.

"Only three million dollars," said Hamza.

"I bet you would have paid him five million!" said Saeed, laughing.

"I would have paid him ten," said Hamza, his eyes twinkling and his voice full of confidence and pride.

It was another beautiful day on Margarita Island, where the temperature rarely rose above 90 degrees, and rarely fell below 70. Day or night, spring or summer or fall or winter, the average temperature was right around 80 degrees. The beaches were always beautiful. The ocean was always a perfect shade of blue.

In the hands of a different regime, Margarita Island could have been among the Caribbean's premier tourist destinations. But in the hands of the heirs of Venezuela's Hugo Chávez, it was ground zero for a different type of visitor: members of Hezbollah, the deadliest Islamist terrorist organization to have a significant presence in the western hemisphere.

Created three years after Iran's 1979 revolution, the Lebanon-based Hezbollah quickly became a proxy for the Quds Force of Iran's Revolutionary Guards Corps. It cut its teeth in the Israel-Lebanon war of the 1980s, when it earned the distinction, retained until September 11, of having more American blood on its hands than any terrorist group in history. By the mid-1980s Hezbollah was expanding beyond the Middle East, setting up new cells in South America, and running a host of criminal enterprises— like drug running, arms dealing, counterfeiting, and intellectual-property pirating—primarily designed to raise money that could be sent back to their operatives in Beirut and Tehran. They also exported their brand of jihadist violence: Iran and Hezbollah are suspected of carrying out the bombing of a Jewish community center in Buenos Aires, Argentina, in 1994 that left eighty-five people dead and hundreds wounded.[1]

For the first few decades of its Latin American operations, Hezbollah's base was the ungoverned area, deep within the continent, where the borders of Brazil, Argentina, and Paraguay meet. But toward the beginning of the twenty-first century Hezbollah began to exploit a marriage of tremendous convenience with Hugo Chávez, Venezuela's virulently anti-American dictator. Before long, with Chávez's enthusiastic consent, Venezuela's Margarita Island was the hub of Hezbollah's hundreds of South American operatives and countless terrorist cells, each comprising propaganda, fund-raising, and operations elements.

Here on Margarita Island, located just fifteen miles north of the mainland and not much bigger than Cape Cod, the brothers Noori ran the show. The oldest of them, Hamza, was head of operations. A native of Lebanon, he was by now a naturalized Venezuelan. Before moving to Margarita, he had served as Venezuela's deputy ambassador to Iran. His middle brother, Saeed, was also a naturalized citizen and had been repeatedly reelected to Venezuela's legislature. He headed up the cell's propaganda division. Their youngest brother, Ali, a banker and financier by trade, oversaw the cell's finances, raising money through a lucrative combination of donations, money laundering, and, most of all, drug trafficking. Like his brothers, he enjoyed powerful connections inside Venezuela's government. Unlike them, he could also boast of equally important connections inside other Latin American governments—and with the most powerful drug cartels of the region.

Of the three, Hamza was the most fanatical—the truest of true believers. "Kill them all" was his favorite mantra, one that he frequently repeated under his breath, almost as a form of meditation. It was a teenage Hamza who had led his adoring little brothers into the fold of radical Islam. He had introduced them to Hezbollah through their local mosque. He had preached to them, and their parents, at the family's dinner table. And he had shown, by his own example, what it meant to be a soldier in the army of their living God. There was not a mission that he had not led from the front lines. There was not a tactic he had ever ruled out, nor a modicum of mercy he had ever entertained.

Hamza had said no to only one thing. He had refused to be a suicide bomber. In his own mind, he justified his decision by saying that the cause needed him alive. He was invaluable. He was indispensable. And Hezbollah had no shortage of foot soldiers eager to die for Allah. But in his heart, he knew his suicide mission was a matter of when, not if.

"Easy for you to say you would have paid him ten," said Ali jovially. "You're not the one who had to raise it!"

The three brothers laughed. Ali, the youngest, had always been the biggest cutup. But the laughter ceased when Saeed asked Hamza, "Enough about the Navigator. Who did you choose for delivery? Who will be making a martyr of himself in the most glorious victory for Allah since the caliphate stretched from Spain to India?"

"Yes," said Ali, "what is the foot soldier's name?"

Hamza paused. The foot soldier's name. The name of the man who would go down in history for triggering the Red Death, the Mahdi in Mecca, and the Day of Allah's Judgment.

"His name," said Hamza Noori, "is Hamza Noori."

TUNNEL BELOWGROUND, MEXICO,
NEAR THE TEXAS BORDER
MARCH 8, 2027

Hamza Noori had not carried a backpack since his school days, and, truth be told, it wasn't the only thing about him that looked a bit out of place. He was among the few middle-aged men marching through the drug tunnel. And despite the guise of casual, somewhat tattered clothes the Navigator had procured for him, he carried himself with the air of a rich and powerful man utterly unlike the dozen drug mules around him.

Despite his fluency in Spanish, Hamza said almost nothing to the men around him, and they knew better than to speak to him. They had no idea what was in his backpack. Neither did the Navigator. Hamza had paid him $3 million to get Hamza into Texas, with the understanding that neither would ever be returning to Mexico. Hamza didn't care where the Navigator fled to—he hoped, for the Navigator's sake, that it was far away from the cartel bosses he had kept in the dark about smuggling Hamza into America—and he suspected the Navigator cared nothing about where Hamza went after they parted ways.

As Hamza walked through the dark dirt tunnel, with wood boards above and beside him to prevent a collapse, he marveled at this little example of how globalization had made the world so much smaller. Decades ago, half a world away in Lebanon, Hezbollah had become among the world's foremost experts on how to dig a secret, safe tunnel that ran for miles below enemy territory. Then, once its alliance with Mexico's powerful drug cartels had matured, Hezbollah used its tunnel-making knowledge as a commodity, for which the cartels paid a pretty penny. And now, here was the Lebanon-born Hamza, unbeknownst to anyone in the cartel except the well-bribed Navigator, using a tunnel built in Mexico with Middle Eastern expertise, carrying a backpack filled with dynamite acquired in Venezuela and spent nuclear fuel acquired from Iran, and heading toward the United States border. The backpack had been made in Taiwan.

As the fourteen men slogged through the tunnel, the Navigator pointed at an X painted on the wooden planks to their left and turned his eyes toward Hamza.

"Welcome," he said, "to the United States of America."

QUDS FORCE NATIONAL HEADQUARTERS
AHVAZ, IRAN
MARCH 15, 2027

On his television set, Ahmad watched a helicopter shot of the city of Houston. The interstate highway was jammed with vehicles. Bundles of belongings, mattresses, bicycles, and all manner of Western consumerist treasures were piled atop the cars. Some people had abandoned their automobiles altogether and were simply running. As he stared transfixed at the CNN footage, Ahmad's first thought had been to praise God, which he did with enthusiasm. His next thought was to see his friend, Behzad.

Making his way down the hallway toward the stairs, he heard

the news spreading throughout the building. Phones were ringing in offices up and down the hall, and his comrades could be heard cheering and shouting, "God is great!"

As he threw open the door to his friend's office and quickly shut it, Ahmad saw that his friend was glued to his television as well. Behzad didn't have to turn around. He knew who had entered. Together they watched and listened.

> "Multiple American media outlets are now confirming high levels of radiation at the port complex in Houston and in surrounding areas of the city . . ."

The newscaster cut to shaky footage that must have been taken from another helicopter hovering over the port. This video was grainy and obviously came from a security camera. But it was in color and clear enough for a quick movement to catch Ahmad's eye, which had been sharpened by years of intelligence training. He saw a small figure kneel down at the base of a stack of shipping containers and back slowly away for a few seconds before a massive cloud erupted and obscured the view.

At this, Behzad jumped up from his seat and walked over to his friend. The two men embraced. There was nothing more to say.

The Red Death was coming. And the Mahdi would soon follow.

After-Action Report to the President on the
Dirty-Bomb Attack at the Port of Houston on 3/15/2027

EYES ONLY

March 16, 2027

LOCATION: White House

AFTERMATH: The City of Houston has been in a state of emergency for over
24 hours. Thousands are thought to have fled the city, while thousands
more remain stranded due to gridlock affecting most roads out.

The radiological device that exploded at the busiest terminal of the Port
of Houston has shut down the second-busiest port in the nation and one of
the country's major energy supply stations.

Casualties from the initial blast appear to be small, but the death toll
from looting and other violent unrest in the city has not been definitively
determined. Multiple hospitals have been sealed off due to the influx of
potentially contaminated patients, and radiation-related casualty figures
cannot be secured as yet.

Coastal communities along Route 146 to the immediate north, south, and
east of the port, as well as numerous industrial facilities to the west, have
been evacuated and remain at the greatest risk for contamination. Residents will remain displaced as these are closed off for several days for
evaluation, and full decontamination could take as long as a year. Alter-
natively, decontamination may prove impossible, which could necessitate
the demolition of entire communities.

Residents from the evacuated neighborhoods are reportedly being
housed in makeshift shelters opened in schools and recreation centers
located farther from the epicenter of the blast. However, as the spread of
radiation continues to be tracked, the area of evacuation may continue to
widen.

Residents in the neighborhoods nearest to the port—and to an indeter-
minate degree, further beyond—can expect to see a higher incidence of
cancer over time.

FEMA, the CDC, and the National Guard have been deployed to Houston to contain, to the extent possible, the radioactive fallout from the explosion. National Guard forces have also been deployed to protect all other major U.S. ports.

It remains unclear how much of the port's cargo was contaminated by the radioactive fallout, and CDC is continuing its evaluation. Regardless of their findings, however, it is likely that consumers' fear of the exposed cargo will reduce its value by several billion dollars.

Thousands of import and export businesses have seen their operations grind to a halt while they wait for the reopening of a port that is first in U.S. imports. Delays of weeks—and perhaps months, along with billions of dollars lost by adjusting to alternative transportation routes—will cause considerable economic damage.

The economic costs to Port of Houston users are expected to ripple strongly into the larger community. Houston's port contributes to more than a million jobs in Texas. Many of them are now in jeopardy.

The Secretary of the Treasury warns that a recession in Houston is likely, which could extend to the overall economy. The stock market has already lost 14 percent of its value.

The price of oil, which is among the most important commodities transported through Houston's port, has increased by 50 percent in the past twenty-four hours. The higher price of energy will have an impact on everyone who drives a car or runs a business. It will have an acute effect on the travel and tourism industry.

Although it is believed that the bomb was smuggled across the border through a narcotics cartel's secret tunnel, all transportation across the U.S.-Mexico border has been halted on your orders until the location of the tunnel can be determined. It is unlikely, however, that the American economy can sustain many more days of this policy, which many people, including many in your own party, are calling drastic.

The United States has recalled our ambassador and staff at our embassy in Venezuela, as well as our ambassador and staff at the interest section in Tehran.

Iran has disclaimed responsibility for the attack. It has also warned against any reprisals by announcing, to the surprise of the U.S. intelligence community, that it has built a nuclear arsenal and will respond to any attack on its territory with "proportional force."

U.S. military assets in the vicinities of Venezuela, Iran, and the Middle East have been placed at the highest alert level, as has NORAD. They await your orders.

SUMMARY: On March 15, a high-ranking Hezbollah operative named Hamza Noori exploded a dirty bomb in a shipping channel of the Port of Houston. Noori was a well-known terrorist leader who lived on Venezuela's Margarita Island, under the protection of the Venezuelan government. It is believed that he entered the United States in recent days through a tunnel built for narcotics smugglers. Hezbollah has long-standing alliances with multiple drug cartels in Mexico, although it is unclear whether any cartel's leadership was aware of the dirty-bomb plot.

After crossing into Texas, Noori, remarkably, appears to have walked the hundred miles to Houston, covering about sixteen miles a day. During that entire time, he carried cash for food and motels, as well as a backpack containing the dirty bomb, which combined dynamite with high-level radioactive waste.

Early reports indicate that the radioactive waste in Noori's backpack bomb came from a nuclear research reactor in Iran, possibly a Chinese-built reactor at the Isfahan nuclear complex. The intelligence community does not know how the material made it to Latin America, although the most likely method of transportation was an unrecorded flight that some intelligence indicates flies between Caracas and Tehran on a biweekly basis. Scattered reports of such a flight have surfaced on multiple occasions, although the Venezuelan state airline announced it to have ceased in 2010. It now appears that the flights probably remained ongoing, or recently restarted.

Shortly after the explosion, Iran's government announced that it was not responsible for the attack. This is, at most, only partly true. At the very least, rogue elements of the government, probably in the IRGC's Quds Force, were complicit in the plot. Recent reports—which have been difficult to investigate further, much less confirm—suggest that radical religious elements within the Quds Force have expressed interest in carrying out unilateral, extra-governmental action designed to draw the West into conflict with Iran in order to bring about the Shiite prophecy of the coming of the Mahdi figure and thereby the apocalypse. Whether this plot also includes elements of Iran's political and religious leadership is not yet known.

Iran's government also announced that it has a nuclear arsenal, which it will use as a deterrent against any American "overreaction." As you know, the intelligence community has been debating for several months whether Iran has a nuclear weapon or weapons. The historic agreement reached between the United States and Iran in 2015 allowed much of the Iranian nuclear infrastructure—including research reactors—to remain intact, and its restrictions on Iran's nuclear program, including inspections, expired two years ago. Within the past two years, Iran could easily have used remaining centrifuges to build a sizable nuclear arsenal.

Knowledge of, or at least suspicion of, Iran's nuclear weapons may have been a key factor in the thinking of Hamza Noori and/or his accomplices. Some analysts believe they were motivated by a desire to spark a world-wide nuclear war as a way to trigger the prophesied "Red Death" of violence that some Muslims believe will, along with the "White Death" of disease, precede the coming of the Mahdi and Islam's version of Judgment Day. The terrorists' motivation, however, may have been limited to a desire to inflict economic damage on the United States.

If the $3 trillion effect on the 9/11 attacks is any indication, the indirect effects of the attack on the American economy may one day be measured in the trillions of dollars.[2]

★★★

Could It Really Happen?

No aspect of the fictional attack described above is implausible. To the contrary, most of the key elements—a powerful Hezbollah presence in Latin America, an alliance between Hezbollah and Mexican drug cartels, and the insecure nature of the U.S. border—are *already* realities. In light of President Obama's disastrous nuclear agreement, this scenario's other crucial element—a nuclear Iran—is highly likely.

Iran, Hezbollah, and Terrorism

In 1979, Ayatollah Khomeini led a band of violent, theocratic extremists into power in Iran. At the time, he promised that the radical revolution—a rule of religious leaders, Sharia law, and no respect for individual liberty—would not stop at Iran's borders. Their goal, he said, was to "export the revolution throughout the world."[3]

Since then, Iran has used any means necessary to further that goal of worldwide Islamist revolution, and its proxy, Hezbollah, has been at the tip of Iran's proverbial spear. Founded in Lebanon in the early 1980s, "Hezbollah clearly acts as a proxy for Iran—specifically, the Iranian Revolutionary Guards Corps Qods Force," which is an Ahvaz-based arm of the Iranian military responsible for international terrorist operations.[4] Although Hezbollah's budget may now be larger, in 2002 its annual budget was "more than a hundred million dollars, provided by the Iranian government directly and by an international network of fund-raisers."[5] Its network of fund-raisers relies on "funding [that] comes from criminal enterprises" as well as direct donations from the "large Lebanese Shiite Muslim diaspora."[6]

The track record for overseas violence by Iran, the Quds Force, and Hezbollah is a bloody one. In 1983, Hezbollah bombed the U.S. Embassy in Beirut, killing 63 people.[7] Later that year, they used a truck bomb to blow up the Marine barracks in Beirut, killing 241 American men and women in uniform. On the same day, not far away, they murdered 58 French soldiers.[8] Two decades later they began a vicious campaign against American military personnel in Iraq and Afghanistan, killing and wounding thousands. Elsewhere, they have murdered Jews because they are Jewish, gays because they are gay, and Christians because they are Christian.

Hezbollah in Latin America

In the mid-1980s, Hezbollah set up operations in South America's Triple Frontier, where the borders of Brazil, Argentina, and Paraguay come together. The region was largely ungoverned, and Hezbollah saw it as a place to raise money by selling drugs, selling weapons, counterfeiting currency, forging documents, and pirating intellectual property. By the mid-2000s, Hezbollah had around 460 operatives in the Triple Frontier and was sending between \$300 and \$500 million from Latin America to Middle Eastern terrorist groups every year.[9]

Before long, Hezbollah cells spread beyond the Triple Frontier. When a new cell is established, Hezbollah often begins by "infiltrating or establishing mosques or 'Islamic centers' to help Hezbollah to spread its influence, legitimize its cause, and promote jihad." Each new cell includes a propaganda arm for recruitment, a fund-raising arm to oversee "illicit and legitimate business activity and relationships," and an operational arm, which "covers logistics, planning, surveillance, and execution of missions."[10]

Overtime, Margarita Island—a Venezuelan island forty to fifty miles wide and just fifteen miles north of the mainland—has taken the place of the Triple Frontier as "the principal safe haven and center of Hezbollah operations in the Americas."[11] The island became a natural headquarters because of the support and protection guaranteed by then-president Hugo Chávez.[12] In 2010 he threw a jihadist convention in Caracas, playing host to top operatives from not only Hezbollah but Hamas and the Palestinian Islamic Jihad group as well.[13] Additionally, Iran and Venezuela were known to collaborate in uranium prospecting operations.[14]

The two countries may have also engaged in a perverse exchange of "best practices" when it comes to repression of dissent. Iranian general Mohammad Reza Naqdi, head of the Basij progovernment militia, reportedly met with Chávez in 2009. That same year, the Basij gained international notoriety for shooting dead an Iranian student, Neda Agha-Soltan, at a demonstration during "Green Revolution" protests against the Ahmadinejad government.[15]

Analysts have linked the Basij tactics and Neda's death to similar repression in Venezuela.[16] In a case with similarities to Neda's death, twenty-two-year-old Venezuelan protester Genesis Carmona was killed at a demonstration in 2014 by the Venezuelan government's own paramilitary force, the *"colectivos."*[17] Joseph Humire of the Center for a Secure Free Society has pointed out that in looking at the deaths of Genesis and Neda, he found "a lot of similarities in the actual results, the killings, [and] there's also similarities in the tactics, clandestine communication techniques that these colectivos didn't have previously, espionage, intelligence, the ability to infiltrate student movements like they didn't before."[18] Venezuela's *colectivos* may have learned repression tradecraft from the Iranian Basij.

Venezuela is not the only Latin American government to embrace Hezbollah. The terrorist group also enjoys "official" support from Bolivia, Ecuador, and Nicaragua.[19] According to investigative journalist Doug Farah, Hezbollah has established a "political financial influence and military presence . . . in concert with the states that are hospitable to its movements and that are replicated in its model, particularly south of the border."[20] In fact, the three fictional Noori brothers—depicted in the account above as operating a Hezbollah cell on Margarita Island with the support of the Venezuelan government—are loosely based on the three Nassereddine brothers. One was a high-ranking Venezuelan diplomat; another lives on Margarita Island and was a member of Venezuela's legislature; the third creates terrorist training centers on the island. Together they operate "a network to expand Hezbollah's influence in Venezuela and throughout Latin America."[21]

The "Aeroterror" Flights

Starting in 2007, Iran and Venezuela were brought even closer together by means of a dedicated regular flight on Conviasa, Venezuela's state-owned airline, between Caracas and Tehran. The flights had only one stop, in Damascus, and usually occurred on a biweekly basis. The idea for the flights was reportedly planned at the highest levels, at a meeting in Caracas between Hugo Chávez and Mahmoud Ahmadinejad themselves. There was even a clever name for it: "Aeroterror."[22] An Iranian source who worked undercover for the CIA went as far as to say that the link was "instrumental in creating an Iranian dominated worldwide terror network that now reaches the United States."[23]

These flights were not open to just any Venezuelan with an urge to see the sights of Tehran. Special government clearance was required to board, but the main purpose of the flights—which took about forty-eight hours round-trip—appeared to be the ferrying of cargo, not people. That cargo, according to a massive expose published in the Brazilian media and verified by U.S. analysts, was often "drugs, weapons, and cash."[24] The stop in Damascus was reportedly for the purpose of collecting forged travel documents for Iranian agents in Latin America.[25] Among those who did make the trip, according to intelligence analyst Peter Brookes, were "a steady stream of elite Al Quds officers from Iran's Revolutionary Guard who were transported to Venezuela . . . and took up positions in the Latin American country's intelligence service."[26]

The intelligence community has had strong suspicions about Aeroterror's connection to Iran's nuclear program. In one instance, a Web site for Venezuelan airline workers posted about "radioactive materials" traveling on the Tehran–Caracas flight, only to be taken offline almost immediately.[27] Since the official manifests for these flights are shrouded in mystery, it is difficult to know what they did or did not carry.

Even the current status of this airborne terror express is hard to pin down. In 2010, a spokesperson for Conviasa told Fox News "we are no longer flying to Tehran and I do not know when the flights will resume."[28] As Conviasa is a state-owned airline, this could be taken to reflect the Venezuelan government's official position.

But that may not have been the final word on the matter. Roger F. Noriega, who served as assistant secretary of state for western hemisphere affairs under President George W. Bush and went on to work on Latin America issues at the American Enterprise Institute, testified before Congress in 2012 that the Aeroterror flights were still in operation in 2012, two years after Conviasa said they were "no longer flying to Tehran."

"The Venezuelan state-owned airline, Conviasa, operates regular service from Caracas to Damascus and Teheran," Noriega told the Senate Committee on Foreign Relations, "providing Iran, Hezbollah, and associated narco-traffickers a surreptitious means to move personnel, weapons, contraband and other materiel."[29]

In addition, Noriega suggested that the difficulty in getting an accurate picture of the dangers of these flights is partly due to willful obstruction within our own government, telling the senators:

> We understand that U.S. executive branch officials have continued to misinform Members of Congress about the existence of Conviasa flights between Venezuela and the terror states of Syria and Iran. Many months ago, we provided U.S. officials the name and contact information of a reliable Venezuelan source with privileged information about those ongoing flights. Unfortunately, that source was never contacted. And Congressional staff members tell us that executive branch officials continue to provide vague or misleading answers to direct questions on this relatively simple subject of whether those Conviasa flights continue.[30]

This is certainly not the only example of the Obama administration's reluctance to be up front with Congress, but when it concerns a possible terror threat in our own hemisphere, the stakes get even higher. Perhaps, as President Obama worked diligently on his legacy project of engaging with Iran, his administration feared the political embarrassment that would come from confirming that Tehran was still running money, drugs, weapons, and spies—and possibly even radioactive material—into Latin America via Caracas.

As the world looks to Iran to show good faith in implementing the Vienna nuclear deal, the American public deserves to know the truth about the Aeroterror flights.

Alliance Between Hezbollah and Mexican Drug Cartels

For many years, Hezbollah has raised money by selling drugs, and it is now increasingly "using the same southern narcotics routes that Mexican drug kingpins do to smuggle drugs and people into the United States, reaping money to finance its operations and threatening U.S. national security."[31] It has made "common cause with drug trafficking networks in Mexico (and elsewhere in the Americas)" and now "relies on 'the same criminal weapons smugglers, document traffickers and transportation experts as the drug cartels.' "[32]

There is evidence that Hezbollah is teaching certain tactics to the cartels. One "disturbing development signaling a growing relationship between Hezbollah and Mexican drug cartels is the increasingly sophisticated narco-tunnels being found along the U.S.-Mexico border. According to investigative journalist Doug Farah, these tunnels resemble the types used by Hezbollah in Lebanon, raising concern Hezbollah is providing drug traffickers the technology to construct [them]." Other lethal technology could also be exchanged between the groups: police in Tucson, Arizona, have expressed concern about cartels making use of Hezbollah's car-bombing tactics.[33]

The Dirty-Bomb Threat

The scenario in Houston described above was designed to show what could happen if a dirty bomb were to be detonated in a high-traffic area, such as a port. We hear the term "dirty bomb" used a lot, particularly in relation to terrorism, but it is important to understand exactly what a dirty bomb is—and what it is not.

A dirty bomb is not a nuclear weapon, though it does make use of radioactive material. It combines that radioactive material—which can be obtained from several sources—with conventional explosives to create what is known as a radiological dispersal device (RDD). While a nuclear weapon can inflict mass casualties and catastrophic damage upon detonation, an RDD in the form of a dirty bomb aims to spread contamination. The immediate effects of the blast itself may be minimal, but the dispersal of radiation in a concentrated area could lead to devastating effects on everything from public health to the economy.

A report from the Congressional Research Service outlines the effects that could come in the wake of a dirty bomb attack:[34]

➤ radioactive contamination of anywhere up to one hundred square miles

➤ closing off of contaminated areas for anywhere from a few days to several years

➤ causing of "significant economic disruption" by, for example, shutting down a city center or—as our scenario envisioned—closing a port

➤ residual economic damage from drops in wages and business in the affected area

➤ decontamination and remediation costs of up to tens of billions of dollars

➤ costs involved with the potential demolition and rebuilding of contaminated buildings

➤ an increase in long-term cancer rates

➤ instilling of "panic and a climate of fear in the target area and far beyond"

This last effect, the "climate of fear," is perhaps the most difficult to quantify but no less destructive than the other consequences. A dirty bomb does not just disperse radiation; it disperses fear. Outright panic in the immediate aftermath and lingering uncertainty afterward could damage our national psyche and even lead to more intrusive restrictions on everyday life. This is one reason why it is so important to prevent this kind of attack from happening on our shores in the first place.

The "Research Reactor" Risk

The radioactive material used to make a dirty bomb could come from any number of sources. Given the extensive medical applications of radiation, a terrorist could potentially obtain radioactive medical waste to construct an RDD.[35] Cesium-137, a radioactive isotope known as a "gamma emitter" that is commonly used in cancer treatment,[36] has shown up on the black market on multiple occasions.[37] Law enforcement stopped attempted sales of this material in Bangkok in 2003 and again in the Crimea in 2004.[38] The simple if scary truth, according to the U.S. Department of State, is that radioactive ingredients for a potential dirty bomb can be found in "widespread use in nearly every country."[39]

One potential source, as we discussed in our scenario, is spent nuclear fuel from a research reactor. Research reactors are a specific kind of nuclear device defined by the nonpartisan Nuclear Threat Initiative as "a small fission reactor designed to produce neutrons for a variety of purposes, including scientific research, training, and medical isotope production."[40] Their purposes are usually benign, but their spent fuel could be even more attractive to someone intent on producing a dirty bomb. In fact, Samuel Brenner of Brown University has pointed out that "it is quite likely that terrorists would look to research reactors as sources of radiological material to construct dirty bombs"[41] because their spent fuel can be pilfered and handled with relative ease.

In *The Four Faces of Nuclear Terrorism*, Charles D. Ferguson and William C. Potter explain why:

> Although spent fuel from commercial nuclear power plants is usually too radioactive for terrorists to handle, spent fuel produced by research reactors may be more vulnerable to terrorist use. The physical security surrounding research reactors tends to be lighter than that for power plants. Moreover, the research reactor spent fuel typically contains fewer fission products than does commercial power spent fuel because of the lower power levels in most research reactors. Thus, research reactor spent fuel may not require as many special precautions to prevent a lethal dose. Because research reactor fuel assemblies tend to weigh much less than commercial assemblies, hauling away the former would be easier than the latter.[42]

Spent fuel from research reactors can be obtained, removed and manipulated with less risk of the terrorists getting sick from radiation before they can carry out their mission. It can also be found in Iran.

Iran operates several research reactors scattered across the country. Ironically, one of these, the Tehran Research Reactor, was provided to pre-Revolutionary Iran by the United States in 1967. Some research reactors at the Isfahan complex—thought to be a major site of Iranian research into nuclear weapons—were supplied by China.[43] It is from here that the spent fuel used in our fictional future weapon originates.

The U.S. Border

Mexican cartels have already smuggled Islamist terrorists into the United States. According to one U.S. official, the "cartels have no loyalty to anyone" and "will willingly or unknowingly aid other nefarious groups into the U.S. through the routes they control."[44] Although there is no evidence that the cartels have smuggled a terrorist who was planning to execute an operation here, the House Committee on Homeland Security found that Hezbollah members "have already entered to the United States across our Southwest border."

For example, Salim Boughader Mucharrafille was a Mexican smuggler and organized-crime member of Lebanese descent who operated out of Tijuana and "smuggled 200 people, reportedly including Hezbollah supporters, into the United States."[45] Similarly, Mahmoud Youssef Kourani, whose brother is one of Hezbollah's chiefs of military operations, traveled to Dearborn, Michigan, to raise money for Hezbollah by way of Mexico. He purchased a Mexican visa from a corrupt diplomat in Beirut and, once in Mexico, crossed the U.S. border.[46] It's no wonder that General John F. Kelly of the U.S. Southern Command has warned that terrorist organizations could easily make use of preexisting drug and human smuggling routes to bring their own operatives or weapons into the United States.[47]

This has not gone unnoticed by America's enemies. ISIS, in fact, has all but threatened to exploit this vulnerability outright, in a scenario similar to the one that we have described here. An article appeared in *Dabiq*, ISIS's official English-language online magazine, in May 2015, which was credited to John Cantlie, a British hostage held in captivity. The article lays out just how ISIS operatives might—hypothetically, of course—first obtain a nuclear weapon and, secondly, surreptitiously transport it into the United States:

> Let me throw a hypothetical operation onto the table. The Islamic
> State has billions of dollars in the bank, so they call on their wilayah
> [province] in Pakistan to purchase a nuclear device through weapons
> dealers with links to corrupt officials in the region. The weapon is
> then transported overland until it makes it to Libya, where the mu-
> jahideen move it south to Nigeria. Drug shipments from Colombia
> bound for Europe pass through West Africa, so moving other types
> of contraband from East to West is just as possible. The nuke and ac-
> companying mujahideen arrive on the shorelines of South America
> and are transported through the porous borders of Central America
> before arriving in Mexico and up to the border with the United
> States. From there it's just a quick hop through a smuggling tunnel
> and hey presto, they're mingling with another 12 million "illegal"
> aliens in America with a nuclear bomb in the trunk of their car.[48]

"Presto." That's how easy ISIS seems to think this would be.
And they've already attempted to move on it. Between 2010 and
2015, authorities in Eastern Europe disrupted four separate attempts by black-market nuke peddlers—some with connections
to Russian security services—to sell radioactive material to Islamic
extremists, including ISIS.[49] If they are already thinking through
how to mount this type of operation, shouldn't we be devoting
just as much time to working out how to stop it?

Nuclear Iran

In July 2015 the United States, along with the United Kingdom,
France, Germany, Russia, and China, reached a deal with negotiators from Iran over the future of that country's nuclear program.
Despite being triumphantly announced by President Obama and
his secretary of state, John Kerry, the agreement promises only
to embolden Iran and, in the long run, will make the world less
safe.

The United States and our allies have made a number of drastic concessions—especially the lifting of sanctions, our only real
leverage against Iran's theocratic regime—in return for an agreement that does not even come close to guaranteeing that Iran will

not produce a nuclear weapon. At the absolute most, all we have done is delay Iran's nuclear ambitions for a limited period.

In return for this limited security, we've agreed to lift sanctions that were actually putting real pressure on Iran. Their state media was understandably excited, crowing as the deal was signed that "all unfair sanctions imposed by the U.N. Security Council . . . are to be lifted."[50] One of the individuals who is set to see these sanctions relax is General Qasem Soleimani, the commander of the Quds Force itself. Given the Quds Force's links to terrorism, it is difficult to see the strategic wisdom in giving relief to their top officer.[51] The flow of Iranian cash resumed by sanctions relief could also mean more funding for Hezbollah operations in Latin America, as in the fictional plot described here.

Even the concessions our side managed to drag from the Iranians are weak. For instance, while international monitors may now be able to inspect nuclear sites in Iran, they are required by this deal to provide twenty-four days' notice before an inspection.[52] A lot of illicit activity can be cleaned up in more than three weeks' time. As Israeli prime minister Benjamin Netanyahu noted, "It's like giving a crime organization that deals in drugs a 24-day notice before checking its drug lab."[53]

Iran did agree to "snapback" provisions that allow sanctions to be put back in place if they fail to hold up their end of the deal. That might sound like a good-faith effort, but the "snapback" may not end up hurting the Iranians very much if it is ever in fact invoked. According to the deal, some investments made in Iran after the initial lifting of sanctions should be able to continue even if the sanctions are reimposed.[54]

Iran is not prevented from continuing to develop intercontinental ballistic missile (ICBM) technology under this agreement. The Iranian military has already bragged about having "thousands of . . . long-range missiles," and that was back in 2013.[55] If they continue to develop ICBMs, it will only contribute to greater danger. "Intercontinental" missiles would not be destined to deliver a warhead a relatively short distance to, say, Israel. Their sole purpose, as their name suggests, is to reach across continents— possibly to the United States. Ayatollah Khamenei has demanded that his country "mass produce" ICBMs, and has called the idea of reducing them "stupid and idiotic." Iranian president Rouhani vowed in 2014 that Iran's "centrifuges will never stop working,"[56] and it looks like that will continue to be the case under this deal. ICBMs and spinning centrifuges in Iran could prove a deadly combination.

Also disturbing are the plans to lift arms embargoes against Iran, letting them once again plunge into the global weapons marketplace. The restrictions on selling conventional weapons to Iran are set to expire after five years. Any of these weapons could end up in the hands of Iran's terrorist allies, making it easier for them to threaten Israel and the entire Middle East region while the Iranian government manages officially to keep its hands clean. That may explain why Hassan Nasrallah of Hezbollah was so relieved that sanctions on Iran would be lifted. "A rich and strong Iran," he said, "will be able to stand by its allies and friends in the region more than at any time in the past." "Allies and friends"—like Hezbollah itself.[57]

These weapons might even make their way to Iran ahead of the five- and eight-year timelines. Frederick W. Kagan of the American Enterprise Institute pointed out in the *Wall Street Journal* that the actual lifting of the arms embargo must be done through the UN Security Council, which could give Russia and China power over the language of the final resolution. According to Kagan, simply lifting the existing sanctions "would allow Russia and China to provide Iran with any military technology they choose."[58] Russia has made no secret of its intention to sell "defensive" missile technology to Iran,[59] and has called for the arms embargo to be "ended immediately."[60] Vladimir Putin's penchant for destabilizing behavior has been discussed elsewhere in this book, and Russian interests in Iran are well established.

In the scenario presented here, the nuclear material used in the dirty bomb was taken from a research reactor, a specific kind of nuclear facility. Research reactors in Iran will continue to operate under this deal, including continued "peaceful nuclear research and radioisotope production for medical and instructional purposes"[61] at the nuclear site in Arak. Furthermore, CNN reports that "inspectors look likely to spend the bulk of their time at Iran's established nuclear facilities like Natanz, Fordow and Arak." We cannot, however, take the risk of ignoring the potential for misuse of research reactors at Iran's other nuclear sites like Isfahan.[62]

★★★

What Can We Do to Stop This?

Iranian personnel using a covert air link to transport a radioactive device to Venezuela, and then having it smuggled across the American border, is a process which would have many moving parts. But the Obama administration has not been doing nearly enough to shut down these parts, and that needs to change.

The following strategies could help disrupt an operation like this—or prevent it from happening in the first place—and all of them would contribute to the greater general safety of our nation:

SECURE OUR SOUTHERN BORDER. This seems like a simple idea. It's certainly been talked about enough. But under President Obama, virtually nothing has been done. The U.S. Border Patrol stopped nearly half a million people trying to cross our nearly two-thousand-mile-long southern border in 2014 alone—and those are just the ones we've caught. I've said many times that it's impossible to know how many people we *didn't* catch, who they were, or what they might have been carrying with them. Enough is enough. Between illegal immigration and the terrorist threat, the reasons to get serious about the southern border are legion. President Obama appears to be unwilling to do anything except issue blanket amnesty to illegal immigrants already in the country—which will only encourage more to make their way here—but that doesn't mean we're out of ideas to secure the border once and for all. Some commonsense components should form the basis for a future border strategy, fashioned by Congress working together with a willing partner in the White House. For instance, we should complete the seven hundred miles of border fence as required by current law, as well as add double-layer fencing in certain areas.[63] But we need a border security plan that's updated for the twenty-first century, too. That's why our plan deploying additional technological countermeasures are essential. Of course, you can't stop a border threat if you can't see it; that's why we should aim for 100 percent visibility on the border using manned and unmanned resources. One method is by making it easier to transfer surplus military assets, like unmanned aerostat surveillance balloons, from theaters of war to the border. Finally, the Obama administration must be kept on their toes with independent border security analysis to make sure they're keeping us safe. Additionally, they will face stiff penalties if they decide not to enforce border security law for political reasons.[64]

GET THE REAL STORY OF THE AEROTERROR FLIGHTS. The American people deserve to know just how closely two nations with distinctly anti-U.S. views, Iran and Venezuela, have been working against our interests virtually in our own backyard. There is no excuse for the administration to "misinform" Congress about these flights and to ignore credible information on them, as former State Department official Roger Noriega pointed out back in 2012. The questions are simple: Are these flights still going on, and if so, what or whom are they carrying? Or, if they have indeed ceased, what or whom *were* they carrying? The administration should not shy away from using diplomatic and intelligence assets to find out the truth.

DEVELOP SUCCESSFUL NUCLEAR THREAT DETECTION CAPABILITIES. The Department of Homeland Security tried to develop new radiation detection technology, only to fail spectacularly $230 million later. Here we have a sadly typical but still disturbing example of government waste that could have real security consequences. The advanced spectroscopic portal (ASP) program was designed to pick up traces of radiation in cargo that arrived at American ports of entry, including the Port of Houston. However, ASP performed dismally during its tests, registering too many false positive readings, among other difficulties. Already over budget, DHS put ASP out of its misery in 2011.[65] To protect against dirty bombs made from radioactive materials, we need to develop and implement this kind of technology, and keep congressional pressure on DHS to make sure it gets done. Our security cannot be held hostage to government's inefficiency.

CANCEL THE IRAN NUCLEAR DEAL ON DAY ONE OF THE NEXT PRESIDENTIAL ADMINISTRATION. The Iran nuclear deal, or Joint Comprehensive Plan of Action, as it's called by diplomats, squeaked by the U.S. Senate in September, in spite of the courageous efforts of several prominent Democrats such as Senator Chuck Schumer, who broke ranks with the Obama administration over what those senators recognized as a bad bargain. Iran's neighbors in the region have opposed the deal because they predict it will lead to a nuclear arms race in the Middle East, a dangerous prospect. By signing away economic sanctions, the international community's only real leverage on Iran, President Obama and Secretary Kerry have put their own political legacy ahead of the security of the entire Middle East region, Israel, the United States, and perhaps the entire world. The deal has effectively green-lit an Iranian nuclear weapons program in ten years, once it expires. The Iranians will continue enrichment to some level, with no reliable safeguards in place to ensure they aren't cheating. Given their past clandestine work with nuclear weapons, an Iranian attempt to circumvent this deal seems likely. The deal allows Iran to maintain its capacity for enrichment and continue centrifuge research, which could put them in a position to produce a bomb quickly once the deal sunsets—if they haven't already done so in secret beforehand. Our next commander in chief, when he or she takes office in January 2017, should arrive at the White House from the inaugural ceremonies, pick up the phone, and send this deal to the same place Ronald Reagan sought to send Communism: "the ash heap of history."

DEMAND REAL VERIFICATION EFFORTS FOR IRAN'S NUCLEAR PROGRAM. At the very least, the Iran deal should include actual avenues for keeping an eye on the regime's activities. As it is, the Obama administration allowed the deal to go through despite the known existence of two secret "side deals" negotiated between the Iranian government and the International Atomic Energy Agency (IAEA). One of these side deals reportedly makes the verification process easier on Iran by allowing them to present their own soil samples from a nuclear site for review, instead of independent inspection. But we may never know for certain what these deals entail because, as an IAEA official told my colleague Representative Mike Pompeo of Kansas, "No American is ever going to get to see them." This is unacceptable. The international community must keep up the pressure on Iran as well as the IAEA to follow through on the strong verification the world was promised when this deal was pushed through. The process should be guided by the principle of transparency and subjected, if necessary, to independent review. Regional—and global—stability demands nothing less.[66]

COUNTER IRAN'S GROWING REGIONAL INFLUENCE. This nuclear deal has only strengthened Iran's position as a regional power in the Middle East and increased the radical theocratic regime's hold on its people. But that deal was only part of a long line of Obama administration policy failures that benefited Iran. By prematurely withdrawing from Iraq, we left a power vacuum in that country that was filled in part by ISIS and in part by Iranian-controlled Shiite militias. Because our country led from behind during the crisis in Yemen, Shia rebels supported by Iran were able to seize the presidential palace in Sana'a. And by drawing "red lines" in Syria that have not been enforced, the U.S. has signaled to Iran's ally Bashar al-Assad that he has nothing to worry about from us. The net result, as Prime Minister Netanyahu of Israel said in March 2015—even before the Vienna accord was signed—is that Iran "now dominates four Arab capitals, Baghdad, Damascus, Beirut, and Sana'a." This requires a shift in our policy thinking toward Iran. Our goal must be to roll back the Iranian threat and to counter Iran's influence wherever it crops up—and that includes influence it exerts through paramilitary allies like Hezbollah. Each Iranian foothold in a new country is a further step toward regional destabilization, which could have disastrous consequences for our allies and for us. We should advance foreign policy goals that support freedom and liberty, and show the Iranian people that there is no place in the modern world for their backward leaders. There are currents of change waiting to bubble to the surface in Iran; President Obama missed a chance to capitalize on them during the 2009 Green Movement election protests by not putting enough pressure on the Iranian regime. Our next president must be prepared to stand with real Iranian reformers against their repressive rulers.

3

The Manchurian Campaign

China Plots to Buy the White House (Again)

NOVEMBER 6, 2024
INTERCONTINENTAL HOTEL
RALEIGH, NORTH CAROLINA
2:06 A.M.

Eddie Farber tried to focus his tired eyes on the anchor on the hotel lobby television.

"To recap," the anchor was intoning, "just over three hours ago, Senator Ben Bradshaw of Connecticut was elected the forty-sixth president of the United States. The result came as a surprise to many. The race had always been close, narrowing significantly in the last few months, but Senator Bradshaw almost always remained behind his opponent, Governor Marcia DeSoto of Nevada, by an average of about two points in most polls. But swing states came out heavily for Bradshaw . . ."

Eddie knew the rest. He had lived it. He had never seen a night like this in all of his twenty-three years, and at this moment nobody could convince him that he'd ever see a night like it again. Certainly he knew—or at least hoped—that many more election nights lay in his future. With a little luck, some might be successful. But none would ever compare to his first—the night he helped make Benjamin Warwick Bradshaw the next president of the United States.

The election had been called by 11:00 p.m. They still had trouble believing it themselves at first. It was true, DeSoto had kept at least a two-point lead over Bradshaw for much of the race—though their internal polls were slightly more optimistic, showing a gap of just one point. Exit polls showed DeSoto ahead by a similar margin. Still, the North Carolina field team had worked hard, and they had hoped those on the ground in the other swing states had done so as well. Eddie and the rest of the field-workers, plus hundreds of volunteers and hangers-on just looking to join the party, had converged on the hotel in Raleigh where the North Carolina for a Fair Future PAC had set up their election night headquarters.

Truth be told, some of the rowdier folks had started the party a little early, right after North Carolina had been called for Bradshaw. It was hard to hold back the jubilation after that. Some of Eddie's volunteers had been among the first to head for the hotel bar. Marianne, the soccer player from NC State with whom Eddie had spent several glorious fall afternoons knocking on doors, had tried to get him to come along; that was hard to turn down. But Eddie was a regional field organizer, and he took his role very seriously. It was his first "real" job, after all, and he wanted to set a good example. But once all the networks *and* the Associated Press had made the call for Bradshaw, he joined in the fun himself.

Now, three hours later, he needed a break from fun. The party was still in full swing and showed no signs of slowing down. The band had long since stopped playing in the hotel ballroom, but the PAC had spared no expense: a DJ had taken over. Streams of revelers were making their way between the bar and the ballroom, but from his vantage point in a comfortable lobby chair, somewhat removed from the noise, Eddie had noticed that a few were beginning to flag. He saw more and more of his fellow party faithful heading toward the exits or the elevators that would take them up to the block of rooms that North Carolina for a Fair Future had reserved in the hotel.

Eddie leaned back in his chair and closed his eyes. Never—not in a million years—could he have seen this coming.

JUST a few months earlier, Eddie had been a typical college senior at a major state university. He'd never been political in his life—never even voted until this election. All through college, he'd had no time for the rallies put on by various student groups; as a matter of fact, he'd generally made sure to avoid them.

But in the spring of his senior year, as graduation was approaching and even Eddie himself was beginning to believe his parents had a point in their incessant nagging about eventually finding a job, he roused himself early from his afternoon nap and headed down to the main quad to a recruitment fair. He shuffled past a number of booths until one stopped him in his tracks with a dazzling display of red, white, and blue: Americans for a Fair Future.

It was a political "super-PAC," the grinning field rep explained to Eddie. It was a term he had heard before. A group of his fellow citizens were coming together, he was told, because they were concerned about the upcoming election, an event of which Eddie had registered a vague awareness. There were chapters being set up all over the country: North Carolina for a Fair Future, Ohio for a Fair Future, dozens more. What caught Eddie's attention was what the grinning man offered him: $18 an hour to knock on doors, with lodging and food provided. Eddie signed on the dotted line, got his parents off his back, became a "committed activist," and found himself in North Carolina.

As it turned out, he took well to his new line of work. He was a natural talker, so it was easy to recite the doorstep sales pitch they got from headquarters praising their candidate, Benjamin Bradshaw. One week it was about health care, the next it was national defense. Eddie handled them all with ease, and always noted the response from the homeowner in the proprietary voter data collection app the PAC had installed on his phone.

Before long, Eddie had worked his way up to regional field organizer, in charge of PAC staffers in several precincts in critical Wake County. That was how he'd met Marianne, the soccer player. Everything was going well. Eddie was spending more time at the Raleigh PAC office now, entering names into voter databases. The higher-ups had told them to sign up as many people as possible: no need to see ID or anything; as long as they were over eighteen, they would be voting, and voting for Bradshaw. Eddie's sections were always the top performers. When he wasn't checking registration numbers, he was signing off on expense reports.

He had hated the expense reports—hated math in general. It was those stupid reports that had given him the one major hassle of the entire campaign. Once they had used the wrong account to pay the rent for the headquarters building or something like that. It hadn't even been Eddie's fault; he didn't even *do* finance. But since he'd been the one to sign off on the report, it came back down on him.

The bank sent a letter with copies of wire receipts requesting clarification. Eddie saw the name of the bank they used in North Carolina, then a bank in New York, and then a receipt from a bank in Shanghai, only about a quarter of which was written in English. He had no idea what that was about, so he went to the office of the field director in charge, Phil, and showed it to him. Phil flipped through the pages, came to the Chinese receipt, and told Eddie to get the hell out of his office. Phil had always been a jerk—one loser in a mostly fun crew. As Eddie left, he had heard Phil pick up his phone and begin dialing.

Eddie didn't think much about expense reports the rest of that day, until the front doors of the office swung open and Frank Dahlgren walked in. Eddie recognized the director of the Americans for a Fair Future PAC—his top boss—from the pictures he'd seen on the Internet. His hair was slicked back and he wore the best-fitting dark suit and shirt combination Eddie had ever seen. With him was another sharp-looking guy, an Asian. Phil ran over to Dahlgren and the other man, holding a stack of papers. They leafed through them, and then Phil led them over to Eddie's desk.

"You Farber?" Dahlgren asked, barely looking up from his mobile phone.

"Yes," said Eddie, unsure whether it would be cooler to call him "sir" or not.

"You know who I am?"

"Yes." Eddie noticed the PAC director was chewing gum.

"You know who this is?" Dahlgren nodded toward his Asian companion.

"No."

"Good," Dahlgren said curtly.

"Please, Francis," the Asian gentleman interjected smoothly, putting a hand on Dahlgren's shoulder. "I am told Edward is one of our top field staffers in North Carolina. Isn't that right?" He had a clipped, almost British accent.

Eddie nodded in agreement.

"Then I'm sure we can trust Edward," the man said. "My name is Mr. Liao." He was now addressing Eddie directly for the first time. Mr. Liao took the stack of papers from Phil. "I would very much like to know if these are the only copies of these receipts that you've received from the bank."

Eddie nodded.

"And nobody else in this, or any other office, would have received any other copies?"

Eddie shook his head. Liao looked to Dahlgren and Phil, both of whom shook their heads as well.

Liao considered for a moment, then stuffed the papers into his briefcase. He smiled. "Edward, how would you like to work in Washington, D.C.?"

Eddie was stunned. So were Phil and Dahlgren, he noticed. He managed to get out "Sounds great, sir." Mr. Liao was definitely a "sir." D.C. would be fantastic—at least it looked like fun on TV.

Mr. Liao's smile broadened. "Excellent," he said. "When Senator Bradshaw wins this election—and I know he will—I'm sure we could find a place for you in the administration. Who knows"—he nodded his head toward Phil—"maybe one of these gentlemen will end up working for you."

Eddie couldn't help but smile back. Mr. Liao's positivity was infectious.

Dahlgren sniffed to himself but lowered his gaze to his phone when Liao looked his way. "The plane is ready," he growled. "We can be back in D.C. in time for dinner." Liao nodded, and the two men turned to leave.

"Of course," Liao said to Eddie, almost as an afterthought, "there's no need to worry about this receipt. We will take care of everything. Thank you for bringing it to our attention, and now you may put it out of your mind." He paused, and his smile seemed to harden before he added, "Entirely." With that, they had swept out of the office. The check and Mr. Liao were never mentioned again.

* * *

THE sounds of breaking glass, accompanied by a joyful shriek, jolted Eddie back to the present. Sitting in the overstuffed chair in the lobby, he was glad to put the business with the expense report out of his mind for good. The election was over and they'd won. Best of all, Liao had made good on his promise. To his amazement, barely a half hour after the race was called, Eddie had received an e-mail from Frank Dahlgren's assistant asking when he could come to Washington for an interview.

As he stood up and headed for the bar, Eddie shook his head and thought how lucky he'd been to meet the sharp-dressing, smooth-talking Mr. Liao.

NOVEMBER 6, 2024
STAMFORD HOTEL & TOWERS
STAMFORD, CONNECTICUT
3:30 A.M.

This was the moment he'd been waiting for. Finally, President-elect Ben Bradshaw of Connecticut was alone at last. Every advisor, every glad-hander, every hanger-on, was gone. His wife and children had gone to bed, and Ben sat alone in the darkened living room of their suite, glass of scotch in hand, and looked out over downtown Stamford.

He could see the building where his father's office had been. *How Dad would have gotten a kick out of this*, Ben thought, and raised the glass solemnly in the direction of the building. Of course, his father's money had made the old man's presence felt. So had his grandfather's, for that matter. He drank a quiet toast to the Bradshaws before him. Just a few hours ago, their progeny had made his victory speech as the next president of the United States.

The speech itself had come much later in the evening than

such speeches typically do. His team had been thrown into a momentary panic. Their opponent, Governor DeSoto, had apparently held off conceding for as long as she could. Rumors flew that her lawyers were frantically casting about to see if there was anything about the election they could possibly contest.

They must have come up empty. Over an hour after the race was formally called, Governor DeSoto finally called Senator Bradshaw to concede. The conversation couldn't have taken more than forty-five seconds, and Ben had to admit that she did sound stunned and shell-shocked. DeSoto had been a tireless campaigner, who Ben had respected for years; now, for the first time, she sounded tired. There was incredulity in her voice, too. She seemed to choose her words very carefully, as if she still didn't quite believe what she was saying. But she was cordial, and promised to help however she could, and that was that.

On the table next to him, Ben's mobile phone buzzed and glowed once again, shattering his peace. It was Lisa, his chief executive assistant. God love that woman, Ben thought, she should be either sleeping or partying like everyone else. He picked up the phone.

"Hello," he said quietly, his casual tone reflecting the many levels of intimacy that made up his and Lisa's longstanding relationship.

From the sound of her voice, she had indeed been sleeping. And probably partying before that.

"He's on his way up" was all she said. Ben winced.

"Who is?" he asked automatically, though he knew full well whom she meant.

"Liao," she said flatly, and he winced again. "They just called me. He came in through the kitchen and he's taking the service elevator up. I suggest you put on a tie."

"Thank you," he said automatically, his mind already racing. Then he added, with some warmth, "You should get some sleep." He heard her laugh quietly.

"Talking to you isn't helping, *Mr. President*," she said smoothly. *For God's sake, not now. Keep it together.*

Ben let himself chuckle contentedly, said good night, and pressed "End." He quickly reached over and flipped on a lamp, got up, and headed to the bathroom. At the sink he wet his hands and ran them through his hair and over his face. As he let the coolness wash over him, he looked into the mirror.

This is your chance, he thought. *You're about to be president of the United States. It's different now.*

At this meeting, he would set the tone for the next four to eight years, and tell Liao how it was going to be from now on. After all, Ben *was* going to be president; what could Liao do to him?

In the mirror, he watched his own face fall. He knew full well what Liao could do. Liao knew about everything. He knew about the parties and the women—in New York, Hong Kong, Macau, and God knew where else. He knew about Lisa. But even if the American public could forgive some extramarital dalliances—it had happened before—Liao also knew how much Chinese money was *really* tied up in the Bradshaw family manufacturing empire, which had given Ben his coveted "business" credentials as a candidate. The Party's finance ministry was basically floating whole divisions now.

No. Ben would have to listen to Liao, put his head down and get to work—as it had always been. *It was all for the best*, he told himself. After all, China's rise to power and prominence had accelerated over the last decade and showed no signs of slowing down. Their money was in everything. The American public was skeptical of their leaders openly cozying up to the Chinese, but it had to be done if America was to keep any standing on the world stage and keep its economy from tanking. Those in power understood that. So it would be done behind closed doors. It would be done by men like himself and Mr. Liao, meeting in the wee hours in darkened hotel suites.

President-elect Bradshaw popped open the pill bottle sitting next to the sink and tossed two caplets into his mouth. Just enough to get through this meeting. As he washed them down with the last of his scotch, he heard the first faint knocking at the door.

NOVEMBER 6, 2024
INTERSTATE 95, SOUTHBOUND
NEAR GREENWICH, CONNECTICUT
5:24 A.M.

The earliest traces of dawn were beginning to break, and found the black Lincoln speeding toward the New York border and Westchester County Airport. They were alone on the highway except for the occasional truck, and Liao Wu Lin had given the driver permission—orders, rather—to exceed the speed limit. They would not have any trouble with the police.

Liao had also given strict instructions about the temperature of the car, and now that it had reached the optimal level of warmth, he allowed himself to relax in the backseat. New England weather, especially in the fall and winter, had never agreed with him. If it had been up to him, he would have gone to Stanford for business school instead of Harvard, but Harvard was what Father, and Father's friends, had had in mind.

Had Liao not gone to Harvard Business School, of course, he never would have met Ben Bradshaw, his old friend who had just been elected president of the United States, and whom Liao had just come from congratulating. Ben Bradshaw, his old friend who barely made a move without Liao's knowledge. He had just fired off a short e-mail to Beijing, a preliminary report on the meeting, which had, of course, been fruitful. His e-mail was encrypted, but that hardly mattered: his country was years ahead of the U.S. in cyber-security measures. Liao had informed his superiors that the soon-to-be president had a good understanding of his administration's first priority: loosening restrictions on the export of missile technology. It was time for unfettered free trade in defense systems. That would be so much easier than having to steal them.

Liao sat back and marveled at how easy it all had been. How seamless. From the beginning, Liao's father, a colonel in the People's Liberation Army intelligence service, had wanted an international education for his son. Anglicizing his name to William Liao, they'd sent him to boarding school in Switzerland and then to Oxford for his undergraduate degree. He learned to move easily among the children of the world's rich and powerful, and when he returned home to visit, the young man enjoyed regaling his father with tales of their foibles and confessed secrets.

The colonel had picked up on his son's eye for detail, and before he left for Harvard Business School, he sat him down to dinner with a few of his old colleagues, and asked him to submit regular reports on his classmates. Liao readily agreed: it was what he had wanted all along. When Liao started sending back a number of reports on Ben Bradshaw, scion of the wealthy Connecticut industrial family, his father took notice. The directive changed: Make him yours. Make him ours.

That, as Liao had once heard in an American film, was the beginning of a beautiful friendship. He and Bradshaw went drinking together, and Liao let his affable but boorish classmate into his exclusive inner circle among the international students. Bradshaw joined Liao at extravagant parties in Manhattan nightclubs, on yachts, on private jets. Ben was hooked.

After graduation, they'd stayed in touch. Ben went to work for his father's company, as did Liao—after a fashion. He officially became an executive at a state-owned manufacturing conglomerate, where he was able to direct the slow takeover of the Bradshaw family companies, but continued his work for the People's Liberation Army intelligence. Ben Bradshaw was his only assignment. The parties continued, including many visits to properties controlled by Liao in Shanghai, Macau, and Hong Kong—with all of Bradshaw's activities duly photographed, of course. Most helpful during Ben's trips to China was the ability to download every shred of data from his mobile phone and laptop.

By the time Ben realized what was going on, it was too late. He had simply acquiesced: no ultimatum had to be given, no threats made. After all, Liao owned so much of Ben's business that they were partners already. Why not, Liao had suggested, become partners in another venture: politics?

The Senate campaign had been a trial run, and it had gone well. Money could be funneled from a number of different directions without attracting attention. Once elected, Ben proved himself loyal. They simply scaled up operations when the decision was made to seek the presidency. A super-PAC provided the ultimate funding solution. With the scaling-up process came its own challenges, however: he still shuddered slightly remembering the close call with the North Carolina bank.

Still, all in all, the mission was a success. Now he was going home for a well-earned rest and maybe some time spent puttering around in the garden with his aging father. As he felt himself beginning to doze, he chuckled once again at the name they'd chosen for Ben Bradshaw's super-PAC: Americans for a Fair Future. Well, at least the future would certainly be fair to China.

OCTOBER 17, 2025
EISENHOWER EXECUTIVE OFFICE BUILDING
WASHINGTON, D.C.
5:19 P.M.

Elsie Zimmerman nearly missed the tweet when it first appeared. She was understandably tired. The twenty-four-year-old White House communications assistant's day had begun at 4:00 that morning, when her two alarms woke her up to begin compiling the morning news clips e-mail to send around to the staff. She loved her job, loved her colleagues, loved working for President Bradshaw—sometimes she still couldn't believe her luck at landing this gig in the first place—but she had never quite gotten used to waking up at 4:00 a.m.

Her eyelids were heavy as she scanned the multiple columns of Twitter postings arrayed on her two computer screens at her cubicle in the EEOB's White House Communications War Room. But one tweet caught her eye just before it slipped out of the frame. It was from the media reporter at one of the inside-the-Beltway trade papers, the "Hill rags." It read:

Sources: NYT to report on suspected fraud in 2024 election

Election fraud? She knew Governor Marcia DeSoto's supporters had been tossing around fraud accusations in the press for months, but why was the *New York Times* now taking it seriously?

She scrolled through other tweets, looking for a reference to this story anywhere else. Moments later a new tweet appeared from the *New York Times* itself:

> Breaking: NYT confirms evidence of massive fraud in 2024 election, possible Chinese government links.

Elsie wanted to call out to the rest of the War Room, but her voice froze in her throat. With a trembling hand, she copied the tweet, pasted it into an e-mail, and sent it around to the rest of the staff.

OCTOBER 17, 2025
SUPREME COURT OF THE UNITED STATES
WASHINGTON, D.C.
6:25 P.M.

Jason Wallace was slipping his tablet computer into his bag and preparing to leave when he noticed the screen begin to glow. He flipped the cover open and saw the Breaking News Alert tweet displayed on the screen:

> NY Times Reports Fraud Confirmed in #Bradshaw Election

He pulled up Twitter and saw a flurry of tweets bearing the same message. He dropped the bag and ran from his desk, down the hallway toward the chambers of his boss, Chief Justice Albert Lang.

The chief justice raised his head from his hands as his clerk burst into his office. "Did you—" Jason began.

"Yes, I saw," the chief justice replied in his quiet drawl. He, like Jason, was a Kentucky native. At Harvard Law School, their shared alma mater, Lang had authored a famous article on tech start-ups for the law review, part of a lifelong tech fascination that continued to amaze his young clerk. Lang held up his mobile phone.

"I think it's breaking the Internet," he said wryly.

Jason looked down at his tablet again. "They posted the full story just now," he said quietly, and sat down in a chair opposite the desk. Silently, each focused on his own screen, Jason and his boss skimmed the story:

> The *New York Times* can independently confirm at least 336 individual instances of election fraud perpetrated in the 2024 campaign, indicating a far-reaching, coordinated effort centered around several chapters of the Americans for a Fair Future super-PAC . . .
>
> . . . incidents focused on swing states, including Pennsylvania, Ohio, North Carolina . . .
>
> . . . enough evidence exists to question the legitimacy of the 2024 presidential election . . .
>
> . . . dozens of constitutional law experts consulted by the *New York Times* all expressed shock and disbelief, and none were able to immediately suggest a course of action for this unprecedented development . . .
>
> . . . speculation continues to swirl around the involvement of William Liao, a Chinese businessman with substantial government and intelligence ties, with the Americans for a Fair Future operation . . .
>
> . . . White House officials had no comment as of press time . . .
>
> . . . attorneys for Gov. Marcia DeSoto, defeated by President Bradshaw last November, have said they intend to file multiple lawsuits as soon as possible.

Jason had almost reached the end when the phone on Lang's desk began to ring. Then his mobile phone went off. Then Jason felt his own phone buzzing in his pocket. He could hear other phones outside ringing as well. He looked at his boss. Lang's face was blank.

Amid the ringing and buzzing, the chief justice of the United States Supreme Court quietly said to his clerk: "I have no idea what to do."

Federal Bureau of Investigation Interim Report to the Director on Potential Chinese Involvement in the 2024 Presidential Election

January 8, 2025

SUMMARY: We are continuing to follow up on the disturbing findings by our financial section involving foreign contributions to a super-PAC operating in support of President-elect Benjamin Bradshaw's campaign. Pursuant to the directive issued by the office of D/FBI on December 14, we have kept this investigation entirely in-house and involved as few Bureau personnel as possible. Internal security is paramount, as information leaking out before evidence is collected could have national and international implications, the severity of which would be impossible to overstate. Below is an updated summary of what we know so far:

We can be reasonably certain that a payment was made from the First Smoky Mountain Bank branch in Raleigh by the North Carolina chapter of Americans for a Fair Future, a pro-Bradshaw super-PAC, using funds that originated in Shanghai, People's Republic of China, and were transferred via Capital Market Bank in New York. We have not, however, been able to find any specific receipt of this transaction, just references in other documents. Furthermore, we have not been able to identify the original Chinese source of the funding: the Shanghai account has disappeared from records entirely.

After finding evidence that pointed to the North Carolina transaction, we began further investigation of Americans for a Fair Future's sources of funding. We have since been able to tie a number of AFF's prominent donors to senior Chinese government or military officials via personal or business connections. A number of these associations were previously known to the Bureau—some were not—but in none of these cases have we been able to definitely identify these Americans' AFF contributions as having originated in China.

We are in the process of following up on several cases of voter fraud alleged to have been perpetrated by AFF units in a number of swing states, including Ohio, Virginia, North Carolina, and Nevada. Some of these allegations have been reported in the press but have been mostly dismissed as partisan agitating. Sources elsewhere in DOJ suggest this is the Department's view as well and that no fraud charges will be filed. Our internal task force, however, believes they may be linked and may be part of a larger AFF effort to commit strategic, easily obscured voter fraud.

Investigation into the inner workings of AFF has proven difficult. Almost immediately after the election, it appears that all hard drives, mobile devices, and even flash drives were confiscated from employees and either wiped or destroyed. We have a cyber-recovery team working to pull any data that may be left on external servers, but access to those appears to be blocked by several layers of security.

We have identified a person of interest: Liao Wu Lin, also known as William Liao. A high-ranking executive at Sheng Holdings, a state-controlled manufacturing and import-export operation, Liao holds both U.S. and Chinese passports and is known to have close ties to Chinese security services through his father, a retired PLA colonel. Liao's father graduated from the PLA National Defense University with Gen. Xi Yuming, current head of Chinese military intelligence, and Xi is known to be a close friend of the family. Liao attended Harvard Business School with Benjamin Bradshaw, and the two are known to have a personal relationship.

A recent piece of evidence has emerged from a source within the Secret Service, which was able to partially download data from President-elect Bradshaw's official and personal mobile phones as well as his personal laptop. All three devices show signs of having been compromised in the recent past on several different occasions. Furthermore, the digital fingerprints left behind heavily suggest the use of technology known to be in the arsenal of PLA hacking units.

It is our preliminary assessment that the President-elect of the United States has—wittingly or not—been compromised by agents acting on behalf of the Chinese government. Furthermore, we believe it highly likely that the 2024 election was heavily influenced by foreign—specifically Chinese—political contributions and thus may have been invalid.

If these allegations are correct, this country risks nothing less than a Constitutional crisis unlike any in our history. The White House, despite several attempts, has not been involved in this investigation. We can release our findings directly to the media, or we can approach the White House first. There is no precedent for this situation. As such, we await the Director's guidance.

★★★

Could It Really Happen?

The idea of a foreign nation exerting influence over the American electoral process is not at all far-fetched, and if any country could pull it off, it would be the People's Republic of China. They've tried it before. From the point of view of this former prosecutor, they have the means and the motive to carry out just such a plan. For one thing, their worldwide intelligence network, along with interconnected state-owned businesses with international presence, give the Chinese government and military a significant clandestine reach.

Why, though, would they need to influence the election directly? After all, China is already one of the largest foreign holders of American debt: we currently owe the Chinese some $1.2 trillion.[1] But the Chinese will do what's best for business. Owning American debt does not automatically translate to influence over American policy toward China or the rest of the world. It would be infinitely easier to have a hand in, or at least keep tabs on, American foreign relations by directly influencing those in power, which the Chinese have a record of doing.

Easier still, however, would be directly helping China-friendly politicians gain or keep power using the most valuable weapon around: money. That's just what high-ranking Chinese officials attempted to do in the 1996 election. Through various intermediaries, money from China made its way to Democratic campaigns, including the reelection effort of President Bill Clinton. I should know: as a federal prosecutor in the Department of Justice's Public Integrity Section in the Criminal Division, I was assigned to the case as part of the department's Campaign Finance Task Force.

Looking back on that case, I find it especially disturbing to think about what happened then and what's happening now.

China and the 1996 Election

It is difficult to say with absolute certainty where and when this story begins. The first public indication that something had gone awry came in a *Los Angeles Times* article on September 21,

1996, which reported that the Democratic National Committee had returned $250,000 from a South Korean national whom DNC officials had personally invited to a Clinton fund-raising event.[2] Some months later China entered the picture when Bob Woodward and Brian Duffy at the *Washington Post* reported that the Chinese embassy in Washington had been a center for coordinating Chinese donations to the Democrats.[3]

Where the Chinese plan originated is still a matter of discussion. However, the most prominent tip of this iceberg was one particular Democratic fund-raiser: a man named Johnny Chung.

Johnny Chung was known as a "hustler."[4] Originally from Taiwan, Chung was a U.S. citizen,[5] an engineer by training who in the 1990s was living and working in California. He had started a company that sent "blast faxes"—the electronic "spam" of the nineties—but by 1994 his business was in trouble. Not only did it bring in less than $20,000 that year, but Chung's investors had decided to take him to court.[6]

It was time for Chung to make some new friends, so he decided to step up his political activity. In August of 1994, he—or rather his company—donated $11,000 to the Democratic National Committee.[7] That may well have attracted some attention, because that same month Chung was invited by a Department of Commerce official to join a trade mission to China. There he met officials of both the Chinese and U.S. governments, including then–commerce secretary Ron Brown. He also met the wife of Yah Lin "Charlie" Trie, another Democratic donor and longtime friend of the Clintons who would also surface in this investigation.

Between 1994 and 1996, Johnny Chung's political stock soared. The *Washington Post* later reported that he visited the White House nearly fifty times between February 1994 and February 1996 and was a regular at Democratic fund-raisers.[8] He portrayed himself to Chinese businesspeople as someone who could get them access to the highest levels of government.[9]

He was able to sustain that reputation. Chung got executives from a Chinese beer company into the 1994 White House Christmas party, where they had their picture taken with the Clintons. Later, in March 1995, he brought several Chinese guests to the

White House to meet Hillary Clinton and have lunch in the White House mess—after he forked over $50,000 to one of the first lady's aides.[10] About this particularly expensive Washington lunch, Chung would later say: "I see the White House is like a subway—you have to put in coins to open the gates."[11]

In 1996, however, Johnny Chung's "hustling" took a far more sinister turn. That year, in Hong Kong, he met Liu Chaoying. Liu was about as well connected to the Chinese political, industrial, and military establishment as one could get. She was a high-ranking executive at China Aerospace International Holdings, which was, of course, run by the Chinese government. Her father, Liu Huaqing, was China's top-ranking general and a member of the Politburo, whose military career had included commanding the People's Liberation Army forces involved in the Tiananmen Square massacre in 1989.[12] Liu Chaoying herself was a colonel in the PLA.[13] As the *Washington Post* explained:

> In many ways, Liu is typical of the favored sons and daughters of China's top political and military families, known as taizidang or princelings. They capitalize on their connections based on their family ties to prosper in the business world, and businesses, in turn, are eager to have them in their management because they can open doors.[14]

At the time she met with Chung, Liu was not only working for China Aerospace but also owned 99 percent of Marswell Investment Limited, a company formed in Hong Kong the previous year. Marswell's actual purpose was obscure, but most of its top executives, including Liu, were shared with China Aerospace.

Chung and Liu must have hit it off in their first meeting; they certainly recognized the value in each other's connections. By the summer of 1996, Chung was throwing his weight around in order to help bring Liu to the United States. He helped get her a visa by putting in a word with the American consulate in Hong Kong. Chung also contacted the DNC to get Liu into an elite Clinton fund-raising event in Los Angeles, where she would end up meeting the president. But these were not simply goodwill gestures.

After Liu received her visa, $190,000 of unknown origin arrived in one of Chung's bank accounts. Shortly after Chung contacted the DNC on Liu's behalf, he followed up by sending the committee $45,000 from that same account.[15]

After her successful visit to Los Angeles, which included a photo op with the president of the United States, Liu and Chung officially went into business together. A U.S. branch of Marswell Investment, Liu's Hong Kong company, was established in California in August 1996. The paperwork was filed by Marswell's vice president, Johnny Chung. Liu Chaoying was the company's president. After that, more money from Hong Kong was deposited in Chung's accounts.[16] At least some of that money is thought to have come from Chinese intelligence sources and was intended to influence the 1996 election.

We know about the Chinese intelligence connection because in 1998 Chung, who was caught in the middle of congressional and Justice Department investigations into fund-raising improprieties in the last election, decided to plead guilty and cooperate. Federal investigators, and later Congress and the public, learned a great deal about China's machinations from his subsequent statements. I learned a lot myself.

I was the lead prosecutor in the Johnny Chung case. Chung testified that Liu Chaoying had set up a meeting for the two of them with General Ji Shengde, head of Chinese military intelligence. To test this claim—which was certainly not implausible, given Liu's network of contacts through her father—we had presented Chung with a number of photographs of Chinese officials and asked him to identify the man he had met with. The director of China's military intelligence service is not generally a well-known, publicly identified figure, but Chung picked out General Ji's picture immediately. He even correctly identified photographs of the general taken several years apart.

Chung stated in sworn congressional testimony that General Ji told him, "We really like your President." The general added, "We hope to see him re-elected. I will give you 300,000 U.S. dollars. You can give it to the President and the Democratic Party."[17] This meeting occurred on August 11, 1996, the same month that

Liu and Chung set up the U.S. office of Marswell Investment, whose parent company in Hong Kong was itself likely an offshoot of state-run China Aerospace.

That same month, the cash was deposited in Johnny Chung's Hong Kong bank account. Chung maintained that the initial source of this deposit was Chinese intelligence, funneled through Liu.[18] The People's Republic of China, of course, attempted to block our access to this account to investigate. But Chung signed a release for his bank records, and upon investigating we discovered some key evidence: the deposit receipt from Liu Chaoying. Portions of this money went to Democratic campaigns in 1996, including the reelection effort of President Clinton, who Chinese intelligence clearly said they "really like."

After the controversy erupted, Chung's contributions were eventually returned. But the fact remained that the funding pipeline had been successfully set up. Because of Chung's cooperation, we had the first concrete evidence of Chinese attempts to influence the American political process. Liu Chaoying and China Aerospace vehemently denied any part in the process—naturally—and the Chinese foreign ministry called the allegations "sheer fabrication."[19]

There were, however, other threads that indicated a wider conspiracy uncovered in our investigation that were not pursued at the time. This was mostly due to bureaucratic hurdles resulting from a "wall" that prevented the sharing of information between the criminal and intelligence sides of the Department of Justice at the time. I would try to follow up on China-related leads with my opposite number on the intelligence side, Jim "JJ" Smith, the FBI's top foreign counterintelligence agent in Los Angeles, but because of the wall that was in place, there wasn't much he could give me. The wall prevented the criminal side from pursuing some promising leads.

Among the many changes that followed in the wake of the 9/11 attacks were the bureaucratic adjustments made as the government came to better understand the terrorist menace faced by the nation. The DOJ came to the conclusion that easier information sharing between their criminal and intelligence divisions would better help connect the dots in terrorism investigations—as the 9/11 Commission recommended—so the wall between the sections came down. But during the Chung case in the late 1990s it was still very much in place.

Interestingly enough, it's possible that information on our investigation was flowing in the other direction—potentially thanks to JJ Smith. Some years later, in 2003, Smith was indicted by his own Department of Justice. Counterintelligence work against China had always been Smith's main focus, but he apparently got a little too close to his work. It turned out that he had carried on a twenty-year affair with one of his "assets," a Chinese-American businesswoman named Katrina Leung. Leung was supposed to be providing intelligence on the Chinese government to Smith, but at the same time she used her association with him to collect sensitive information for her other handlers in China. At the time that JJ Smith was working on the Chung case from the intelligence angle—while I was handling the criminal side—he was in the midst of an affair with a woman working for the Chinese government.[20]

Someone did try to pressure Chung not to cooperate with federal authorities. He was approached during the investigation by an individual claiming a connection to Liu Chaoying who advised him not to discuss his dealings with General Ji.[21] This individual presented to Chung what the *Los Angeles Times* would later call "a carrot and a stick": Chung was offered a bribe if he kept quiet but threatened if he continued to cooperate.[22] Chung was induced to go to prison rather than keep working with investigators. This individual promised that he would have influential help. He even brought up the possibility of an eventual pardon from the president himself.[23]

Furthermore, the individual was making reports back to high-ranking military officers in China. My recommendation was to bring charges of obstruction of justice against this individual. But the matter was soon reassigned to the U.S. Attorney's Office in Los Angeles and therefore was out of my jurisdiction. Shortly thereafter, I returned to the Public Integrity Section in DOJ's Criminal Division. No charges were ever brought against the individual who tried to intimidate Johnny Chung, and who had possible links to the Chinese government.

But later threats against Chung were still taken very seriously. The FBI was concerned enough at one point to move the entire Chung family into federal protective custody, hiding them in a succession of Los Angeles-area hotels for a twenty-one-day period in May and June of 1998.[24] One of Chung's daughters had to be accompanied to her high school graduation rehearsal by a federal agent.[25] During this time, the FBI was monitoring the activities of several Chinese travelers in Southern California, concerned that at least some of them may have been assassins targeting Chung— but no attack materialized.[26]

Through Johnny Chung's cooperation, we were able to establish a connection between the Chinese government and efforts to help President Clinton win the 1996 election. When Chung was sentenced following his guilty plea, the judge took his extensive cooperation into consideration and gave him a lesser sentence.

There were indictments filed against other individuals with Chinese connections as well. Yah Lin "Charlie" Trie, the Clinton friend and donor from Arkansas whose wife met with Chung during his trip to China with the Commerce Department, was found to have gone to Beijing and actively solicited $1 million for political activities from people in the Chinese government. Trie's accounts would receive more than $1 million in wire transfers from an associate in Macau who had links to Chinese officials,[27] but no concrete connection was established. Trie's contributions to the DNC and to President Clinton's legal defense fund—which totaled about $1 million—were returned.[28] Trie initially fled to China but eventually returned to the U.S. and pled guilty to one felony and one misdemeanor.

Another individual, John Huang, also had ties going back to the Clintons' days in Arkansas, having first met then-governor Clinton in Little Rock in 1980.[29] Huang had worn many hats: American director for the Indonesia-based Lippo Group, official in the Clinton Commerce Department, and professional fund-raiser at the Democratic National Committee. Huang would later plead guilty to guiding illegal campaign contributions from his former Lippo colleagues, but his dealings with Chinese officials also came to light. Huang was recorded discussing political donations with staff at the Chinese consulate in Los Angeles,[30] but his money was never traced directly back to the Chinese government.

The strongest link was still Johnny Chung and his connections to Liu Chaoying—daughter of the most powerful general in China—and the director of Chinese intelligence, General Ji Shengde. An American intermediary was given money by one of the highest-ranking officials in the Chinese government with the intent of seeing it land in President Clinton's reelection war chest.

Our investigation of Chung proved the official connection, and we tried to widen the probe. During the course of the investigation, it appeared that Chung was linked to a wider circle of intelligence operatives. But again, because of the wall between the criminal and intelligence divisions at DOJ, our efforts to expand the inquiry into the so-called China Plan were frustrated. There were some calls for an independent counsel—even the FBI director, Louis Freeh, wrote in 1997 that he found it "difficult to imagine a more compelling situation for appointing an independent counsel"—but no such counsel was ever appointed.[31]

A report issued by the Senate Committee on Government Affairs in 1998 suggested that focus on political goals led to carelessness. This report found numerous fund-raising irregularities perpetrated by Democrats in the 1996 elections. "In the frenzied drive to raise such large amounts of campaign money," it stated, "the Democratic Party dismantled its own internal vetting procedures, no longer caring, in effect, where its money came from and who was supplying it."[32]

Another, more simple question was: Why? What did the Chinese hope to gain from trying to tip the scales in an American election? As it turns out, their goals may have reflected the interconnected nature of business and politics in China's heavily state-subsidized economy.

"Clinton Coup" Parts I and II

In his first presidential campaign in 1992, Bill Clinton notably took a tough line on China. He blasted President George H. W. Bush for being too soft on those whom Clinton called "the butchers of Beijing."[33] He had made several trips to China's nemesis nation, Taiwan, during his tenure as Arkansas governor and went on to invite Chinese dissidents to the White House in his first term.[34] But the Chinese government would not be easily dissuaded: they began a concerted effort to use their intelligence services to work toward changing Clinton's mind.

Beijing began by identifying Clinton administration officials who were in favor of more engagement with China, including high-ranking individuals on the president's economic team, the Department of the Treasury, and National Security Adviser Tony Lake himself.[35] Once the targets were pinpointed, the influence offensive began. Business interests friendly to China were enlisted to help.[36] The efforts paid off: by late 1993, the administration was already shifting to a more pro-China stance. The Chinese reportedly call this "the Clinton coup."[37]

If the Chinese had been successful in their "Clinton coup" by leaning on the president's own advisers, it is not difficult to imagine their desire to maintain this good relationship with Washington by keeping the now-friendly president in office. That could explain a very high-ranking Chinese official telling an American donor in 1996: "We really like your President." Chinese intelligence had worked hard to leverage sympathetic staff in the Clinton administration; it was to their advantage to keep these people in their jobs for the upcoming term. Donating to their boss, the president, would help ensure that.

But there was another angle to the 1996 efforts: an attempt at a second "Clinton coup." The Chinese were also after American technology, including rocket systems. And they attempted to insert themselves into our political process in order to obtain it any way they could, from influencing trade policy to actively swiping government documents.

At the center of this, Liu Chaoying emerges once again. She

worked for China Aerospace, which benefited from a friendly—
and controversial—Clinton administration trade policy toward
China. In March 1996, for instance, five months before Liu went
into business with Johnny Chung, the Department of Commerce made a decision to ease some restrictions on the use of
Chinese technology to launch American satellites. This was good
for China Aerospace.[38] In addition to working with Liu to fun-
nel money from Chinese intelligence and set up a subsidiary of
her China Aerospace–linked company, Marswell, in California,
Johnny Chung also sought to get her meetings with American
aerospace executives during her visits to the United States.[39] Liu,
General Ji Shengde, and others in China's defense community may
have thought of political donations as extra insurance to maintain
friendly trade policies.

Another connection to the Commerce Department was John
Huang, the Commerce official turned DNC fund-raiser. While at
Commerce, Huang got hold of secret government documents and
hid them away in a safe in his office. The topic? Exporting American defense technology to the Chinese.[40]

China has and will continue to have a great deal to gain by
maintaining an influence over American policy. The Chinese see
the United States as a major obstacle on their path to global su-
perpower status, and want to neutralize our ability to stand up to
them as much as possible. They've shown willingness and ability
to influence the American political process before: What better
way to do it than holding sway over the president themselves?

What Can We Do to Stop This?

From the point of view of this author and former federal prosecutor, we should be concerned about a direct Chinese threat to
our democracy, as well as the instability that would result when
an investigation into foreign influence on a presidential election
undermines public confidence in our institutions. If we are going
to protect our political process against foreign interference, this
needs to be considered as part of a broader strategy of counterbal-
ancing China's influence. Despite a much-hyped "pivot" toward

Asia in its foreign policy, the Obama administration has avoided standing up to China, which in turn only seems to have emboldened Beijing.

A new administration could improve on these policies by following some basic guidelines when dealing with China:

WORK WITH OUR ALLIES TO RESTORE ORDER IN THE SOUTH CHINA SEA. Chinese aggression in the South China Sea will continue to be a flashpoint in U.S.-China relations. China has carried out a campaign of churning out artificial islands in disputed territory, some of which could serve military purposes. They have "reclaimed" thousands of acres, threatening the delicate balance of power in the region.[41] Yet, President Obama offered only an anemic, noncommittal observation that made sure to praise the Chinese for good measure:

> And the truth is, is that China is going to be successful. It's big, it's powerful, its people are talented and they work hard. And it may be that some of their claims are legitimate, but they shouldn't just try to establish that based on throwing elbows and pushing people out of the way. If, in fact, their claims are legitimate, people will recognize them.[42]

Secretary of Defense Ash Carter has taken a slightly harder line, calling for "an immediate and lasting halt to land reclamation by all claimants,"[43] but the Chinese military was still invited to participate in the "Rim of the Pacific" (RIMPAC) multinational military exercise in 2016, giving them a chance to size up the forces of not only the United States but of many of their Asian neighbors who are already threatened by Chinese territorial encroachments.[44] We need to show China that if it can't play by the rules, it will not be treated as an equal partner in the Pacific community. Already nervous about falling under Chinese domination, our Southeast Asian allies should be reassured of America's commitment to standing with them. We should continue to project naval power in the region and increase engagement with joint naval exercises and more port visits with known allies in the region. Making sure we have a strong enough navy to accomplish this is paramount.

TAKE A FIRM LINE AGAINST ALL FORMS OF CHINESE SPYING AGAINST AMER-ICA. The Chinese intelligence network is massive, and includes a significant presence here in the United States. As just one recent example, six Chinese citizens, including three college professors, were arrested in May 2015 on charges of economic espionage. Two of the professors met while conducting research in California funded by the Defense Advanced Research Projects Agency (DARPA) and went on to steal technological secrets from American companies for whom they later worked and passed them on to their government.[45] Assistant Attorney General for National Security John P. Carlin describes the situation as "powerful, dedicated nation-state activity focused on our private sector with the goal of stealing as much as they can"—and economic espionage like this is estimated to cost hundreds of billions of dollars every year.[46] But the Chinese aren't just out to steal trade secrets: they've also gone after individuals. In an operation that was at one point code-named "Dancing Panda," Chinese hackers broke into the private e-mail accounts of U.S. government officials. This is known to have occurred around the time that then–secretary of state Hillary Clinton was conducting most of her business on a private e-mail account.[47] But that was minor compared to the hack attack on the Office of Personnel Management disclosed in the spring of 2015, in which over twenty-two million Americans had their personal data compromised. China has been identified as the perpetrator, but the Obama administration still refuses to publicly acknowledge this.[48] If we can't stand up to Chinese spying in cyberspace, how can we be expected to stand up to them on the world stage? A good first step toward protecting against Chinese spying is publicly holding them accountable.

RECOGNIZE CHINA'S REFUSAL TO PLAY BY ECONOMIC RULES. China has continued to flex its economic muscles as well as military ones, and is attempting to circumvent the United States in this arena as well. Their initiative to establish the Asian Infrastructure Investment Bank is a clear attempt to spread China's economic power as a counterweight to America's.[49] Even our allies are on board: Britain, South Korea, Germany, and others all joined the AIIB over American objections, calling into question the Obama administration's influence when it comes to checking China's economic expansion. But Beijing's worst fiscal offense is their currency manipulation, which has allowed their yuan to rise 33 percent[50] against the U.S. dollar over the last ten years, benefiting their own economy while costing American jobs.[51] But President Obama has not seen fit to even call out the Chinese for their obvious currency manipulation. The next president of the United States should make clear that all countries should respect the global economic rules of the game.

BE CAREFUL OF CHINESE MONEY CIRCLING AROUND U.S. POLITICS. What Johnny Chung attempted to do on behalf of the Chinese government was blatantly illegal, and he was caught and convicted. The Federal Election Commission is very clear that "it is unlawful to knowingly provide substantial assistance to foreign nationals making contributions or donations in connection with any U.S. election," including serving as "conduits or intermediaries," as Chung did.[52] But there are other ways for the Chinese to curry favor with American politicians without making direct political contributions. For instance, the Chinese seem to have remained on excellent terms with the Clintons. Former president Bill Clinton received $200,000 to speak at a conference sponsored in part by Chinese government agencies in October of 2011, while his wife was in the midst of unveiling the Obama administration's plan to "pivot" toward the Pacific.[53] The Clinton Foundation—which has come under fire over contributions from foreign governments—received a pledge of $2 million from a single Chinese company, Rilin Enterprises, in 2013. Rilin's head, Wang Wenliang, is a member of China's legislature and has close links with the government.[54] Another Chinese billionaire, Yan Jiehe, founder of the China Pacific Construction Group, paid Bill Clinton $550,000 for a speaking engagement in Shanghai[55] and has donated between

$250,001 and $500,000 to the foundation.[56] Yan, whose office, according to Bloomberg News, is located "in a military compound that's separated by a wall from the Communist Party's top training center," has confidently predicted Hillary Clinton's success in 2016, claiming: "Hillary Clinton will become the next president, there's no one in the U.S. who could compete with her." She will be "friendly" to China, Yan said.[57] It's not hard to hear in this echoes of General Ji Shengde's "We really like your President" comment about her husband in 1996. But the Clinton case brings up a serious issue. It is important to make sure that Chinese or other foreign donations to charities—especially those with already spotty records of disclosure—do not find their way into funding presidential campaigns. The advent of super-PACs in today's elections makes for additional avenues of funding, and we must make sure these as well as traditional campaign fund-raising efforts stay free of foreign contributions.

4

Black Friday

Massacre at the Mall of America

MINNEAPOLIS, MINNESOTA
FRIDAY, APRIL 24, 2020
7:17 P.M.

Omar Othman Ali was not a devout Muslim. Not yet. His faith was important to him, but not *that* important. He didn't pray five times a day. He had no plans to make a pilgrimage to Mecca. And he did not fast during Ramadan, the holiest month of the year, which was beginning today.

However, Omar was a believer. Sure, he figured there's probably a God. And sure, Muhammad was his prophet. Might as well believe in something. And might as well follow the faith of his parents, who had left war-torn Somalia for the United States while his mother was pregnant with him a quarter century ago. But if Omar had to describe himself, he'd probably identify as a Minnesota Vikings fan before he'd think to identify as a Muslim.

As Omar walked aimlessly through the mosque on this Friday evening—his parents had taken him to prayers for the first day of Ramadan since he was a child, and he kept up the tradition—he ran into an old friend from Roosevelt High School.

"Omar," said Abukar. *"Salaam Alaykum."*

"Wa-Alaykum," replied Omar, without enthusiasm. He wasn't used to the traditional Arabic greeting, but he remembered that Abukar had always been something of a zealot. Back at Roosevelt,

he had studied Arabic, quoted verses from the Koran, and complained to anyone who'd listen about the blasphemy of Western movies, music, and clothing.

"Where are you going?" asked Abukar.

"Just heading home," said Omar. Home was a studio apartment in Minneapolis's Cedar-Riverside neighborhood that Omar paid for—barely—by driving a taxicab. With fourteen thousand residents of Somali background, Cedar-Riverside, popularly known as Little Mogadishu, hosted the largest concentration of Somali-Americans in the United States.

"Why don't you join us for a movie?" said Abukar, with excitement. Omar wasn't sure who "us" were. "You'll be sorry if you miss it," Abukar added. "And it's about to start." When Omar hesitated, his face full of skepticism, Abukar said, "It's only forty minutes. Just down the hall. What do you have to lose?"

Back in high school, Omar wouldn't have even considered Abukar's invitation. Back then, Omar had been "one of the cool kids": he'd been busy and usually surrounded by friends. But times had changed. Omar was frequently bored, from both driving the cab for loud, obnoxious Minneapolis conventioneers and spending his quiet hours at home. He had few friends now, and he often felt directionless. Now, all of a sudden, here was Abukar, promising at least a bit of a reprieve from his boredom, as well as some human company—maybe even the prospect of friendship. Omar figured, *Why not see what Abukar's so excited about?*

SANTA CLAUS, INDIANA
SUNDAY, APRIL 26, 2020
2:04 P.M.

The Voyage was the reason Bryan had driven Anthony the three hundred miles from their home in Peoria to Holiday World, the most famous (and only famous) tourist attraction in Santa Claus, Indiana. Holiday World boasted the best wooden roller coaster in America—the Voyage—and Anthony had been begging his dad for months for a trip to the theme park.

"Are you sure you're not scared of it?" Bryan teased his son. He knew the answer. Anthony was a roller coaster junkie. He had been only six years old when his dad took him to the Six Flags in Gurnee, Illinois. Anthony had loved everything about it, except for the height limits on the roller coasters. Now that he was—barely—forty-eight inches tall, he was determined to ride any and every rollercoaster he could find.

It had taken five hours to drive from Peoria to Santa Claus. And it meant Bryan would have to use one of his vacation days for the trip back tomorrow.

But Bryan would do anything for his son.

Especially today. His birthday.

MINNEAPOLIS, MINNESOTA
SUNDAY, APRIL 26, 2020
11:47 P.M.

The movie had made an impression on Omar. Quite an impression. So had the battle scars and war stories Abukar shared from his time in Somalia. Omar dreamed about the heroes of the movie on Friday night. He spent most of Saturday searching online for more information about its protagonists. And he returned to the mosque on Saturday evening, not just to pray, but to look for Abukar, whom he had found.

Friday night's movie had profiled three Somali-American jihadists from the Twin Cities. It was called *Minnesota's Martyrs: The Path to Paradise.* The film, which Abukar explained was made in 2013 and was hugely popular in certain social media circles, followed the three jihadists from Minnesota to training camps in Somalia, and then finally to their deaths. One had studied engineering at the University of Minnesota. Another had gone to Omar's high school, Roosevelt High. They were among the dozens of Minnesotan Muslims who had joined the Harakat al-Shabaab al-Mujahedeen, a Somalia-based terrorist organization allied with Al Qaeda and determined to create an Islamist caliphate in East Africa. And they appeared to be having a good time doing it. "This is the real Disneyland," one of the film's subjects had said into the camera. "You need to come here and join us!"

Omar wasn't ready to join the hundreds of foreign recruits fighting alongside the thousands of Somalis in al-Shabaab. But he was intrigued. All day Sunday he immersed himself in Shabaab's social media postings from the past weeks, months, and years. He had always assumed that jihadists were backward, living in the Stone Age, holed up in caves and swinging on monkey bars at desert training camps a thousand miles away from the nearest Internet connection. But, to Omar's surprise, Shabaab was extremely active on social media. They boasted a sophisticated media operation whose material was entertaining and inspiring.

Reading tweets and blog entries dating back more than ten years, Omar laughed as al-Shabaab taunted their Somali and African Union enemies. "Your inexperienced boys flee from confrontation & flinch in the face of death," said one tweet. Another boasted, "Europe was in darkness when Islam made advances in physics, Maths, astronomy, architecture, etc." In response to a threat by Somalia's transitional government to bomb suspicious donkey caravans, al-Shabaab jabbed, "Your eccentric battle strategy has got animal right groups quite concerned."

Why did he think this was funny? Omar never imagined himself caring much about a war halfway around the world, much less laughing at jokes the soldiers made about it. But something about what he was reading on the al-Shabaab sites spoke to him. He wasn't quite sure just how, but something within him had stirred. Yes, he had stuck to his daily diet of Vikings fan blogs while surfing the Internet that boring Sunday, but somehow he always found himself switching back to the al-Shabaab pages. Maybe he was starting to feel that connection with his homeland his parents had always talked about. Maybe the men he read about really were the ones who were going to save that country. He could see why they wanted to be part of such a grand design.

It was the videos that captivated Omar the most. He found a large number of videos like *Minnesota's Martyrs*, each well produced, with exciting footage, charismatic personalities, and inspiring music. The videos, like the tweets and blogs, were usually in English, designed to appeal to donors and potential recruits in the United States, particularly in American cities like Minneapolis with large numbers of Somali-Americans. None of the videos mentioned that in the 1990s and early 2000s, before graduating to bigger and higher-profile acts of terrorism, al-Shabaab made a name for itself by stoning women, sawing off hands for minor violations of Sharia law, and keeping food away from starving victims of a famine that killed tens of thousands of Somalis, most of them Muslim.

BEFORE Omar knew it, the clock on his laptop said, MON 2:47 AM. Time had flown. But Omar wasn't ready for bed. He had just found another way to connect to al-Shabaab. It was a more direct way to communicate with the men he was so quickly beginning to admire. And it was a far more dangerous step than any he had taken since running into Abukar on Friday evening.

Omar pulled up one of al-Shabaab's most active Twitter accounts, the one that shared the best stories and articles from the front lines of the war. Omar opened up the Direct Message box, typed "hey - do u know where i can read any more?" and pressed Send. No harm in seeing what would happen, he thought.

As it turned out, he didn't have long to wait. He brushed his teeth, got ready for bed, and paused to check his computer one last time, when he noticed his Twitter message had received a reply. The al-Shabaab account had written: "Glad to help brother - follow this link. Then we can talk more." Omar clicked on it and was taken to another site with download instructions for TOR, a different kind of Web browser that promised to be more secure.

The download was easy, fast, and free. A few minutes later, another message from Twitter appeared: some search terms. Within a few clicks, Omar had found and joined an Internet chat room frequented by al-Shabaab propagandists and potential recruits. Too excited to think about sleep, Omar immediately set up a profile under a nom de guerre, one he took from a nearly decade-old movie in which a Somali pirate tells Tom Hanks's character, a captured American sailor, "I'm the captain now."

"Hi," he typed. "Salaam Alaykum." Then he paused before adding, with a flourish reflecting a confidence and purpose unimaginable just a few days ago, "They call me the Captain."

TAMPA, FLORIDA
SATURDAY, DECEMBER 26, 2020
8:12 P.M.

Anthony could still remember his mom, although sometimes he wasn't sure if the happy image of her warm smile and blond hair came from the countless hours he spent with her before the car crash, or from the photographs his dad kept all over their house.

It had been nearly five years since her death—almost as much time without her as he had been with her. And there wasn't a night, alone in his bed in a darkness broken only by his Batman night-light, that he didn't think of his mom. She was so smart, Daddy always said. And so much fun. And although she hadn't planned to leave them—hadn't planned to be run off the interstate by a drunk driver—she had left Anthony in good hands.

Anthony's dad was an amazing parent. Every hour Bryan wasn't working on the factory line, he spent it with Anthony—coaching Little League, going to superhero movies, and, whenever possible, traveling to theme parks for roller coasters. They had no extended family. And although Anthony had plenty of friends, Bryan didn't. Certainly no best friend. And certainly no girlfriend. Anthony was not just his son; he was his life.

Every Christmas vacation since the accident, Anthony and his dad had spent a couple of days at a theme park. This year's destination was the farthest they've ever trekked—the first to require a plane flight. Busch Gardens in Tampa, Florida. Home to the Scorpion, Montu, Kumba, Cheetah Hunt, and, at twenty stories tall and reaching speeds of seventy miles per hour, the scariest coaster of them all, SheiKra.

Anthony knew that his love of roller coasters wasn't shared by his dad, who, Anthony suspected, might even be slightly afraid of heights. But what Anthony didn't know was that his dad enjoyed their trips to theme parks as much, maybe even more, than Anthony did.

Nothing in the world made Bryan happier than seeing his son have fun.

SOUTHERN SOMALIA
SATURDAY, JANUARY 16, 2021
11:34 A.M.

The cost of Omar's flight to Mogadishu had been funded through the donations of Minneapolis's Somali-American community, who believed Abukar and his associates when they said the money would pay for famine relief work. Abukar had even arranged for a fake itinerary that Omar showed his parents and described to his neighbors in Cedar-Riverside. They thought he was visiting cousins he'd found online, using money he'd made driving his cab.

Omar's real destination was a training camp several hundred miles southwest of Mogadishu. His job there was straightforward: to learn how best to place and detonate a roadside bomb. Load and fire an automatic rifle until he could do it with his eyes closed. Become comfortable with the other weapons of choice among al-Shabaab fighters: grenades, mortars, surface-to-air missiles, and car bombs.

He had a chance to put these skills into practice, too, and not just in skirmishes with African Union soldiers in Somalia. Al-Shabaab was on friendly terms with a number of Al Qaeda–aligned militant groups in Syria. So, to give their new recruits a taste of real action, Omar and others were packed up and sent on a trip to the front lines of the jihad.

They took a circuitous route, flying first to Egypt, then traveling by boat across the Mediterranean to Greece. From Greece they crossed into Turkey, and from Turkey they were able to slip into northern Syria. The senior al-Shabaab men who accompanied them said this was one of several indirect routes they used to get to the front: the more complicated your route, the harder you were to track.

Omar met brothers from all over the world during his short tour in Syria. He made friends from France, Britain, Belgium, Germany, even a number of other Americans. Nothing about your background mattered—not race, not country, just commitment to Allah. It was the camaraderie among this international group that sustained Omar through his only real moment of crisis on the trip—just after they ambushed members of a rival militant faction, some so-called moderates supposedly trained by Americans. For U.S.-trained fighters, they turned and ran awfully easily. Still, when Omar fired at their pickup as it drove away, and saw one of them slump forward and tumble from the bed, he had a moment of doubt, a moment of weakness. But his friends congratulated him, and feted him that night. "First blood," they said. Now he was truly a member of their family.

When Omar thought back to the days before he ran into Abukar at the mosque—before the movie; before the chat rooms; before the safe houses in Mogadishu; before the stretch of nearly impassible roads out of the city and into the desert—he couldn't believe how different his life had once been. The once-friendless cabdriver was now a holy warrior surrounded by hundreds of comrades. He also had a target for his newfound zeal: the enemies of Islam.

Hate was what drove Omar forward now. It was an emotion that had been unfamiliar to him before he entered this world, but he realized he had only been blind to its power. His life before had been listless, boring, devoid of almost any emotion at all. Things had merely rolled off his back. But what had put him over the edge was the discovery, thanks to al-Shabaab, that he had an enormous capacity for hatred. Hatred for those who threatened his family's homeland of Somalia, and hatred for those who slandered his God and Prophet around the world.

In the nine months since he first watched *Minnesota's Martyrs*, Omar had learned to hate those who stood in the way of al-Shabaab's African caliphate. They included Somalia's Transitional Federal Government—in war-torn Somalia, the government had been "transitional" for more than a decade—and its allies, like Ethiopia and Kenya; the peacekeeping forces of the African Union; and the United States, which occasionally launched drone strikes against key al-Shabaab leaders.

But beyond Somalia's civil war, Omar had learned to hate the culture of the nation he had been born and raised in. He hated Hollywood movies. He hated pop music. He hated miniskirts and high heels; J.Crew and the Gap; and perhaps most of all, perhaps most indicative of a poisonous and polluting culture, Victoria's Secret. The men who watched such movies, listened to such music, and shopped at such stores had no honor. The women who did so had no shame.

Today, Omar listened attentively as an al-Shabaab leader who had once fought as a senior commander for Al Qaeda in the Arabian Peninsula read the words of the greatest martyr of them all, Osama bin Laden. "The war which has been taking place on your soil," bin Laden had proclaimed to al-Shabaab fighters before his death, "is a war between Islam and the International Crusade." The devout soldiers of Somalia should "continue their steps on the path of Jihad." They were among the most "important armies in the Mujahid Islamic battalion."

As Omar gazed across the desert landscape, he felt that he was a part of a glorious history—a history that included the conquest of Christian Spain, the defense of Jerusalem from the Crusaders, and the fall of the Twin Towers.

He had been a small boy on September 11, 2001, but he remembered the fear and the panic it caused among the infidels. How glorious to have been a hijacker on that greatest of all days. How happy those martyrs must now be, in Allah's paradise.

WASHINGTON, D.C.
SUNDAY, AUGUST 15, 2021
12:19 P.M.

FBI agent Larry Bancroft didn't normally work weekends. But this weekend was different. As were the previous six. Since taking charge of the interagency "Dark Web Task Force," Bancroft had not taken a single day off work.

How could he? The Presidential Daily Briefing's "Threat Matrix" was showing more chatter, potential plots, and imminent attacks against the homeland than at any time since the early 2000s. Bancroft had no doubt that America's enemies were planning something big. And he was equally sure that they were using a little-known part of the Internet to do it: the Dark Web.

If a computer user runs a search through mainstream search engines like Google or Yahoo, he'll never find the Dark Web. It is only accessible through anonymity-protecting browsers like TOR—originally called The Onion Router because of the layers it employs to protect identities. Created by the Naval Research Laboratory to protect the anonymity of covert military communications, intelligence agents, political dissidents in foreign countries, and law enforcement personnel attempting to set up sting operations, TOR is a free, easily downloadable browser that routes users' Internet traffic through several different countries before the user arrives at the desired Web site. Traffic intended to be sent from a computer in Los Angeles to a computer in San Francisco might go from L.A. to Vienna to Oslo to Kiev before finally arriving in San Francisco.[1]

The result is that an Internet user can search for—and find—narcotics, illegal guns, hacking software, child pornography, sex slaves, and even professional assassins, all without leaving a trace of the Internet user's identity. It leaves no browsing history on a computer. It sends no identifying information to a tech company. As one analyst explained, it is as if the online black market were a masked costume ball, and "TOR provides the costumes."[2]

Agent Bancroft's job for the last six weeks was to lead the latest federal government effort to crack the Dark Web. There was of course some irony in the fact that the FBI, the DEA, the ATF, and the NSA were working together to pierce the anonymity made possible by a browser created *and still funded by* the United States government—whose Departments of State and Defense still believed it did more good than harm. And there was frustration on Bancroft's team that the task force was so understaffed by their agencies and underfunded by a Congress that did not take seriously the threats posed by the Dark Web.

But regardless of any irony and any frustration, Bancroft was a true believer in the importance of his mission, and that sense of purpose kept him working round the clock, seven days a week. He knew that the next 9/11 could be plotted and planned in the chat rooms and underground markets of the Dark Web. And he felt sure that time was not on his side.

MINNEAPOLIS, MINNESOTA
FRIDAY, SEPTEMBER 17, 2021
8:04 P.M.

By now the chat room felt like a second home to Omar. It was the same room he had found on that first weekend after watching *Minnesota's Martyrs*. And the same room he returned to when he came back to Cedar-Riverside from his training and fighting in Somalia. With battle scars and war stories to rival Abukar's, Omar—still calling himself the Captain online—talked with his brothers in the chat room, including many of those he had fought beside in Somalia like the veteran he was. A veteran whose biggest battle was still ahead of him.

"Salaam Alaykum," he typed to the Somali-side commander of the mission he had returned to the United States to plan and execute.

"Wa-Alaykum," replied the commander, who went by the purposefully innocuous-sounding nom de guerre "Student31102065." The numerals were randomly chosen.

After a few pleasantries, the Captain and the Student turned to business. They had only ten weeks left. The Captain still needed more guns. And more money. And more men.

The money was easy. In recent years, an increasing number of merchants—especially on the Dark Web—had begun accepting Bitcoin, a virtual currency that was as untraceable as a TOR Internet search. And with the imminent transfer of Bitcoin would come the means to buy the guns on the latest version of the black market Web site, shut down and reopened dozens of times in the past decade, originally known as the Silk Road.

But the men were another matter. The plan was for each of them to be American citizens. Each had been recruited from a Somali-American neighborhood and trained in Somalia, just as Omar had. There were several dozen to choose from. But the Student's first two choices to join Omar and his Minneapolis team had been killed that summer by enemy forces in Somalia. Another had been stopped in transit back to the United States because his name was on a watch list. He eventually made it home, but the Student couldn't be sure that the would-be martyr wasn't under surveillance. They couldn't risk including him in the mission.

As soon as it was time to talk business, Omar picked up a book next to his computer, a common, easy-to-obtain English-language biography of the Prophet Muhammad. Today was the two hundred and sixtieth day of the year, so he opened to page 260. The first letter of the first line was *w*. On a piece of scrap paper that he kept in the book, Omar had written out the twenty-six letters of the alphabet, beginning with *w* and ending with *v*. He had then written the alphabet, beginning with *a*, above it. His scrap paper read:

```
abcdefghijklmnopqrstuvwxyz
wxyzabcdefghijklmnopqrstuv
```

Because the first letter of his next message to the Student started with *n*—the message was "Name?"—Omar typed the letter *j* in his message in the chat room, because *j* was directly below *n* in the two lines.

This method of encrypting a message was centuries old, and its genius was that it only required the sender and receiver to have the same seemingly innocuous book—in this case, the Muhammad biography. But unlike code writers of the past, Omar and the Student had to fear the possibility that a federal agent would read their messages and use a computer program to look for patterns that revealed the code. So Omar and the Student moved to a new letter of the book for every letter of every message. Therefore, because the second letter on page 260 of the book was *h*, Omar had written on his scratch paper:

```
abcdefghijklmnopqrstuvwxyz
hijklmnopqrstuvwxyzabcdefg
```

And because the next letter in his message was *a*—n-a-m-e-?—he typed onto the computer screen the letter *h*, which sat directly below *a* on the two lines on his scratch paper.

It took a couple hours to write enough scratch-paper lines to use for a brief chat room conversation, but Omar and the Student always wrote hundreds of lines out before they entered the chat room. They would then chat briefly, using several hundred encrypted characters. Then they would return to plain English for anything that could be discussed without using the code.

Today was no different. The encrypted conversation lasted only a few minutes. Omar had learned what he needed to know: the name and location of his last foot soldier, another Somali-American from Cedar-Riverside. Omar guessed that he, too, was probably recruited by Abukar at the same mosque.

It was all coming together perfectly, just as Omar and his commander had planned it when they first hatched the idea in Somalia. He lit a candle, held the day's scratch paper over the burning flame, and watched the paper disappear before his eyes. Even if the FBI burst through his door at that moment and seized everything in the apartment, they'd never find the key to Omar's code.

When the last corner of the paper disappeared over the candle, Omar felt the rush of adrenaline that he had come to crave like a drug. He felt supremely confident. He felt immensely proud.

And with his work online completed, and the next task in a long line of battle preparations ahead of him, the Captain signed off.

WASHINGTON, D.C.
SATURDAY, SEPTEMBER 18, 2021
4:42 P.M.

Eleven weeks into his command of the Dark Web task force, Larry Bancroft was seething. He had in his hand a screen shot of a discussion from a chat room frequently visited by al-Shabaab terrorists. It was less than twenty-four hours old. It should have been invaluable intelligence, probably even actionable. Instead, it was worthless. The conversation was written in a code no one on the task force could crack. And—more to the point—the identities of the men calling themselves "the Captain" and "Student31102065" were unknown and unknowable, all because the task force, like every task force before it, had made far from sufficient progress in breaking through TOR's power to hide the identities of the men and women who use the Dark Web.

Bancroft stared at the indecipherable messages.

Why, he asked himself, wasn't the executive branch throwing ten times more personnel at this most critical of missions?

Why, he asked, wasn't Congress funding the mission with enough money to hire the best hundred—or hundreds of—cybersecurity experts in the world?

And why was this nation—which, in the wake of 9/11, had vowed to move heaven and earth to prevent another attack on its homeland—tolerating a government that relegated the protection of our homeland to a second-tier priority?

He did not know why so many people were making so many mistakes, but he did know that those mistakes would have consequences. And he was afraid those consequences would be all too apparent, all too soon.

MINNEAPOLIS, MINNESOTA
FRIDAY, NOVEMBER 26, 2021
10:51 A.M.

The SpongeBob SquarePants Rock Bottom Plunge was not the scariest roller coaster Anthony had ever seen. Not by a long shot. A highlight of the Nickelodeon Universe, a kid-themed amusement park in the middle of Minneapolis's Mall of America, the roller coaster was tame by Anthony's standards. But he loved the animated SpongeBob show. And besides, who cared if the coaster wasn't wild? It was inside a mall! How cool was that?

Anthony had begged his father to take him to Mall of America, and Bryan figured there was no better time than Black Friday. Thanksgiving was always more bitter than sweet, since they had no other family to celebrate it with. It made sense to both of them to spend it traveling, on the latest of the road trips they loved taking so much. With Dad in the driver's seat, Anthony had been yesterday's navigator, calling out directions he found using the Google Maps app on his dad's iPhone 12.

Of course, the mall was packed this morning, because of all

the discounts at each of the mall's 520 stores. Even at a place that was seven times bigger than a baseball stadium, Anthony and his dad felt cramped.

Still, they were together and they were having fun. Anthony leaned against his father as they waited in a long line for the SpongeBob roller coaster. Then he heard an unexpected series of sounds.

First came the loud *rat-a-tat-tat* of what he first guessed were firecrackers. Maybe some kind of holiday show.

Then, from a distance, came screaming.

And then it grew louder and closer as hundreds and then thousands of shoppers and theme park patrons came rushing toward him.

Before he knew what was happening, Anthony felt himself flying through the air as his dad grabbed him like a sack of potatoes and ran from the screaming mob. He still had no idea what was happening. No idea that four gunmen, marching into the mall like gunfighters heading to the O.K. Corral, had opened fire at one end of the building, causing a stampede away from them that spread toward and then swarmed over Nickelodeon Universe.

Thousands of people were scrambling toward any exit they could find.

Some chose wisely.

Others did not.

Anthony and his dad were among the many who did not.

They ran toward one of the five exits where five other gunmen were waiting for them. One at each exit. Just waiting for hundreds of people, flying from the first four gunmen, to run right into their lines of fire.

Like lambs to the slaughter.

★★★

After-Action Report to the President
on the Terrorist Attack of 11/26/2021

November 27, 2021

LOCATION: White House

KILLED: 267, including 4 local police officers (1 off-duty)

WOUNDED: 1,191, including 12 local police officers and 2 FBI SWAT agents

AFTERMATH: The Mall of America is closed. It will likely remain closed for weeks, perhaps months.

A curfew and travel restrictions have been imposed on Minneapolis and St. Paul, because the gunmen's suspected co-conspirators remain at large. Federal and local law enforcement agencies are conducting a manhunt for Abdullah Bahdoon, Adam Othman, Khalid Gutaale Guleed, Samatar Waabberi, and Abukar Ali Mohammed.

Eight gunmen have been killed while one, Hassan Arale, remains at large. Security footage recorded him entering the Mall of America with three other gunmen. Amid the chaos of fleeing shoppers, Arale then exited the mall.

Law enforcement in the Twin Cities has been authorized to stop, frisk, and question anyone on the streets. Checkpoints have been set up at every unclosed road leading out of the metropolitan area. The Somali-American neighborhood of Cedar-Riverside—aka Little Mogadishu—is in lockdown, with residents prohibited from leaving their homes and law enforcement officials going door-to-door searching for suspects. Until the state of emergency is declared over, the police and FBI have been authorized to search homes in Cedar-Riverside and elsewhere without a warrant or probable cause. The Attorney General believes such searches are permitted pursuant to the Fourth Amendment's "exigent circumstances" exception, but the Department of Justice's Office of Legal Counsel has not yet issued a formal opinion on the matter.[3]

Roving mobs of vigilantes have targeted Somali neighborhoods across the United States. Most of their violence has been limited to vandalism:

throwing rocks through house and apartment windows and burning cars. However, on at least 27 occasions, Muslim-Americans, usually Somali-Americans, have been assaulted. On at least one occasion, Muslim-Americans retaliated against a suspected vigilante. Thus far, none of the assaults have been fatal.

International travel to and from the Middle East and East Africa has been suspended.

Additional Marines have been sent to guard U.S. Embassies in East Africa.

Many Americans appear afraid to shop at malls. Early projections indicate that retail sales during Thanksgiving weekend and the subsequent holiday season could be 10 to 25 percent less than expected, for a loss to retailers as large as $175 billion. Other sectors of the economy will undoubtedly be affected by this severe blow to Christmas shopping.

SUMMARY: Intelligence indicates that the attack on the Mall of America was funded, planned, and executed by Harakat al-Shabaab al-Mujahedeen and Al Qaeda. They entered into a formal alliance in 2009 when al-Shabaab issued a statement to Osama bin Laden declaring, "At Your Service, Osama." Since then, al-Shabaab has continued its decades-long terror campaign in Somalia and elsewhere in East Africa while also making threats against the United States' Western allies and the American homeland.

The date, Friday, November 26, was chosen because it was known to be the busiest shopping day of the year. Al-Shabaab's goal was to murder as many shoppers as possible, while also maximizing their attack's economic impact. From their perspective, they could not have chosen a better day.

They also could not have chosen a shopping center with a higher profile. The Mall of America is the nation's most famous mall. It was likely chosen in part because, as a home to popular clothing stores, a movie theater, and a television station's amusement park, it represents American culture, which al-Shabaab believes is helping to corrupt the Muslim world.

Early reports suggest that the attack was planned in Somalia and Minnesota. No state has a larger Somali-American population than does Minnesota, with a population of more than 25,000. Most of them live in Minneapolis's Cedar-Riverside neighborhood, as did most of the gunmen. The gunmen are among the scores of Cedar-Riverside residents who have traveled to al-Shabaab's training camps in Somalia in the past two decades. Many were attracted to al-Shabaab through social media.

Each of the gunmen trained at terrorist camps in Somalia. As American citizens, they returned to their homes in Minneapolis on commercial airliners, using American passports. None were on the no-fly list. After returning to Minneapolis, the attack's perpetrators communicated with al-Shabaab commanders in Somalia through online chat rooms using the Dark Web, which hides their identities from law enforcement and national security officials.

On the morning of the attack, four gunmen entered the mall together wearing dark trench coats. Once inside, they drew their AK-47s and opened fire. One fired straight ahead. One shot to the left. One shot to the right. And one protected their rear. Using 30-round magazines and wearing body armor, each man reloaded dozens of times over the next two hours. Among the victims were several first responders, who arrived at the scene without adequate backup and without training in SWAT situations.

Shoppers fled away from the first four gunmen. However, many of them ran toward five exits where five additional gunmen were waiting for them. After killing as many people as possible, these five gunmen met up with three of the original four gunmen near the first floor's Victoria's Secret. The fourth of the original gunmen shed his coat and weapon and exited among the panicked shoppers. Several of the remaining eight gunmen went store to store, rounding up shoppers who had sought hiding places behind clothing racks, under counters, inside ventilation shafts, and in dressing rooms. Meanwhile, other gunmen protected their perimeter. Among their tactics were a series of booby traps they had placed to slow down law enforcement officials.

On occasion, when a shopper looked like he or she might be Muslim, the gunman administered a quick exam, asking, for example, for the name of Muhammad's mother. Anyone claiming to be Muslim who failed these exams was quickly executed.

After rounding up hundreds of shoppers, the gunmen took them hostage, holing up in the mall's Apple Store. A standoff ensued, delayed in part by several remote-controlled bombs that the gunmen had placed in the mall's common areas, particularly the spaces near the Apple Store. After an unsuccessful negotiation with FBI agents who had training in hostage situations, a dozen hostages were executed. One was beheaded. Images of the murders were immediately posted on Twitter, and they spread quickly around the world through social media. Soon after the hostage executions, a SWAT team stormed the Apple Store. They were met with automatic rifle fire and grenades. Each of the eight gunmen was killed. Five additional hostages were also killed by the gunmen's crossfire.

★★★

Could It Really Happen?

Every element of the fictional attack described above could happen. In fact, much of the details are, as *Law & Order* used to advertise, "ripped from the headlines." Omar's character is based on a real jihadi from Minnesota. The al-Shabaab propaganda is taken from actual videos and social media messages. The Dark Web exists. Even the attack on the Mall of America is based on an attack by al-Shabaab on a mall in Nairobi, Kenya.

A Dangerous Threat: Al-Shabaab

Al-Shabaab has been terrorizing Somalia since the 1990s. Its self-styled jihadists chop off hands, yank out teeth, flog, amputate, kidnap, behead, stone, starve, assassinate, and blow up anyone in their way. The group's goal is to build an Islamic caliphate in East Africa where sharia law is strictly enforced and where Western culture is censored.[4] As recently as 2008, Somalia had the fourth-highest number of terrorism-related deaths in the world, behind Iraq, Pakistan, and Afghanistan. In 2009, among Sunni terrorists, only the Taliban was responsible for more fatal attacks.[5]

Al Qaeda is known to operate in Somalia as well. As Matt Olsen, President Obama's head of the National Counterterrorism Center, said, "Beyond al Qaeda senior leadership in Pakistan [and] its presence in Yemen . . . probably the next most significant terrorist threat may emanate from the al Qaeda presence in Somalia in terms of the willingness and apparent ability, or at least the intent, to strike outside of that particular country."[6]

For several years, until 2011, al-Shabaab controlled large amounts of Somalia's territory, including much of its capital, Mogadishu. It also controlled most of the south-central part of Somalia.

Beginning in the mid-2000s, an African Union force, supported by the Kenyan and Ethiopian militaries and with limited U.S. assistance, began to liberate Mogadishu from al-Shabaab. However, around that time, al-Shabaab became an even bigger threat to the region and to the United States. As it was uprooted from the Somali capital, it began a campaign of terrorist attacks outside of Somalia that frequently targets Christians and has included the murder of 76 people in 2010 in Kampala, Uganda; the murder of 67 people in 2013 at the Westgate Mall in Nairobi, Kenya; and the murder of 148 people in 2015 at Garissa University College in Garissa, Kenya.[7] It thrives on what the Congressional Research Service identifies as the "region's porous borders, proximity to the Arabian Peninsula, weak law enforcement and judicial institutions, pervasive corruption, and, in some cases, state complicity in terrorist activities, combined with the almost 20 year absence of central authority in Somalia."[8]

A Threatened Target: Mall of America

In early 2015, al-Shabaab issued a call for an attack on the Mall of America.[9] Analysts believe this "new threat by al-Shabab extremists to attack the Mall of America in Minnesota could serve as a call to arms for disillusioned Somali-Americans."[10] According to former U.S. attorney W. Anders Folk, "There's certainly some precedence for the idea of a terror group putting out ideas in the public sphere to influence people who are on the fence."[11]

Al-Shabaab has already attacked a large mall somewhat similar to the Mall of America. In an attack quite similar to the fictional attack described in this chapter, al-Shabaab killed sixty-seven people at the Westgate shopping mall in Nairobi, Kenya, in September 2013. At least eight al-Shabaab terrorists—the precise number is unknown—laid siege to the mall for eighty hours. At the start of the attack, four gunmen approached cars as they made their way to the mall's entrance. Less than two football fields away, a second wave of terrorists drove their vehicle through a barrier, jumped out, and assaulted those nearby with small-arms

fire and grenades. The attack was planned so that fleeing shoppers, according to news reports, "ran straight into the firing line of
two militants." Some shooters held an assault rifle in each hand.[12]

Later, I heard testimony at a House Foreign Affairs Committee hearing describing how shoppers who were unable to escape
"hid in toilet stalls, behind mannequins, in ventilation shafts, and
underneath food court tables."[13] The terrorists fought off an initial
attempt by law enforcement to stop them, and they rearmed using
weapons they had previously stored in the mall.[14] At times, the
shooters separated non-Muslims from Muslims, our committee
was told, by asking "captives to recite specific Quranic verses and
to name the relatives of the Prophet Muhammad, killing those
who failed."[15] During the siege, al-Shabaab released statements
through Twitter.[16]

Homegrown Terrorists from Minneapolis

Minnesota is home to twenty-five thousand Somalis and
Somali-Americans, which is a third of their population in the
United States. Around fourteen thousand of them live in Cedar-
Riverside, a neighborhood in Minneapolis.[17] It is a "large, tight-
knit and culturally isolated Somali-American community."[18] And
the vast majority of its members are hardworking, peaceful, law-
abiding men and women.

However, in recent years, about two dozen Minneapolis residents have been among the forty Americans who have joined
al-Shabaab and the fifteen Americans who died fighting for the
terrorist group. Primarily because of this, the House Committee
on Homeland Security can call the United States "the primary ex-
porter of Western fighters to al-Shabaab." There is not another Al
Qaeda—allied terrorist organization in the world, according to our
research, that "has attracted anywhere near as many American
and Western recruits as Shabaab."[19]

The character Omar described in the fictional account above is
loosely based on Cabdulaahi Ahmed Faarax, a Somali-American
from Minneapolis who was nicknamed "Smiley" in high school.

Like the fictional Omar, he graduated from Roosevelt High School. Like Omar, he had been "well-adjusted and popular" in school. Like Omar, he was a Vikings fan. Like Omar, he was not particularly devout when he was a student. Like Omar, in his early twenties, Faarax began making more frequent visits to his local mosque, the Abuubakar Islamic Center in Minneapolis, which has sent nearly a dozen recruits to al-Shabaab. Like Omar, he traveled to Somalia for training with al-Shabaab. Like Omar, he lied to his family about why he was traveling to East Africa. Like Omar, he returned to Minneapolis—using his American passport—with experience on the front lines in Somalia and the "battle scars" to prove it. (One day before the FBI filed terrorism-related charges against Faarax, he entered Mexico, and he has not been heard from again.)[20]

In other ways, Omar's profile is based on homegrown al-Shabaab recruits in general. Like many jihadist recruits, the fictional Omar is motivated in part by "boredom, idleness, and thrill-seeking impulses among youth."[21] And like other Minnesotans who joined al-Shabaab, he stays at al-Shabaab safe houses in Somalia until arriving at a training camp where he receives instruction by "top Shabaab leaders including . . . a senior Al Qaeda operative."[22]

Al-Shabaab even appears to have some competition in recruiting from disaffected youth in this community. Six young Somali-American men were caught trying to leave the country to join ISIS in April 2015. The government estimated that 15 others from Minnesota had managed to successfully leave the U.S. to do just that over the previous year.[23]

The "Foreign Fighter" Threat

The term "foreign fighter" might sound vague, but in the national security sphere it has a very specific meaning. These are individuals who are inspired or recruited to travel to a terrorism hot spot from another country, receive training, and potentially participate in actual fighting there, and then return to their home countries to carry out further attacks. The fictional Omar in our story is one such foreign fighter, who spends time with al-Shabaab in Somalia but also with allied groups in Syria.

There is a disturbingly steady flow of foreign fighters like Omar leaving home to fight in the global jihad, and their numbers are only increasing. One UN report said that foreign fighters increased by 71 percent between 2014 and 2015.[24] A surprising number of these come from Western nations. According to data released by the Office of the Director of National Intelligence in July 2015, some 25,000 foreigners from more than 100 different countries have gone to fight in the war embroiling Iraq and Syria. About 4,500 of these are believed to come from Western nations. This includes hundreds of Americans: some were stopped before they could leave, but many managed to travel successfully to the conflict and have since returned to the U.S.[25]

It's not just U.S. passport holders we need to worry about. The United States does not require an entry visa for citizens from many countries, including much of Europe. There are thousands of Europeans fighting with jihadists on Syrian battlefields who could eventually gain easy entry into the United States to put their training to use on our shores.[26]

Ideally, our law enforcement and counterterrorism officials would be able to track these individuals and stop them, either from leaving to join the jihadists in the first place or from returning after their time in the fight. But serious security gaps exist, particularly in Europe, and foreign fighters exploit these to travel to the front lines. They often go by roundabout routes, known as "broken travel," which has been described as "hopscotching between countries by different modes of transportation to avoid detection." Omar's group entered Syria by traveling first to Greece and then to Turkey before crossing the Turkish border into Syria. A twenty-three-year-old Ohio man took a similar route on his way to receive training from an Al Qaeda–aligned group in Syria. He flew to Greece on a one-way ticket, then to Turkey, then to Syria. And despite a history of showing support for extremists on social media, nobody stopped him along the way.

A Talent for Social Media

The RAND Corporation's Seth Jones reports, "Social media has helped terrorist groups recruit individuals, fund-raise, and distribute propaganda more efficiently than they have in the past."[27] Al-Shabaab's tweets and news releases have included the following taunts and boasts, several of which were quoted in the fictional story above:

➤ "Your inexperienced boys flee from confrontation & flinch in the face of death."[28]

➤ "Europe was in darkness when Islam made advances in physics, Maths, astronomy, architecture, etc. before passing on the torch."[29]

➤ "Your eccentric battle strategy [of targeting donkey caravans] has got animal rights groups quite concerned, Major."[30]

➤ "You now have a choice to make. Either you call for the immediate withdrawal of your troops from our country or you shall receive the bodies of your remaining sons delivered to you in bags. Think long. Think hard."[31]

Al-Shabaab also uses Twitter, Facebook, and other social media to highlight "alleged abuses by [enemy] forces"; "U.S. support for Ethiopian military operations"; and "civilians casualties purportedly resulting from U.S. airstrikes or from retaliatory [enemy] military strikes."[32] In addition to short posts, its media arm produces "slick propaganda videos"[33] like *Minnesota's Martyrs: The Path to Paradise*, a forty-minute movie about three Twin Cities Americans who died fighting for al-Shabaab.[34] The organization also uses Internet chat rooms, an official Web site (written in Somali, Arabic, and English, for maximum appeal), quiz shows for kids (with grenades and automatic rifles as prizes), YouTube, and traditional news releases to reach and appeal to as many people as possible.[35]

The Link Between Al Qaeda and al-Shabaab

Osama bin Laden once operated out of East Africa, and Al Qaeda and its allies have been active in the region for decades. The eighteen U.S. soldiers killed in the "Black Hawk Down" incident in Mogadishu in 1993 were killed by militants who were, according to Al Qaeda, trained by bin Laden's organization.[36]

In 2009, Bin Laden told al-Shabaab, "You are one of the important armies in the Mujahid Islamic battalion."[37] He also said that "the war which has been taking place on your soil for these years is a war between Islam and the International Crusade," and he encouraged them to "continue their steps on the path of Jihad."[38]

That same year, al-Shabaab formally declared allegiance to Bin Laden and Al Qaeda by issuing a statement entitled "At Your Service, Osama."[39] Since then, al-Shabaab has forged even closer operational links with central Al Qaeda and with the Al Qaeda in the Arabian Peninsula (AQAP) splinter group in Yemen, just across the Gulf of Aden from Somalia. The House Committee on Homeland Security has been able to identify a number of these links:

➤ Al-Shabaab has shown public support for AQAP and its former cleric, Anwar al-Awlaki.

➤ Al-Shabaab has been known to fly the Al Qaeda flag at its rallies.

➤ Al-Shabaab has sent personnel to fight with and receive training from AQAP.

➤ Al-Shabaab provided safe haven for Al Qaeda operatives such as Fazul Abdullah Mohammed, who was in Mogadishu during the 1993 "Black Hawk Down" battle with U.S. Special Operations Forces, and helped mastermind the 1998 U.S. embassies bombings.

➤ After Osama bin Laden's death, al-Shabaab vowed revenge, saying of the U.S.: "So, let them rejoice for a few moments since they will cry much afterwards, because the lion Osama left behind him huge armies of mujahedeen."

➤ Al-Shabaab's propaganda has increased in production value, appearing similar to messages produced by Al Qaeda's "As-Sahab" ("The Clouds") media wing and AQAP's *Inspire* magazine.

The Dark Web

When most of us surf the Internet, send e-mail, and engage in social media, we do so without complete anonymity. Whether we realize it or not, the reality is that a lot of our activity—where we go and what we look at—is somehow traceable. So, too, is the location from which you're browsing.[40] Unless, of course, you've entered the depths of the Dark Web.

Despite the wealth of information available at our fingertips via a simple Google search, there is still a large part of the Internet most of us cannot access—and wouldn't want to. Called the Dark Web, it can only be found using a browser like TOR, where users can browse freely under a cloak of almost total online invisibility.

The Dark Web's most infamous Web site was called the Silk Road. Until it was shut down in 2013—and soon replaced by imitators—it was a sort of black-market version of Amazon.com where buyers could use Bitcoin, the anonymity-protecting virtual currency, to purchase illegal drugs, hacking software, and other contraband.[41] In less than three years, $1.2 billion in illegal goods were sold on the Silk Road, netting $80 million in fees for the Web site's creator, Ross Ulbricht.[42] Fond of calling himself the "Dread Pirate Roberts" (after a character in the 1987 film *The Princess Bride*), Ulbricht was finally identified and arrested by federal agents in 2013.

The Dark Web is an ideal marketplace and method of communications for the traditional criminal element to exchange everything from stolen goods, child pornography, drugs—even expertise and services for carrying out a murder. But we know that terrorists lurk in some of its corners as well. The problem is finding them.[43]

★★★

What Can We Do to Stop This?

To prevent foreign fighters from launching a deadly Westgate-inspired attack against an American shopping mall on a crowded day, we should focus our efforts on disrupting several terror processes. We need to stem the flow of foreign fighters, and there are steps that can be taken to do that at home as well as abroad. In addition, we must track them not only in person but also in the seedy underbelly of cyberspace.

To better protect ourselves across these many fronts, we must:

CATCH MORE FOREIGN FIGHTERS IN THE UNITED STATES. The Obama administration has not been able to develop and articulate a serious strategy for dealing with the threat of foreign fighters coming into and out of this country. In addition, their efforts to counter radicalization among Americans in the first place have been lacking.[44] A comprehensive strategy to catch foreign fighters before they leave our shores or as soon as they return can be based around four basic principles: identification, prevention, detection, and disruption. First of all, we develop intelligence to figure out who is looking to leave the country to fight for a jihadist group. This often happens at the local level, which can lead to the second line of defense: educating communities about the reality of the war in Iraq and Syria. Impressionable would-be recruits need to know that they aren't headed for paradise—they're headed for prison. If they are still determined to leave, we try to stop them with detection. American and foreign border agencies must know who is entering and exiting their country (see below). Finally, once the individual has been detected, we disrupt—i.e., arrest and indict him or her. Hopefully, with the help of local intelligence, this will happen before the individual even leaves the United States.

CATCH MORE FOREIGN FIGHTERS ABROAD. This is not just America's problem—it's a worldwide threat. And other nations, especially in Europe, are lagging woefully behind in both the mentality and capabilities to protect against foreign fighters. Italy, for instance, is largely unwilling to deal with the tens of thousands of illegal aliens from North Africa and the Middle East, including Syria, who arrive in their country every month after crossing the Mediterranean. ISIS has boasted of their success in transporting their personnel to Europe this way. Once there, travel is easy, as European border checkpoints have been virtually nonexistent for decades. European intelligence agencies also suffer from a lack of resources and a reluctance to share information with one another, undermining the kind of coordination necessary for tracking international terrorists. Most disturbingly, Europe does not make use of technology that could make it easy to catch these fighters: passports are rarely checked against fraud databases to see if they are forged or stolen, and EU law makes it difficult to check Europeans' names against international terror watch lists when they travel. As foreign fighters crisscross the world, the United States cannot afford to worry about just our own borders. We need to defend outward, and that means working with our European allies to bring their terrorist-tracking capabilities into the twenty-first century.

SHINE LIGHT ON THE "DARK WEB." There is no shortage of strange things on the Internet, but few corners of the Web are as dangerous as those utilized by terrorists under the cover of "dark space." Terrorists have learned to adapt and make use of the Dark Web as well as apps designed to encrypt and otherwise hide their communications. We need to adapt our ability to fight back, and that means going after those who misuse technology while protecting the rights and civil liberties of law-abiding Americans. This is in everyone's best interest, and it is an area where the public and private sector can and should work effectively together. Companies that develop this technology don't want to see it used to wreak havoc. That's why it's critical for Silicon Valley and Washington to work together to create a framework for tackling terror online.

This is a dialogue that must continue and will lead to concrete results.[45]

USE CONVENTIONAL MILITARY RESOURCES TO TARGET ONLINE COMMANDERS. ISIS-related accounts send out some two hundred thousand tweets per day,[46] many designed to inspire violence against the U.S. homeland and other Western targets. ISIS commanders in the field are no longer the only ones issuing orders to their followers. Osama bin Laden planned his terror campaign from caves using couriers. Today's generation of terrorists uses sophisticated social media strategies to radicalize their followers—including many already in the United States. Terrorism has gone viral. Nobody even has to travel to Syria or Iraq to receive training and instructions to carry out a terror attack—they can be radicalized at home. At each end of every online ISIS communication sits a human being. Someone sends and many receive. This means ISIS's top social media experts are as much of a menace as their operational commanders. In order to figure out who they are, we need to upgrade our human intelligence capabilities in the Middle East and elsewhere. If we can find out who is sending ISIS's tweets, we can stop them. One success in this area was the killing of Junaid Hussain, a.k.a. Abu Hussain al-Britani, a British-born jihadist active in ISIS's "Cyber Caliphate," by a U.S. air strike. The continued draining of ISIS's talent pool of social media jihadists should be a priority along with draining their talent pool of executioners and bomb makers.

5

Going Dark

Cyberstrike on the World's Financial Capital

GERMANY
SOUTHEAST OF BERLIN
AUGUST 15, 2020
4:14 P.M.

Markus Reinicke swore and slammed on his brakes as he realized the turn had snuck up on him yet again. He incurred the wrath of several of his fellow motorists on Bundesautobahn 113, and the sounds of screeching tires and belligerent horns assailed him as he veered into the industrial park, his coffee mug threatening to tip out of the Audi's cupholder.

The entrance was virtually unmarked, identified only by a small sign that was difficult to see until a car had already turned onto the service road. The discreet location was, of course, necessary for Markus and his colleagues. They had moved their base of operations out of Berlin to this nondescript location just south of Berlin Schönefeld Airport and about twenty miles south of the city itself, specifically to avoid prying eyes.

It was all about the work. That was all that Markus had the bandwidth to think about these days. They were getting so close, and tonight, if all went according to plan, the operation would finally kick off. He had been running the preparations through in his head all during the drive from Berlin. He hadn't been able to use the Audi's GPS, knowing full well those systems could be too easily tracked. Markus could track many types of them himself; any good hacker could.

As he drove through the rows and rows of warehouses, storage units, and low, squat office buildings, Markus focused again on his goal. After tonight, the world would, quite simply, never be the same. Granted, most of the sheep who had spent seventy-odd years roaming its surface consuming and breeding and dying would have no possible conception of the significance of the change, but it would be radical and irreversible all the same. He, Markus Reinicke, would have pulled off the world's first quantum hack.

"Quantum computing": it still sounded to Markus like something out of science fiction—which, of course, it had been until great advances in the field a few short years ago, the "golden era" that some said began back in 2015.[1] There were a few prototype machines in various stages of development now, and the tech press was positively singing of their promises in fields like research and medicine.

Some quantum machines the public knew about, and some they didn't. But the international online underground was all-knowing, and for hackers like Markus the trade in rumors and expertise was wide-ranging, if conducted with a certain wariness. It was as if even the international hacker community was aware that they were playing with fire.

Markus thought about the idea of the "hacker community" and scoffed. It was this same "hacker community" that had expelled him more than a year ago after calling into question what they had the gall to refer to as his "ethics."

Markus had once belonged to one of the largest hacker collectives in Europe. Based in Berlin, they called themselves the Digital Justice Ministry, and they made it their goal to go after "big fish": Big Government, Big Business, Big Banks. They wanted to keep them honest, to remind them that the constituents and customers they served were real people and deserved respect. If that meant occasionally publishing the details of secret government programs, well, that was all for the greater good.

Markus had always liked to run his own operations on the side—simple digital snooping on a cheating spouse or a rival company, the odd fraudulent wire transfer—for any customers willing to pay him enough. Hacking was hardly a "day job," he reasoned. He had to make money somehow, if only to keep a roof over his head, maintain his computer equipment, and ensure a steady supply of Club-Mate, a caffeine-heavy soda that hackers employed as an essential fuel.

But that soon became too much for the senior DJM members. They didn't like how Markus made his extra money—too many disreputable clients, they said—so he was out. Simple as that. They would not turn him in to the authorities—that was another precept of their code—but they wanted nothing further to do with Markus Reinicke. And now it was his turn to show them all.

Markus pulled the car up to the warehouse he had rented and got out. He keyed the code into the lock on the warehouse door and felt the door give way.

The cavernous space within was brightly lit and significantly colder than outside. Markus quickly put on the sweatshirt he had brought in from the car. The area was sparsely furnished. There were a few folding tables and chairs, a couple of mini-refrigerators—stocked mostly with Club-Mate—and a microwave. At the far side of the room, where it was slightly warmer, there were three cots and a space heater against the wall for when they had to work late. Tonight would be one of those nights.

Markus saw Klaus and Gerhard get up from their laptops set up on folding tables and head toward him. They were the faithful—the only two who had followed Markus out of the DJM. Together, the three of them had formed Guardians of Destruction—GOD—and launched themselves into the project that had made the men friends in the first place: building a quantum computer. The only trouble had been money. But they had soon sorted that out.

Soon after his departure from DJM, Markus made a new contact in an online forum who had offered a tantalizing commission. When Markus told him how well a "quantum hack" would work for his purposes, and how Markus was just the hacker to make this happen, he had essentially been offered a blank check. Though his new benefactor had hidden himself behind several layers of identity protection, Markus easily identified the original source of his

IP address: Tehran, and a government building no less. After the sanctions were lifted, the Iranians had money to burn.

Now Markus, Gerhard, and Klaus were standing before the fruits of their labor. A large plastic cubicle loomed in the center of the room. Inside, under many protective layers designed to keep temperature and magnetic noise levels low, was their quantum processor. The processor was connected to a dedicated server they had set up in a data rack outside the cubicle, next to the system's cooling unit. On a wheeled desk next to the system, hardwired into the server, was a laptop computer.

"We ran the first series of tests this morning," reported Klaus. "Everything seems ready, but we thought you'd want to run the last series yourself before tonight."

"I do, yes," replied Markus. "How is the cooling system?"

"Holding steady," said Gerhard. "No fluctuations in the last hour."

"Excellent."

Markus went over to the mobile desk and sat down in front of the laptop. This was where he would harness a quantum processor to do a hacker's bidding for the first time. The processor chip itself—no bigger than a thumbnail—Markus's contact had sent him via a late-night rendezvous in a Frankfurt parking lot. The man who passed it to him had said nothing, but some of the packaging bore Chinese characters. Markus had known better than to ask questions.

It really was a thing of beauty. Instead of working in the binary "zero and one" language of bits, tonight Markus would deploy qubits—quantum bits—that could function as a zero, a one, or even both. With qubits, Markus could be nearly everywhere at once. He would need to be, if he was going to hack hundreds of U.S. government servers in just a matter of hours.

GRAND VICTORIA HOTEL
SINGAPORE
AUGUST 16, 2020
10:09 P.M.

It was quiet—finally quiet. Still, Celeste Matheson had a buzzing in her ears that she couldn't shake. Maybe it was because her
entire day, from the moment her alarm had woken her up that
morning, had been taken up with noise. There was the noise when
the phone and tablet buzzed simultaneously all through breakfast
in her room. There were the excited noises of her staff members
at their morning briefing. There was noise from the press who
hounded her on her way into and out of the negotiation sessions.
And then there were the sessions themselves: seemingly intermi-
nable lectures on American economic imperialism coupled with a
request for handouts. But what had she expected from the North
Koreans?

The secretary of state kicked off her shoes and sat down on the
bed. It was littered with papers, as was virtually every other surface in the suite. The evening briefing with her staff had just broken up, and Secretary Matheson didn't have the energy to clean
up yet.

Maybe there was time to call her husband. Of course, she realized, he'd be at work. It was just after 10:00 a.m. there, twelve
hours behind. He was probably in the partners' meeting at his law
firm just then, and there was no sense in trying to tear him from
that. She'd worked in high-powered firms—in fact, she'd met her
husband at one of them—but this was the most fun Celeste had
had in her entire professional life. Even more fun than the Senate.
She relished being the country's top diplomat, relished being the
first secretary of state in decades to deal directly with the North
Koreans.

"Dynamic," the papers called her, even "ruthless." Both she
took as equal compliments.

She had to be both dynamic and ruthless in the current negotiations. North Korea had finally been brought to the table by virtue
of a famine that had, according to the best intelligence estimates,

already killed tens of thousands. The North Koreans were demanding the lifting of sanctions plus food aid but had, until now, been unwilling to scale back their nuclear program in exchange. At least, that was the basis on which these talks between North Korea and the United States, along with China, South Korea, and Japan, had been called in the first place. But at the meetings themselves the North Koreans had been steadfastly unwilling to make any concessions at all, preferring to harangue instead. It was as if they were stalling, but for what? The end of the famine?

It was early yet. Celeste still had a few days to figure them out. Maybe the bottle of white wine chilling in the suite's refrigerator would help her clear her head.

But as she made her way toward the refrigerator, her phone began buzzing yet again. Reluctantly, she reached back to the bed and picked it up. It was Gwen, her chief of staff.

"Ma'am, have you seen the *Post*?"

Celeste sighed. "No, I haven't. Can we just go over the editorials in the morning?"

"No, ma'am, this can't wait. They've got hold of everything."

Unsure what her top aide meant, Celeste pulled over her tablet and went to the *Washington Post*'s Web site. As it loaded, she asked Gwen tiredly: "Everything good or everything bad?"

"Everything, period," Gwen answered.

Then Celeste saw it. Splashed across the main page, posted only minutes ago, was a story on the Singapore negotiations. Celeste only had to skim the first few paragraphs to know the level of detail the *Post* had obtained: specific quantities of food the North Koreans had asked for, troop withdrawals they had demanded along the DMZ—they really did have everything. Celeste was shocked, and then she was angry.

"Who the hell leaked this?" she said into the phone through clenched teeth. "If it was one of ours, God help—"

"Ma'am," Gwen cut her off, "it looks like it came from your e-mail. They have you quoted as calling the North Korean foreign minister 'a bug-eyed toad of a man.' "

Celeste froze. She'd only written that in one e-mail to one person: her husband. And that had been on her personal e-mail, not her government address. But how could anyone have gotten to either?

As she was about to ask this of Gwen, her chief of staff came back on the line preemptively: "Check the *New York Post*," she said in an even more agitated staccato.

"Do they have it already?"

"They published something on the negotiation leak a few minutes ago; it looks like all the major papers did. But I'm just now getting a tweet . . ." Gwen trailed off for a moment, then came back on, more quietly this time:

"They have the mug shot from your DUI in law school."

KOREAN PEOPLE'S ARMY JOINT CHIEFS
CYBER WARFARE UNIT 121
FACILITY NO. 1
PYONGYANG, NORTH KOREA
AUGUST 17, 2020
3:13 P.M.

Pak Min-chol sat at his computer desk, quite unnerved by the sound that emanated from the row of desks behind him. It was laughter—raucous, uproarious laughter—and at work no less. The boys behind him were asking for trouble. But still the laughter continued.

Finally, Pak decided he could no longer stand it. He got up from his desk and turned around to see what all the fuss was about.

Less than a year ago, he would never have dared to get up from his computer in the middle of an assignment. But that was different. In his student days at Command Automation University, and even before then, going all the way back to Geumseong Middle School, the rules had been rigid, designed to train him to hack with precision and speed.

Pak was a graduate now, and had been funneled directly into Bureau 121, the North Korean military's elite hacking unit. Here he had found his reward for years of dedication to his craft. The government had moved his entire family down from their home in Musan, a mining town in the bitter cold of North Hamgyong province. They had been given choice accommodations in

Pyongyang—which was just as well, because reports suggested the famine was hitting North Hamgyong especially hard. Pak himself was housed in an even nicer apartment block in the company of his fellow hackers. All because a conscientious teacher at his primary school in Musan had noticed Pak's talent with computers.

Now, as a fully fledged—albeit rookie—member of Bureau 121, Pak enjoyed certain freedoms. He and his hacker comrades got unfettered access to the Internet in their personal apartments—although Pak knew it was monitored—which meant they could watch as many Western films and as much television as they wanted. And they could occasionally take breaks to gather around someone's tablet computer and share a laugh, as was happening now.

Pak's friend, Ri Yong-sun, called him over. Ri was holding the tablet and a cluster of other young men, all in identical gray tunics, were gathered around.

"Come and look at this," Ri said. "It just keeps getting better and better."

They were scrolling through a series of headlines from the United States from the last twenty-four hours:

Secretary of State's Personal Memos from NK Negotiations Leaked

Analysts: American Position in Singapore Severely Weakened

But it wasn't just the negotiators who had been hit:

Supreme Court's Online Habits Detailed, Adult Web Sites Among Those Visited

United States Senators Find Online Bank Accounts Depleted

Work and Home Servers of Government Personnel Reported Breached

News like this had been coming in all day. Someone was really giving it to the Americans this time. Pak only wished it had been them. All they had been doing for the last few months, stuck in this room in the basement of the Ministry of Post and Telecommunications, was routine hacks against unidentified targets. He wanted to know what it was all for. He was ready to get into some real action.

Pak laughed along with the others as Ri scrolled through more American embarrassments, until two swift claps stopped them all cold.

Standing in the elevated entryway to the room was General Hong Se-yun, the overall commander of Bureau 121, whom Pak had seen on only a few occasions. Surrounding him were several of the senior hackers, all wearing black tunics. It was one of them who had clapped to get their attention.

Another man, bearded and wearing a gray Western-style suit with no tie, stood out in their group. Pak had seen him before on occasion, touring the lab with the senior hackers. He had never been introduced to any of the men in Pak's unit, and never spoke to anyone directly, but Pak had once overheard him referred to as "Comrade Abbas" and "a brother from Tehran." Comrade Abbas wasn't the only foreigner who had visited the lab in recent days—a technology officer from the Chinese embassy in Pyongyang had arrived for two "inspection tours" in the last month, and Pak had noticed a lot of the code they'd been working on showed signs of interaction with Chinese IP addresses.

But Pak knew better than to ask questions.

General Hong stepped forward and gripped the railing of the entryway. His chestful of decorations glistened, and even from his distance Pak could recognize the Order of Kim Il-sung medal.

"Take your seats, gentlemen, for today we send you into battle for the glory of the Republic," the general said. Pak and the others scurried back to their desks as their seated comrades began clapping in unison.

With a calming hand motion, the general quieted them down.

"You have no doubt seen the reports. You know the Fatherland needs your help. Out there, in your hometowns, your countrymen are dying. And why? Because the imperialist aggressors in the United States and the West are willing to *let* them die. They want to keep food from our children's mouths to try to force us to give up our natural right to nuclear power.

"Today you will show them—*we* will show them—that they cannot hold our people hostage. Today we will show them what it means to have your world torn apart by catastrophe. We will show them the weakness, the meaninglessness, of the dollars they hold so dear. Today, in the name of the Supreme Leader, we will plunge America into darkness to match the darkness of the American heart."

The clapping and cheering lasted, by Pak's count, for at least six minutes.

CATHCART INVESTMENTS
WEST TWENTY-FIFTH STREET AND SIXTH AVENUE
NEW YORK CITY
AUGUST 18, 2020
9:44 A.M.

Ed Benedetti noticed something odd shortly after trading began at 9:30. The Cathcart offices were quiet, as they usually were. Few phones rang, and there was little chatter among the traders. Nobody had to shout orders across a room, after all. At high-frequency automated trading firms like Cathcart, all the trading was done by computers. Their algorithms scanned news reports and other online sources and filled orders accordingly, all without the awkward, bumbling involvement of humans.

The humans in the office, like Ed, were not the typical hot-shot economics or business majors one tended to find at trading firms. They were mostly programmers or mathematicians by training. Ed's own background was in engineering. Each of them sat at a desk with four computer screens arrayed in front of them, watching the orders tick by. They were there mostly in case a client needed help or in case something went wrong.[2]

Now Ed was getting a sinking feeling that something was definitely wrong. The day had started out robust—more than 20 million shares in the first two minutes—but nothing out of the ordinary. However, as Ed watched, in the first ten minutes of trading, the pace picked up. He watched the number of shares climb higher and higher, and the orders placed stream across his screens faster than he could read them. Where were they all coming from?

He looked over at Rajiv Agarwal, a Stanford statistics PhD, seated at the next desk.

"Raj, are you seeing this?"

"Oh, yeah. Weird, right? And I just got a text from my buddy at Pierce Edmunds. Sounds like they're seeing the same thing over there."

Ed's brow furrowed as he watched his screens. Already his mind was taking unpleasant trips back a decade, to the "flash crash" of 2010. On that awful day in May, one enormous trade spooked a lot of the high-frequency traders, and for a brief moment there hadn't really been a stock market at all.[3] If something was going wrong, and that happened again . . .

Rajiv was looking down at his phone again. He had a lot of friends in a lot of places.

"It looks like a bunch of the big auto-trading firms went crazy right out of the gate this morning. It's going on all over."

He looked up and grinned at Ed, then knocked on his wooden desk for luck. "I guess it's going to be a really good day."

Or a really bad one, Ed thought.

MIDTOWN BAGEL & PHO
WEST FORTY-NINTH STREET AND EIGHTH AVENUE
NEW YORK CITY
AUGUST 18, 2020
10:03 A.M.

Jane Truong shook her head as she scrolled through the day's news on her mobile phone, leaning on the counter of her family's deli in midtown Manhattan. What was going on in D.C.?

For the last two days, leak after leak had been cascading out courtesy of hackers breaking into politicians' home and work e-mail accounts. The hackers had uploaded all the embarrassing information and photos they had found onto a Web site and left them free for the taking. First the blogs had bitten, then reputable news sites.

Jane had read all about the questionable browsing history of the Supreme Court justices and the illegitimate children of no less than three cabinet secretaries. It seemed that the most embarrassing revelations were coming from security clearance documents that had been discovered and widely distributed.

Public figures weren't just being embarrassed by the massive hack. The morning before, most members of the United States Senate had woken up to find their bank accounts wiped out. This morning the same had been done to some three-quarters of the U.S. House of Representatives.

As she scrolled through the latest D.C. hack story, a breaking-news alert flashed on Jane's phone:

New York Stock Exchange Reports Trading Day Begins with Flood of Flash Trades

So now Wall Street was losing its mind, too. Jane remembered earlier "flash trade" scares and felt a nervous pang in her stomach. She reminded herself to call her family's broker later that day: he probably had his hands full at the moment.

Jane figured the politicians and financial wizards would eventually find a way to get themselves out of whatever mess they'd created, but what made her angrier was what the North Koreans were getting away with in Singapore. The hack news had thrown a massive wrench into the nuclear negotiations, and now the talks had all but imploded. Jane wanted to see North Korean nukes dismantled once and for all, and food aid for their famine finally presented the leverage to get it done.

Before joining the family business, Jane had studied foreign affairs at NYU, and she made sure to keep up with the news. But more than that, this was personal. It was the communists who had forced her grandparents to flee South Vietnam in 1975. Her grandmother had been pregnant, and Jane's own father had been born at sea on a U.S. aircraft carrier just days after the fall of Saigon. Jane had grown up with stories of communist oppression, and she had hoped the U.S. could use these negotiations to weaken the North Korean regime and eventually free that country's people.

But now everyone was more concerned about the snide remarks Secretary of State Matheson had sent her husband about the North Korean foreign minister, although it was his government that put money into nukes instead of feeding its own people. It burned Jane to see the communists getting the upper hand.

Her mind jerked quickly back to the present as the door opened and the bell above it clanged. The morning rush of customers had petered out already, but here, right on schedule, was Carlo. Carlo worked in IT and didn't have to show up until 10:30, so he usually stopped in for a bagel on his way. Jane's husband, Ted, who worked at a bank downtown, had been at work since 8:00.

"Morning, Carlo," Jane called warmly. "Want the usual?" She began unwrapping a bagel.

"Yeah, thanks, and large iced coffee" said Carlo, wiping sweat from his forehead. "It's a scorcher out there. Hey, I should tell you, your ATM's not working for some reason." Carlo gestured toward the front door.

Jane frowned and came out from behind the counter. They'd never had a problem with the ATM outside before.

"What's the problem?" she asked as she went outside to take a look. Carlo was right. It was brutally hot—a real New York August.

"Beats the heck out of me," Carlo replied as he followed her, clearly baffled by the ATM's antiquated technology. "The screen's just frozen."

Jane tried and, sure enough, none of the buttons worked.

"The weird thing is," Carlo was saying, "I tried to use the ATM at my bank two blocks back, and theirs was busted too."

As Jane watched, the machine's frozen screen went blank.

Behind her, she suddenly heard the screeching of tires followed by a scraping crash of metal on metal. She wheeled around and saw two taxis and a delivery van tangled with each other at the intersection of Forty-Ninth Street and Eighth Avenue. She soon saw why: the traffic light was out. As the other traffic struggled to avoid the pileup, Jane heard the dull crunch of several other fender benders.

Carlo ran straight for the accident with Jane close behind him.

As she reached the curb, she was conscious of something else going on around her. People on the sidewalk were pointing frantically, not at the accident, but at the buildings around them. Jane turned back toward her restaurant just in time to see all the lights go out. As she watched, every storefront and window on the block went dark.

She heard a low rumble, as if the hum of the city itself was powering down. The jackhammer around the corner on Forty-Ninth went silent. Here and there she could hear people screaming.

Jane thought immediately of her husband and their daughter, Marilyn, in the third grade. Ted's work was closer to her school; she had to call him. She pulled out her phone, but of course there was no service. No Internet, either.

She ran back to the restaurant. The lights were out, and so were the fans. The lights were off in the drink and meat coolers, too, she noticed; the food wouldn't last long. She tried the phone on the counter: dead.

There were more screams outside now. She could see people running now. Jane looked up and down. She couldn't see a single lighted window. When she was in high school, in 2003, the city had gone through a blackout. It had made for an annoying few days without power, but everything had turned out all right. Was it happening again now, or was this something worse?

Jane had a decision to make. She had no way of getting in touch with her husband and no way to reach their child—that is, unless she went to them. But she was the only person working at the restaurant, and someone had to watch the family business in case things got . . . dangerous. Then it hit her. This was a family business, but "family" came before "business" for a reason.

Jane grabbed her keys, ran out of the restaurant, and locked the door behind her. Then she took off running down Eighth Avenue toward her daughter's school downtown.

August 20, 2020

LOCATION: The White House

AREA AFFECTED: 15 states, including the New York City and Washington, D.C., metropolitan areas

AMERICANS WITHOUT POWER: Approximately 93 million

CURRENT STATUS: Much of the Northeastern United States remains without power for the third straight day, including the cities of New York, Philadelphia, Boston, Baltimore, and Washington, D.C.

Initial death tolls are low but appear to be increasing as civil unrest grows and spreads, particularly looting in the evening hours. A heat wave and lack of air-conditioning due to the outages have accounted for the deaths of dozens of senior citizens.

Hospitals in the affected area are reporting difficulties resulting from inadequate or strained generators.

Ports along the Eastern Seaboard have been shut down due to the inability to operate most of their equipment.

The New York Stock Exchange was forced to suspend trading for a day, but backup power is now in effect. Trading has been complicated due to a massive influx of high-speed automatic trades before the blackout, and the markets continue to drop.

Major metropolitan airports have reopened, under reduced schedules, but smaller regional airports remain closed.

Cars stuck in traffic jams, some taking days to move a few miles, have been reported on eastern U.S. highways as panicked citizens, mostly cut off from reliable information, attempt to flee cities.

Governors in all 15 affected states have deployed National Guard units, and FEMA and other federal resources have been mobilized.

Units on the front lines report increasingly hostile crowds. Sources on the ground suggest that public trust in government has taken a substantial hit in the wake of recent leaks targeting public officials.

In much of the Northeast region, however, some communities are expected to be without power for between 2 and 3 weeks.

Note: A 2015 Cambridge University study provides additional guidance on what can be expected to transpire. A number of the following effects have already been reported across the affected area:

"Companies, hospitals, and public facilities with backup generators are able to continue in operation, but all other activities requiring power are shut down. This includes phone systems, Internet, television and radio, street lights, traffic signals, and many other facilities."[4]

Generator failures at hospitals compromise treatment equipment, and as the summer heat bears down on the elderly, "a rash of deaths [are] reported in nursing homes."[5]

Citizens fall ill due to water pollution resulting from industrial accidents or by eating spoiled food.[6]

"Water supplies are impacted during the blackout due to the loss of power to pumps. Supplies of potable water become limited across the affected area."[7]

"Cash quickly becomes the only accepted form of payment but the shortage of serviceable ATMs means that many citizens are unable to obtain paper money."[8]

Widespread communication breakdown: telephone lines are "overloaded"; mobile services manage only a few more hours of operation on generator power; 911 centers are kept running by generators but few can use phones to contact them; the Internet is down; "emergency radio and word-of-mouth are the primary means for people to receive information."[9]

"Factories and commercial activity responsible for 32% of the country's economic production" come to a halt.[10]

Traffic lights fail, causing "a sharp spike in road accidents and gridlock."[11]

Gas stations shut down and "a run on vehicle fuel" ensues.[12]

Impact Estimates (based on 2015 Cambridge University Study)[13]

Scenario	Power Outage Duration	Economic Costs
Standard	2–3 weeks	$243 billion
Extreme	4 weeks	> $1 trillion

SUMMARY: At present, our intelligence strongly suggests that multiple cyber-attacks perpetrated against American targets in recent days should be viewed as interrelated and coordinated.

On August 16, social media sources and various blogs reported that significant amounts of data had been disclosed by a previously unknown German hacker outfit calling itself the "Guardians of Destruction," or "GOD." On a website which they apparently set up to host this data, they refer to this hack as "The Wrath of GOD."

This hack constituted a massive breach of U.S. government servers, in addition to private servers storing government officials' personal data. Their single greatest haul appears to be several decades' worth of federal security clearance and background check files, which include potentially compromising information on federal personnel going up to Cabinet-level. Senior officials' e-mail communications were also revealed on a large scale, and a number of personal bank accounts were made to display a "zero" balance, though no money appears to have been stolen or transferred.

Federal forensic computer experts are still in the early stages of cataloging the material released by the hackers and piecing together the specific nature of their attack. These efforts have been further hampered by the subsequent blackout. Our teams have, however, been able to establish that the Guardians of Destruction were able to breach a large number of secure servers over a very short period of time—apparently a matter of a few hours.

This suggests the group is in possession of an advanced example of extremely powerful technology still in the research phase in most sectors: the quantum computer. A separate report on quantum computing will be submitted separately, but in short, quantum computing could allow hackers to break the codes for government servers in a fraction of the time that it would take a conventional computer.

This is thought to be the first "quantum hack," and if this is confirmed, it will necessitate an urgent reconsideration of the United States' entire cyber-security strategy. The sophistication involved in quantum computing, particularly the production of the necessary quantum processor, suggests that the German hackers may not have acted alone. China is known to be conducting its own serious research into quantum computing for strategic purposes, but no link between China and the Guardians of Destruction has yet been established.

In the midst of the scandal generated by this mammoth disclosure of data, a separate cyber-attack was launched on August 18. This attack does not appear to have been perpetrated using a quantum computer, but it has caused widespread damage nonetheless. Over 90 million Americans across 15 states were initially left without power, and some 30% of the nation's economy was compromised. Certain areas have seen at least partial restoration of power by this point, but others may remain dark for weeks.

The first signs of trouble appeared at the New York Stock Exchange, which was overwhelmed with high-frequency trades as soon as the trading day began. Several high-frequency trading firms are reporting that their trading software has been compromised, suggesting that hackers were able to tamper with their trading algorithm and set off a flood of activity. The market was beginning to show signs of reaction to this when the full second wave of the attack hit, temporarily halting trading altogether.

It appears that the main assault targeted the control systems at several power stations across the United States with a malware program. This bug was able to place successful "logic bombs" that, when triggered in an obviously coordinated strike, exploited critical holes—called "zero day vulnerabilities"—in control systems to take control of approximately 50 power generators in a number of locations. The program increased the generators' rate of spin, and though it sent back data which suggested normal operations to anyone monitoring from the control room, the generators effectively spun themselves out of control and blew apart. At some power plants, affected generators caused fires which led to the entire facility being taken offline.

It has been easier to make an informed assessment as to the perpetrator of the second attack. A failed attempt to breach the security system of a power station in Los Angeles several weeks ago bore several similar hallmarks to the recent East Coast attack and was eventually traced back to a facility in Pyongyang, North Korea. Other elements of the attack suggest the specific involvement of hackers from Bureau 121, North Korea's specially trained cyber-warfare unit. Though no formal communication or claim of responsibility has been received from Pyongyang, analysts suggest that this attack may be intended to strengthen North Korea's hand during the ongoing nuclear negotiations in Singapore.

Unrest is growing in the areas remaining without power, as well as in areas with power as the latter are being flooded by anxious citizens in search of staple items such as food and water. State and federal emergency management units are responding, but report that citizens appear less inclined to comply with their instructions.

We have been hit, it appears, by a "perfect storm" of cyber-attacks. However, our attempts to link them remain conjectural. If, as our analysts believe, the North Koreans intended to make a show of force to shore up their negotiating position in Singapore, it is likely not a coincidence that some of the first data posted by the German "Guardians of Destruction" hackers targeted Secretary of State Celeste Matheson, our lead negotiator. But we know of no link between the German hackers and Pyongyang, which suggests coordination at another level.

Chinese involvement cannot be ruled out. Indeed, there exists the possibility that North Korean hackers are acting as a "front of shop" operation for a larger Chinese plot. The North Korean government is known to lease IP addresses from China, including some linked to previous cyber-attacks. In addition, unverified reports from South Korean intelligence have suggested an increased presence of both Chinese and Iranian nationals in Pyongyang serving in "advisory" capacities for the government's various telecommunications programs. This may serve as cover for hacking coordination, but these South Korean reports are still being vetted.

★★★

Could It Really Happen?

So much of our world relies on a very simple principle: when we flip on a light switch or turn on any sort of device, we expect power to be there. We expect the light to turn on or the device to start working. Most of our everyday activities require the use of some sort of power, usually electrical. We take it for granted. But what if, one day, it wasn't there? What if we found ourselves plunged into a literal—if temporary—dark age?

A serious cyberattack on the power grid would constitute a major national security threat on its own, but what if it came on the heels of an assault on the financial sector? Or a major hack targeting sensitive government data in which officials' personal information was used to compromise their professional work? Government servers, especially when they contain classified information, are supposed to be secure. If they cannot be protected adequately, that could threaten our entire national security infrastructure.

We can begin by breaking down the elements of this hypothetical attack in roughly the order in which they occurred in the scenario.

Compromising Government Data

If the United States government is going to be responsible for the security of this nation, it should be able to protect its own critical data from outside attacks. Unfortunately, high-profile hacking incidents suggest it has a long way to go. Additionally, irresponsible actions on the part of individual high-level government officials can result in improper handling of classified information. Officials' personal data and classified information can be dangerous if it falls into the wrong hands, as our scenario shows. Recent examples prominently highlight these deficiencies.

In the summer of 2015, millions of Americans had their personal information exposed after two cyberattacks were launched against the Office of Personnel Management (OPM), the government agency responsible for keeping records on all federal employees. The first of these hit OPM records stored on servers at the Department of the Interior and resulted in the theft of records on 4.2 million employees.[14] That would have been bad enough, but the hackers weren't through yet. They soon struck again, this time directly at OPM's own system, and stole files on 21.5 million individuals. These were not mere employment records, however: they were files related to these workers' security clearances.[15]

When someone applies for a government job that would involve handling sensitive information, they need to obtain a security clearance, which involves a lengthy application process and a background investigation. Applicants are required to provide a complete picture of their life since the age of eighteen, including every place they've lived, listings of their family and neighbors, and anywhere they've traveled outside the United States. In the wake of the OPM hack, it appears that anyone who made such an application since at least 2000 has had their information compromised.[16]

The 21.5 million people affected include not just current and former federal workers, but their family, friends, relatives, and others who may have been listed on their applications.[17] Because I am a former federal prosecutor who held a security clearance, it's likely the hackers know plenty about me!

So who are they? Who now holds all the information they'd care to know about millions of federal workers at all levels? Government officials—although they'll only say so privately—have pinpointed China as the source of the hacks, which were apparently part of a "strategic plan" of Beijing's aimed at beefing up their data-gathering efforts.[18] Big-data theft on such a massive scale, specifically targeting government employees, is not carried out to commit fraud crimes like identity theft. There can be only one motive for one state to steal another's government data: espionage. And Chinese spies now have a deep well of information about our government workers, including many in sensitive positions, and their families.

Sometimes sensitive government information can be exposed even without the involvement of foreign actors. Sometimes high-level federal officials decide to sacrifice security in the name of convenience.

Former secretary of state Hillary Clinton appears to have done just that while serving as our nation's top diplomat. While working in government, Secretary Clinton opted to make substantial use of a private e-mail account hosted on a private server located at her house in New York, not her office in Washington. It was out of "convenience," she said.[19]

Internal investigators, looking at some 30,000 e-mails on Mrs. Clinton's private account, found that potentially "hundreds" of them could contain classified information.[20] For her part, the former secretary of state, U.S. senator, and first lady—then in the midst of her second presidential campaign—insisted that she "did not send nor receive anything that was classified at the time."[21] Charles McCullough, inspector general of the intelligence community, disagreed, pointing out that a sample of forty of the Clinton e-mails revealed that "at least four" did contain "information [that] was classified at the time that the e-mails were sent," according to Reuters.[22] Clinton's only response was that she had "no idea" about the e-mails in question.[23] In addition, it was revealed that, as part of these investigations, the State Department itself managed to publicly release one e-mail that included classified information.[24]

This generally cavalier attitude toward classified material being trafficked through a private server raises a number of disturbing questions. For instance, just how secure was this personal account? If Secretary Clinton's own carelessness allowed classified material to be exposed, it is not difficult to imagine the even greater level of damage that could be done if a trained hacker was able to break in, as our scenario suggests.

The Hacker Community and Its Complicated Ethics

In the scenario above, U.S. government data and e-mails were stolen by a German hacker who sold his skills to the highest bidder, a practice that got him kicked out of a larger hacking collective. This larger group, the fictional "Digital Justice Ministry," is loosely based on a real hacker organization based in Germany, the "Chaos Computer Club," or CCC.

The CCC, founded in 1981, is one of the world's oldest hacking groups.[25] Members gather at its Berlin headquarters under posters bearing messages like "Liberty waits on your fingers" and even drink Club-Mate, as do our fictional hackers. CCC hackers are known to be talented, and they have their own distinct ethos. A 2011 *Guardian* report, which calls CCC "a hub of political activism," says their values include "transparency of governments, privacy for private people and the removal of excessive restrictions on sharing information."[26] Sometimes their hacks are benevolent and point out weak spots in the security used in consumer technology.[27] But they have also been known to strike when they feel their ideals have been violated: in October 2011, they exposed a German government online surveillance program in a move that, according to German media, "triggered a political shockwave in the country."[28]

As far as we know, the CCC has rejected overtures from jihadists and other groups to carry out attacks on their behalf.[29] The hackers' own ethics probably have a lot to do with this. But we present the entirely possible scenario that a member of this community with different ideas, who has no problem working on behalf of one state against another, could go rogue and carry out such a cyberattack as we describe. Groups like the Chaos Computer Club contain many accomplished hackers, and only a few need be lured away.

Quantum Computing: The Next Cyber Threat

The fictional hacker in our scenario uses a prototype "quantum computer" to break through security barriers on multiple government servers in a relatively short period of time. Quantum computing, which is still being researched, will allow computers to work at speeds much, much faster than we can imagine today. It will also have profound implications for cybersecurity.

Standard computers today operate using "bits," which transmit information in sequences of zeros and ones. In this binary code, 1 means a bit is "on" and 0 means a bit is "off." Using this simple language, which actually dates all the way back to early computing in the 1930s, our computers can perform calculations or perform whatever task they are programmed to do. The problem is, some tasks can take a long time. Quantum bits, or "qubits," speed up the process exponentially. This is because unlike a standard bit, which can only be on or off, a qubit can be on, off, or what's called a "mixed state" in between the two.[30]

A qubit, therefore, can essentially be many places at once. That means a computer running on quantum bits—a quantum computer—can perform far more calculations at far greater speeds than traditional computers today.[31] Vivek Wadhwa, who holds research positions at Stanford and Duke Universities, puts it this way: "Imagine being able to open a combination lock by trying every possible number and sequence at the same time."[32]

Taking this analogy only a small step further: Imagine that this theoretical "combination lock" is in fact the layer of security protecting a government server. This is how, using a quantum computer, our fictional hacker was able to break in. It's no wonder that Wadhwa refers to quantum computing as "the technology equivalent of a nuclear weapon."[33]

Mark Ritter, an IBM researcher, announced in April 2015 that we were "entering what will come to be seen as the golden age of quantum computing research."[34] IBM is just one of many companies working on quantum computer technology; Google and Microsoft are in the arena as well, along with the defense industry.[35] One company in Canada, D-Wave Systems Inc., has already built a quantum computer, and it was the physical description of D-Wave's machine that informed the description of the one used by our fictional hacker.[36]

While the United States remains the world leader in quantum computing research, we may have some competition—from the Chinese. The private security firm Stratfor reports that the Chinese government has "dedicated significant funds" to this endeavor.[37] Stratfor points out that China was able to catch up with the United States in developing supercomputers, and as such they cannot be discounted in the race to master the next generation of technology, quantum computers, as a nation security resource.[38]

The Chinese factor into our quantum computing scenario as the source for the quantum processor used by our German hacker. Chinese media reported on experiments with quantum processors at the University of Science and Technology of China in April 2015,[39] and our scenario posits that in the near future

Chinese-made quantum processors will find their way onto the black market—with or without government collusion. This prospect is uncomfortable but hardly unimaginable.

Forcing the Markets into a "Flash Crash"

Trouble begins again in our scenario with the start of the trading day on Wall Street, when several high-frequency trading firms notice a marked increase in orders. High-frequency trading is all automated: large amounts of shares change hands at high speeds, usually with minimal human involvement.

The danger here, of course, is that trading done by machines can be vulnerable to cyberattacks against these machines' programming. The algorithms they rely on can be altered, for instance, or preset risk limits removed. And because these high-frequency trading firms can be wired into many stock exchanges around the world, the repercussions would be felt not just in the United States.[40] A trader in the UK flooding the market using illegal trading methods helped cause a "flash crash" in 2010 that caused high-frequency traders to temporarily stop trading. When that happened, one former high-frequency trader said: "Basically, we saw the market just disappear. It vanished."[41] The disruption was temporary, but the Dow Jones industrial average still lost 600 points before recovering.[42]

As a CNN report pointed out, in automated trading "the machines don't feel obligated to step in during a crisis."[43] Hackers targeting these machines in their algorithms could cause serious damage in a short period of time, and erode confidence in the markets well after their initial attack. But in our scenario, the entire stock market soon shut down on its own.

When the Lights Go Out

If the second wave of this cyberstrike begins to crest with the attack on the markets, it comes crashing down when it takes out the power grid. This phase of the scenario is based on a hypothetical attack designed by the University of Cambridge's Centre

for Risk Studies. An analysis of this fictional attack and its subsequent economic impacts was published in July 2015 in a joint
report issued by Cambridge and global insurer Lloyd's of London. Using "several historical and publically known real-world examples," the Cambridge scenario provides an up-to-date picture
of what a massive cyberattack against the United States might
look like.[44]

In this fictional attack, hackers working for an unnamed "hostile actor" were able to implant a malware bug into the systems of
control rooms at U.S. power stations. The bug looked for and located "zero-day vulnerabilities," holes in the security system that
the developers don't know about and, once discovered, must be
fixed as soon as possible, ideally in "zero days."[45] The report notes
that the implanting of the bug and the laying of its "logic bombs"
could be achieved in a number of ways, including by compromising devices used by plant personnel with access to the network or
by breaking into systems via remote access.[46]

The bug then enters a dormant period, where it transmits information back to the hackers, allowing them to analyze the power
systems and see how best to gain control of individual generators.
The attackers time their attack for the hot summer months, aware
that "an attack in the summer will cause widespread disruption."[47]

When the attack is initiated and the malware attempts to take
over individual generators, the Cambridge report factors in security measures that protect many of the infected devices. Still,
in our scenario, the infection was so widespread that, across the
northeastern United States, fifty generators were hacked through
their plants' own control systems and made to self-destruct. Once
in control, the Cambridge model imagines, the hackers would
speed up the generators to cause them to burst into flame and
blow themselves apart, which also causes additional damage at
the plants.[48] This is similar to an earlier simulated attack in 2007
known as the Aurora Generator Test, when experiments at the
Idaho National Laboratory showed that a generator could be
hacked remotely and made to self-inflict damage in this way. The
basis for the Cambridge scenario contends that, despite increased

security since then, some 10 percent of U.S. generators remain vulnerable to this kind of attack.[49]

When fifty generators go out, the effects are profound. The short- and long-term consequences hypothesized in the Cambridge scenario are far-reaching. Immediately, 93 million people across fifteen states and Washington, D.C., would find themselves without power. While the initial attack would cause few casualties, deaths would ramp up due to accidents and civil unrest. Infrastructure would shut down, public services become unavailable, and communications crumble. Social unrest would increase as periods without power drag on, along with food and water shortages. It would be several weeks before power could be fully restored.

Airports would be temporarily shut down, in an echo of a real-life event in which nearly a thousand flights were disrupted in August 2015.[50] Though this was determined to have been caused by a technical glitch in an FAA flight-routing system, a strategic cyberattack against a similar system could produce a similar result. On 9/11, of course, flights all over the country were grounded on purpose, and the 9/11 Museum in New York today features a haunting graphic display showing what that looked like. Lights representing each flight are arrayed over a map of the United States on the morning of 9/11. They crisscross the map brightly at first, but a time-lapse effect shows them starting to disappear around 10 a.m., until the map is mostly dark. The sky is emptied, just like it could be in a cyberattack.

The Cambridge scenario has a number of different variants, which affect the length of the blackout and the eventual total cost. The "standard" versions of the scenario involve fifty power generators being affected, resulting in a blackout lasting two to three weeks in some localities[51] and inflicting an economic hit estimated at $243 billion.[52] In the "extreme" scenario, which imagines one hundred generators impacted, power could be out for as long as a month[53] and the economic costs could exceed $1 trillion.[54]

The Cambridge-Lloyd's report does not speculate on the final human toll of such an attack. An earlier study, however, may provide at least a ballpark estimate. In 2007 the National Academy of Sciences presented a report on power grid vulnerabilities to the Department of Homeland Security, but it remained classified until 2012. According to that report, we can expect "hundreds or even thousands of deaths" if such an attack were to be launched in already-excessive weather conditions such as summer heat.[55]

North Korea's Cyberwarriors

We imagine that North Korea is behind the attack on our power grid as part of a plan to demonstrate its capabilities and hold the United States hostage during negotiations over its nuclear program when the country is in the midst of a famine. Could this hermit kingdom, where only a tiny fraction of the population has Internet access, really pull off such a sophisticated attack? In fact, when it comes to cyberwarfare, the North Koreans are much more capable than they may seem.[56] According to security expert Richard Clarke in his book *Cyber War: The Next Threat to National Security and What to Do About It*, "while North Korea may not have invested much in developing an Internet infrastructure, it has invested in taking down the infrastructure in other countries."[57]

North Korea has at least four dedicated agencies within its government and military structure devoted to cyberwar, the most prominent of which is the Korean People's Army Joint Chiefs Cyber Warfare Unit 121,[58] also known as "Bureau 121."[59] Reportedly, this elite force is made up of approximately 1,800 hackers,[60] and a 2014 analysis by Hewlett-Packard cited South Korean sources[61] that ranked Bureau 121 the third-largest cyberwarfare unit in the world, behind those of Russia and the United States.[62]

According to one North Korean defector, for his former country "the strongest weapon is cyber . . . it's called the Secret War."[63] And they make sure to recruit only top talent to serve on the "secret war's" front lines. Another defector, a former computer science professor, describes "a pyramid-like prodigy recruiting system, where smart kids from all over the country—students who are good at math, coding and possess top analytical skills"[64]— are identified early on. Like our fictional North Korean hacker recruit, they are sent to Geumseong Middle School in Pyongyang. Later they attend one of the country's elite colleges, such as Command Automation University, where, according to Richard Clarke, "their sole academic focus is to learn how to hack into enemy network systems."[65]

Hacking for the regime comes with many perks. Defectors report North Korea's cyberwarriors are well paid and can bring their whole families from their hometowns to live in the comparative luxury of Pyongyang.[66]

North Korean hackers have launched several high-profile attacks against South Korea and the United States in recent years. Serious alarms were raised in July 2009 when U.S. and South Korean government Web sites were attacked over several days.[67] In April 2011, 30 million subscribers of a South Korean bank were shut out of online banking and card services.[68] More banks in South Korea were hit in 2013.[69] North Korea was also behind the attack on Sony Pictures in 2014, which cost the company at least $15 million.[70]

The 2009 attack is perhaps most relevant to our scenario. In multiple waves of "distributed denial of service" (DDoS) attacks starting July 4, hackers succeeded in temporarily shutting down the Web sites of the U.S. Departments of State and Homeland Security, and servers at the U.S. Treasury, Secret Service, and other agencies. South Korean government and corporate Web sites were hit even harder.[71]

Richard Clarke notes that "the damage was contained" but that the attack, "though not devastating, was fairly sophisticated," and the order to proceed, according to many analysts, came from the country's then-ruler Kim Jong-il himself.[72] North Korea also launched multiple rockets at the same time, projecting force in two battle spheres simultaneously, with the cyberattack being far more effective. Barely two months after the attack, former President Bill Clinton was in Pyongyang for a meeting with Kim Jong-il to secure the release of two imprisoned American journalists.[73]

As in our scenario, North Korea has shown itself willing to use cyberattacks as diplomatic leverage.

There is also the question of North Korea's coordination with other countries in cyberwarfare efforts, particularly China. For instance, some North Korean hacker units are known to have operated cells out of hotels in China.[74] South Korean intelligence reported that an IP address linked to the 2009 attacks was traced to the North's Ministry of Post and Telecommunications and that the address itself was leased from China.[75] Finally, we include an Iranian operative among the North Korean hackers. Iran's own past cyberwarfare activities include attacks against oil companies in Saudi Arabia and Qatar and financial institutions in the United States. Given the countries' well-documented exchange of nuclear scientists—Iranians have reportedly traveled to observe multiple North Korean nuclear tests[76]—coordination in other areas, such as cyberstrategy, is not difficult to imagine.

★★★

What Can We Do to Stop This?

The 9/11 attacks horrifically exposed America to a new reality of war in the twenty-first century. We have not, thankfully, had a massive cyberattack that caused direct damage to American citizens on that kind of scale. But I believe that we are still stuck in a pre-9/11 mentality when it comes to facing the uniquely twenty-first-century threat of a massive cyberattack. That is a mentality we need to shed before something drastic forces us to do so.

Just like any cyberattack our nation might face, this scenario had many moving parts. Broad changes in our national cybersecurity policy can go a long way to preventing these kinds of attacks in the first place. Toward this end, we should:

ESTABLISH CYBERWARFARE "RULES OF ENGAGEMENT." Cyberattacks can easily be used as instruments of war against the United States and can be just as devastating as missiles or bombs. We need to establish how responses to cyberattacks will fit within the continuum of force escalation as a part of our larger defense policy. To do that, we must work out answers to a number of questions. For instance: When is a cyberattack a crime versus an act of war? How is cyberwar defined if the enemy is unclear? Do international agreements such as the North Atlantic Treaty apply in the event of cyberattacks? Only when solid consensus is reached on answers to these and other questions will we have a cyberpolicy truly worthy of the twenty-first century.

STEP UP RESEARCH INTO QUANTUM COMPUTING. Albert Einstein referred to certain aspects of quantum mechanics as "spooky action at a distance."[77] Our own distance from a quantum future is closing fast, and we need to run to meet it to avoid being spooked. This means the United States must be far and away the world leader in quantum computing research. Because of the cybersecurity implications for all Americans, there is a role for government in this process as well. Whether through increased government research, partnerships with private industry, or a combination thereof, we must take the lead not only in advancing quantum computing but also in constructing the toughest defenses against its less benevolent uses.

TRAIN AND RECRUIT THE NEXT GENERATION OF CYBERWARRIORS. Cyberspace is our newest battlefield, and we must have trained fighters ready to deploy—cyberwarfare roles not just in the military but in civilian agencies like the Department of Homeland Security as well. The traditional military makes it a priority to inspire young Americans to serve in its ranks, and makes sure they pick the best. Our civilian cyberdefenders should be of the same caliber. DHS should review their cyberworkforce periodically to make sure they have the training they need to respond to any sort of online emergency and should strive to recruit top talent. But this goes beyond encouraging young, tech-savvy Americans to serve in government; it starts even earlier, with the support of STEM (science, technology, engineering, and math) education in our schools. More STEM education in schools means more students will get the tools and motivation they need to pursue college degrees in the telecommunications field. One of those students could go on to discover a zero-day vulnerability in some critical software and prevent a cyberattack.

RECOGNIZE THE RISKS OF INCREASED CONNECTIVITY. Technologists like to talk about "the Internet of Things": the idea that more and more devices will become interconnected over time. Some estimate that as many as 100 billion devices will be linked to some kind of network by 2020.[78] Naturally, greater connectivity can bring greater risk of attack. A hacker exploiting a weakness in one device could potentially take down a much larger network. Government and the private sector should work together to make sure that security protections are built into our networks and products as we develop and connect them. This caution can also be applied to policies that lead to increased connection. For instance, President Obama wants to integrate America's power grid and make it even more digitized with the Smart Grid Initiative. Grants to accomplish this will be administered by the U.S. Department of Energy. Unfortunately, it is not clear that power companies applying for this government money will need to make any improvements to their systems to keep an increasingly digitized grid safe from cyberattacks.[79] Serious security requirements, or at the very least a greater measure of transparency, would improve this White House policy.

INCREASE PROTECTION FOR GOVERNMENT NETWORKS. After the Chinese hacked the Office of Personnel Management and stole the personal data of over 22 million Americans (including, most likely, my own as a former employee of the Department of Justice), it became clear that our civilian federal networks have serious security vulnerabilities. Their protections should be brought more in line with those employed by the Department of Defense to secure military networks. For instance, civilian networks should employ more advanced cybersecurity programs and be provided with additional technical support to detect incoming threats. And as soon as threats are detected, no bureaucratic hurdles should prevent responding to them right away. When a zero-day vulnerability is discovered, there's not a second to spare.

**PROMOTE MORE AND SAFER SHARING OF INFORMATION AND BEST PRAC-
TICES BETWEEN THE PUBLIC AND PRIVATE SECTORS.** Our enemies have launched, and will continue to launch, cyberattacks against government agencies and businesses alike. Everyone shares risk, and that means everyone shares the responsibility to help mitigate that risk. The Department of Homeland Security has an agency specifically designed for this purpose called the National Cybersecurity and Communications Integration Center (NCCIC), which the government and the private sector use to interface on cyberissues. Many companies remain leery of handing over their information to the federal government, and understandably so. Regrettably, this causes most cyberattacks against companies to go unreported. Reporting cyberattacks can provide vital clues to stopping hackers in the future. That is why NCCIC is and must remain strictly a conduit for sharing information: it is not a regulator that will use the information a company submits against it, nor will it harvest data on the company's customers. Built-in privacy protections, for companies and private citizens, should remain a key part our information-sharing structure. President Obama supports this kind of cooperation, but he expects too much from businesses and does not offer them the kind of liability protection they need and deserve. The next administration must respect the concerns of members of the business community when they turn additional information over to the government, and must offer them real protection and incentives to report attacks. Eighty-five percent of America's critical infrastructure, like the power grid, is controlled by the private sector, which only underscores how critical their buy-in really is. But the flow of information need not be just one way. Businesses should be encouraged to share cyberattack reports with each other as well; a timely report of an attack by one bank could alert the whole financial industry in time to avert a major crisis. Best practices—such as strategies for multifactor authentication for critical systems—could also be exchanged. The sooner we make it easier for businesses and the

government to work together efficiently while respecting the privacy of all involved, the sooner we will be able to defend against the kind of cyberattacks fictionalized here. The good news is, some progress is already being made on this front. The Center for Strategic and International Studies (CSIS) has convened a cyberpolicy task force, of which I serve as a cochair. With one working group based in Washington and another in Silicon Valley, our task force brings together the best and brightest minds in the public and private sectors to meet this challenge head-on. That's the kind of cooperation we should see at all levels between government and the business community.

6

The Threat We Can't See

Bioterror in the Magic Kingdom

MIAMI GARDENS, FLORIDA
JULY 14, 2019
2:32 P.M.

Just a few streams of light were making their way into the small guest bedroom where the three women sat and waited. The blinds were drawn, of course, and even the brilliance of the South Florida summer sun was not enough to penetrate the gloom.

Ayesha sat on the bed and looked from one of her companions to the other. Fatimah sat on a chair near the door, and Safiyyah was seated at a small computer desk in the corner.

Ayesha liked her two companions, but she was still not sure she could fully trust them. Her husband, Osman, had said that was probably a good thing. She would have to remain on her guard and not get complacent. If she was too comfortable with the others, there was always the chance she might miss something. A suspicious glance at a mobile phone, a period of lapsed contact—these could mean trouble the closer they got to the mission itself. It could mean one was preparing to back out or, worse, inform.

Still, they all knew each other well enough from the mosque. Ayesha and Osman had chosen the other two with confidence after staying up late many nights going through lists and lists of prospective candidates. They had plenty of time, but they had wanted to make sure everything was going exactly as planned.

When Osman had first told Ayesha that he'd heard from his

cousin Farouk—with whom no one in the family had had any contact for years—somehow she knew that this was where it would lead. Farouk had been an active member of their local mosque, though "active" was perhaps too weak a word. He had been known to argue with other congregants, and even the imam, about "complacency" in the community. South Florida Muslims, he complained, weren't pulling their weight in the global struggle. Most of their friends ignored Farouk, finding his ramblings tiresome. But Osman, to whom he'd always been close, always heard his cousin out. Part of that was because of the urgings of his wife.

Ayesha had always been drawn to Farouk. Not in any way that compromised her loyalty to Osman: her husband was a good man, a good father, and she would love him eternally. But Farouk, she felt, had something she'd never seen before, a holy fire that burned brighter and brighter the more animated he became when he would sit around their dinner table expounding on their duty to support their brothers and sisters in jihad. When Farouk stopped visiting their house and stopped showing up at the mosque, everyone seemed to feel they were well rid of him. But Ayesha knew that if he left without a word, there must have been some higher purpose.

So when Osman told his wife that Farouk had reached out unexpectedly by e-mail but that he was hesitant to respond, she insisted that he do so. "After all, he's family," she said. So Osman wrote back, and Farouk revealed he'd been in Pakistan for over a year. He had made contact with others as committed to the jihad as he was, and it sounded like he'd made his way into their inner circle fairly quickly. They had come up with an idea: a plan to strike a new kind of fear into the infidels, one they wouldn't be able to shake. Farouk asked for Osman's help, and more specifically he asked for Ayesha's.

There was a knock at the door, and Ayesha stood up to answer it. Saffiyah and Fatimah had just enough time to exchange a nervous glance before their friend returned, leading her husband, Osman, and a small, nervous-looking man in glasses who held a briefcase tightly under his arm. He set the case down on the desk in front of Saffiyah and cast his eyes sideways at Osman.

"This is Dr. Aziz," Osman said. "He says that everything is ready and we can get started."

As Dr. Aziz began to open his briefcase, Osman looked over at his wife. These, he realized, were the last moments he might have to convince her not to go through with Farouk's plan, not to forfeit her life and the lives of their friends for a scheme they weren't even sure would work. She had been so determined, and the strength of her faith had always been something he had loved about her, but this . . .

Osman knew he had to say something. But the words caught in his throat. Maybe if he was able to look at Ayesha, just to make eye contact, he could get the message across. He looked at his wife, but her eyes were fixed straight ahead in a steely gaze. Osman knew there was no going back.

Meanwhile, Dr. Aziz had removed a cloth from his briefcase and was unfolding it delicately. He revealed three hypodermic syringes, which he held up and inspected, each in turn.

"Come, sisters," Ayesha said, and gestured to the other two women.

Fatimah and Saffiyah both got up and joined her on the bed. Ayesha began rolling up her left sleeve, and the other women followed suit. Osman leaned against the doorway and watched as Dr. Aziz checked the needle once more and then injected Ayesha in the upper arm.

Ayesha barely flinched as the needle went in. As Dr. Aziz picked up the second syringe and moved to inject Fatimah, Ayesha closed her eyes and spoke some words from the Quran:

> But the transgressors changed the word from that which had been
> given them; so We sent on the transgressors a plague from heaven . . .[1]

MILLEDGEVILLE, GEORGIA
JULY 21, 2019
8:17 P.M.

Brad Galvin drummed his fingers on his desk as he scrolled through the credit card bill displayed on his computer screen. Things didn't exactly look great. A combination of planned and unplanned expenses appeared to be setting the Galvins up for a pretty lean month. They had to send in the next installment of fees for Brad Jr.'s summer soccer camp—all his friends were doing it, and it really wasn't fair to keep an eleven-year-old cooped up in the house all summer—and Brad and his wife, Jenny, had hoped that would count for June's main extravagance. Of course, that was before their minivan decided to start leaking oil.

The van had to be repaired as quickly as possible, not just because it was the main method of ferrying Brad Jr. and his nine-year-old sister, Cassie, around to all their various activities, but also because it was essential to the Galvins' upcoming summer vacation: a trip to Disney World.

That was what was really making Brad nervous. The trip was looming over his head like a tree branch swaying in a strong wind. And Brad knew exactly when it was going to snap. At the end of this week, the whole family was going to pile into the van and make the five-hour drive to Florida.

It wasn't the prospect of the trip itself that disturbed Brad—far from it. It had been an annual Galvin family tradition for the last three years, and the kids looked forward to it almost as much as Christmas. And Brad loved spending this time with his family; working the hours that he did, he didn't get to see them as often as he liked. Neither Brad nor Jenny had been able to go on vacations like this when they were kids, and they were glad to be able to give Brad Jr. and Cassie as many opportunities as they could.

The simple fact was that when the Galvins had decided to visit Disney World three years ago, times were just a little bit better. Brad had a good job managing a franchise for a car rental company, and Jenny had been able to do some freelance editing work online while she was at home with the kids. But as the children got older and got into more and more things, Jenny found she just couldn't make the time to take on new projects anymore. Brad still had his job at the car rental company, but the national chain, after years of rumors, had had to switch their health insurance carrier thanks to convoluted federal law. The effect on Brad and his coworkers, however, had been very simple: everyone's premiums had gone through the roof.

It hadn't proven a catastrophe, at least not so far. The Galvins still lived in a nice house on a nice street. They had the minivan and the sensible sedan that Brad drove to and from work. Nobody in their house would go hungry. But, like many Americans, they had entered a phase—hopefully temporary—when they were having trouble making ends meet. Brad knew that the Disney World trip was going to put a strain on their finances. He had gone for one of the most affordable trip options, but it would still end up costing them around $3,000.

Jenny was putting the kids to bed. In a few minutes Brad would get up to go kiss them good night. After that, he and Jenny would sit down and go over the numbers. They both knew they had to make this work. The look on their children's faces would be worth it.

WALT DISNEY WORLD RESORT
LAKE BUENA VISTA, FLORIDA
JULY 29, 2019
4:41 P.M.

Fatimah emerged from the women's restroom next to the "City Hall" building in the Magic Kingdom's "Main Street, U.S.A." area at Disney World. She felt a bit better after having splashed some cold water on her face, but was still feeling faint. She fumbled in her purse and pulled out a handheld electric fan that sprayed water, which she used to spray the air all around her. Before she put it away, she made sure to turn around and spray the bathroom door handle.

Fatimah joined the throngs of people making their way down the "Main Street." She was not going anywhere in particular. Her job was simply to make a few ambling circuits of the park, maybe wait in some lines for a few minutes, visit the restroom, and generally spend time in areas where she found a high concentration of people. All she had to do was breathe, cough when she felt like it, and remember to use her spraying fan.

She sprayed wherever she could, making use of the multiple refill cartridges she kept in her purse. She innocuously sprayed wherever crowds were thickest, whenever she lingered at food carts, and whenever she went through a doorway. The spray was refreshing, but it wasn't just water. It was a solution made from the serum Dr. Aziz had supplied, and it carried a deadly strain of smallpox.

Fatimah was glad to be feeling at least somewhat normal again. The last few days had been particularly uncomfortable. As Dr. Aziz had explained, however, this was how everything was supposed to work.

The strain of the smallpox virus with which they had been injected, and which each carried in her spraying fan, was designed to follow a strict progression of symptoms. When the disease occurred in nature, there was some variance to the length of each stage, making it harder to tell how and when it would advance in an individual. Fatimah, Saffiyah, and Ayesha had been injected with a version Dr. Aziz had customized himself, so he knew which symptoms would hit when.

Each of the women had followed his estimates so far: a ten-day period of incubation with no symptoms, and then three days of fevers and pain all over. Then, yesterday, the three women—all of whom had been staying at Ayesha and Osman's house—woke up to find their fevers had gone down. For the most part, at least: Fatimah's temperature was still running a little high. More importantly, they had each felt and seen small red bumps emerging in their mouths. The following day, today, those bumps had turned into open sores. That was when Dr. Aziz had said they were at the peak stage of being able to spread the virus. This meant it was time to put the final phase of their plan into action.

Osman drove the women the three and a half hours up the road to Disney World. Nobody said much on the ride. Fatimah, who still had a slight fever, slept for much of the ride. When they arrived, Osman handed each of the women a ticket for the Magic Kingdom Park and led them all through the gate. The women made sure to flip on their fans as they went through the turnstiles. Once they were through, everyone split up without a word. Fatimah went in one direction, Saffiyah in another, and Osman and Ayesha in a third.

After a few hours of walking and spraying, Fatimah now found her headache returning. *I must just be tired*, she thought. Seeing a bench nearby, she walked over and sat down. The movement made her head swim all over again.

WALT DISNEY WORLD RESORT
LAKE BUENA VISTA, FLORIDA
JULY 29, 2019
4:43 P.M.

"Look, Daddy!" Cassie Galvin exclaimed, pointing through the Main Street, U.S.A., crowds. "That lady just fell over!"

Brad Galvin stared, a bit lazily, into the distance. What on earth could his daughter be talking about? There wasn't a lot more he could process right now. It was all he could do to keep up with his kids as it was. He could tell Jenny was flagging as well. This was their first day in the Magic Kingdom park, having spent the last two mostly at the Animal Kingdom. Epcot was still a day off.

Still, Brad and Jenny had known right away that going lean for another month or two would be worth it. Cassie and Brad Jr., who fought plenty at home as brothers and sisters tend to do, were not only getting along but seemed to be enjoying each other's company, going off to explore different areas together and leaving their parents panting to catch up. Brad even noticed that during the whole five-hour drive from Milledgeville the kids hadn't even zoned out with their headphones. They'd talked the whole way down, all four of them.

Standing in the middle of Main Street, U.S.A., Brad wondered whether the person his daughter had seen "falling over" was one of the wandering performers putting on a show. However, as he looked down the wide avenue with the trolley clanging down the middle, he saw it: a small heap curled up on the ground in front of a bench a few yards ahead.

When he saw that, he leapt into action. Still holding his daughter by the hand, the former lifeguard, current Boy Scout lifesaving instructor, and only CPR-certified employee at his workplace headed at a fast walk toward the still form. It was a woman, he saw as he drew closer, with one of those water-spritzing fans clutched in her right hand.

Brad knelt down beside her. He grabbed her wrist, took the fan out of her hand, and felt for her pulse. It was faint but present. He put his ear down close to listen for a heartbeat. There it was. He could also hear her breathing steadily.

Just as Brad was wondering what to do next, the woman came to. She saw Brad and Cassie kneeling over her and her eyes went wide. She stood up and began brushing at herself frantically as Brad tried to calm her down.

"It's okay," said Brad. "I think you just had a fainting spell. Want to wait for somebody to come get you?"

The woman shook her head. She muttered something in a language Brad didn't understand, then she hurried away. The Galvins, along with the handful of other patrons who had wandered closer to see what the excitement was about, found that it was over before it had really started. At least there hadn't even been time for the park staff to get involved, which, Brad had to admit, was a relief: they could keep moving.

"Good eyes, Cass!" Brad said as he watched the woman walk away—perhaps, it seemed to him, a bit unsteadily.

"My hero," said Jenny as she put her hand around her do-gooder husband's waist. He smiled sheepishly, and together, hand in hand, the four Galvins kept walking down Main Street, U.S.A.

FORT LAUDERDALE-HOLLYWOOD INTERNATIONAL
AIRPORT
BROWARD COUNTY, FLORIDA
AUGUST 12, 2019
8:16 A.M.

Osman sat in the departure lounge with his head in his hands. The fever had dropped, but he was still reeling. Even if it wasn't the sickness he could feel overtaking him, the emotional toll of the last few days had been staggering.

After their return from Disney World, Osman and Ayesha had asked Osman's brother to watch their two children for a while. They wanted to go on a retreat with some friends from the mosque, they said. Ayesha was too sick to come say good-bye; the raised bumps had begun to appear all over her body. But when

Osman waved as the kids drove away with their uncle, it hit home that this would be the last time he would ever see them. At least in this life.

His good-bye to Ayesha had been worse, but hadn't lasted very long, since she kept slipping in and out of consciousness. He left her lying on their bed, covered in the horrible pustules. She couldn't have more than a few days left.

Now Osman was fulfilling the final part of her and Farouk's plan. He could feel the sores developing inside his mouth. He wondered how long it would take for him to get as bad as Ayesha was. At least he'd be able to get to his destination.

"Final boarding call for Flight 872 to John F. Kennedy Airport, New York City," he heard over the public address system. "Repeat, this is your final boarding call."

Osman stood up and walked toward the gate. At least this part was easy, he told himself. All he had to do was breathe.

MILLEDGEVILLE, GEORGIA
AUGUST 12, 2019
10:12 A.M.

Brad Galvin was just glad to be back at work. He had felt bad about taking a few days off last week, especially right after his Disney World vacation, but his coworkers had understood. Besides, his fever had been especially nasty. Nothing like he'd ever had before. Brad wasn't the type to get sick often, especially not in the summer. And when he did come down with something, he usually powered through without missing any workdays.

Last week though, he'd been flat on his back for several days. Worse, he was afraid Jenny might have caught whatever it was. She seemed a bit under the weather now as well. What a fine "Welcome home" present this bug was.

At least their trip had been a success. They'd managed to visit nearly every park, and both kids and parents had kept up impressive energy levels the entire time. The kids hadn't been able to stop talking about it: Brad had heard his son on the phone the other day describing all the big rides in detail to one of his friends.

He smiled to himself at his desk. Now it was time to get back to the grind. There were bills to pay, after all.

As he turned to focus on his computer again, his tongue started to poke idly at the little bumps that had recently appeared in his mouth.

CENTERS FOR DISEASE CONTROL AND PREVENTION
ATLANTA, GEORGIA
AUGUST 13, 2019
8:29 A.M.

Phones were ringing, screens were flashing, and staffers constantly rose from one monitor to huddle over those of others. For Lisa Borowitz, who had worked in the CDC war room for only a few weeks, it was unlike anything her training had prepared her for.

Despite the studied calm, she was very aware of the undertones of panic running through the entire operation. She had known yesterday that something wasn't right. Senior staff had been in and out of the war room several times, but she hadn't been able to figure out what exactly was going on. It wasn't until this morning that she first heard the word she and her colleagues feared more than almost any other: "smallpox."

All the reports were coming out of the southern United States. A huge digital map at the front of the room had been zoomed in to show the Southeast, highlighting the areas where cases had been reported or confirmed. Lisa glanced up at the map again: four cases in Miami; seven in Orlando; six in Raleigh; even two in Milledgeville, less than a hundred miles away. As she watched, another incident indicator flashed up on the screen: three cases reported in Charlotte.

Lisa did some quick math in her head. From what she knew about smallpox, the people showing up with symptoms now would have been exposed about two weeks prior. They would likely have been contagious for at least some of that period, and many would have sought treatment right as the bizarre symptoms, like the all-over rash, first showed up. That was the most dangerous phase.

She knew what must be going on at the higher levels now.

Stockpiles of the vaccines would be raided and sent to the hot spots as quickly as possible, if they weren't already on their way. If the pockets were isolated enough, maybe the disease could be contained.

They were blessed, Lisa thought, that nothing had shown up yet in any major cities. In smaller cities and suburbs, exposure patterns might be easier to track, but if cases started showing up in major urban areas, like New York, Los Angeles, or Washington, where millions of people lived in close quarters and made heavy use of public transportation, the dangers would increase exponentially.

But maybe that was needless extrapolation. Maybe these were isolated incidents that could still be contained. Lisa remembered the case of a smallpox outbreak at a German hospital in 1970: that hadn't ended up spreading. But the question remained: Where had this come from? Smallpox had been eradicated decades ago.

Lisa knew the answer, even if she was afraid to think it. There was little to no chance smallpox was cropping up naturally again all of a sudden. This outbreak had to have been caused by man. It had to be terrorism.

There was enough vaccine in the U.S. to handle it. Lisa knew that. But she also knew that it was most effective up to seven days after initial exposure. How long had the virus been circulating already? How much of a head start did it have?

With a jolt, Lisa realized that everyone around her was sitting straight up at attention at their monitors. The CDC director had marched into the war room, accompanied by a squad of aides. She stood in front of the massive map as it continued to flash its bad news.

"Ladies and gentlemen," she announced loudly but calmly, "in case it is not already apparent, we are in the midst of a national emergency here."

September 1, 2019

LOCATION: The White House

INFECTED: 3,321

KILLED: 1,022 (smallpox); 27 (civil disturbances)

ONGOING EFFECTS: More than 3,300 Americans have been hospitalized with confirmed cases of smallpox in 19 states. There are thousands of additional reported cases of smallpox-like symptoms which have yet to be confirmed.

Over 1,000 Americans have been confirmed dead from smallpox.

A massive vaccination program is under way. While there exist sufficient reserves of smallpox vaccine, difficulties have emerged in strategically identifying areas where the virus is next likely to spread. Anticipating the contagion pattern is proving problematic.

Staff at local hospitals in major hot spots—mostly in the southern United States—are reporting an inability to deal with the influx of cases and are consistently requesting assistance from state and federal authorities, putting a strain on present resources.

Hospitals have been forced to remove patients to different wards, and in some cases transfer patients to other facilities, in order to effectively isolate smallpox patients whenever possible.

In at least five localities, entire hospitals have been closed off in order to treat the inordinate number of smallpox patients present.

Emergency training and instruction materials have been distributed to hospitals and first responders nationwide in order to make them aware of the symptoms of smallpox that occur prior to the readily apparent rash.

Governors in all 19 affected states have mobilized National Guard units, which have been engaged in protecting vaccine shipments, quelling civil disturbances, cordoning off hospitals and attending to other duties as necessary.

At least 200 cases of violent civil disturbances have been reported. Confirmed deaths associated with these actions currently stand at 27.

Martial law has not been declared on a national level as yet, but the Attorney General and Department of Justice are currently reviewing options to present in the event this course of action becomes necessary.

The European Union, Russia, China and 31 other nations have issued travel warnings or outright bans to prevent their citizens from traveling to the United States until the situation has been stabilized.

SUMMARY: The United States is in the grip of a smallpox epidemic unlike anything seen in decades. Our public health infrastructure is struggling to cope with the stress, and many local health facilities have been overwhelmed with cases. We appear to be nearing the end of the first wave of the outbreak—if our estimation of the time of the disease's introduction is correct—but it is impossible to say with certainty whether our vaccination efforts will entirely stop the spread, and if so, how quickly. We do have some preliminary guidance based on the Johns Hopkins Dark Winter war game exercise of 2001. The chart below shows their worst-case estimates after an infection of approximately three thousand with approximately one thousand deaths.

We remain hopeful that our vaccination efforts will prevent our seeing casualties on this scale.

The U.S. Intelligence Community has had a difficult time pinpointing exactly when and where the disease was introduced in the United States, but we can say with a high degree of confidence that this is an incident of bioterrorism. The perpetrators have yet to be determined, but there have been several potential links established between the communities in which some of the first cases were reported: Miami Gardens, Florida; Orlando, Florida; and Milledgeville, Georgia. We cannot state with certainty whether the virus was introduced in a single location and subsequently radiated out via human carriers, or was introduced in multiple locations.

A gas station clerk in the Miami area was, we believe, one of the first to be infected. He visited a local emergency room complaining of a high fever, was given antibiotics, and was subsequently sent home. Days later, he presented with a rash and was admitted. That same day, a park attendant at the Magic Kingdom Park at Walt Disney World presented with a rash as well. The following day, a middle-aged man in Milledgeville, Georgia, who had recently traveled to Disney World with his family, also showed a rash

Clinical Infectious Diseases

Smallpox epidemic projections, worst-case scenario (in the absence of disease-containment measures or new vaccine delivery), reported to the National Security Council meeting 3 (December 22, 2002) as part of the Dark Winter simulation exercise.

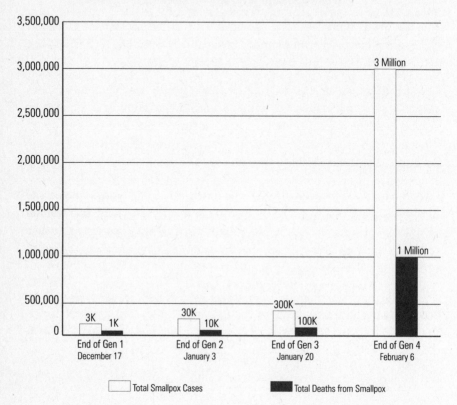

Tara O'Toole et al. Dis. 2002; 34:972–983 Clin Infect © 2002 by the Infectious Diseases Society of America

and was admitted to a local hospital. Two days after the Milledgeville man's admission, his wife complained of a high fever and was admitted herself. The smallpox diagnosis was confirmed in all of these cases.

In another, possibly related incident, a mailman reporting a strange smell emanating from a home in Miami Gardens, Florida, led police to discover the body of Ayesha al-Jabbari, age thirty-seven. The discovery was made on August 20, and Ms. al-Jabbari appeared to have been dead for several days. The coroner determined that she died of smallpox, which required the immediate vaccination of all personnel who had come into contact with the body. Despite this, two police officers became infected, and one of them died.

Ms. al-Jabbari's husband, Osman, has not been located. He is believed to have purchased a one-way ticket from Fort Lauderdale–Hollywood International Airport to John F. Kennedy Airport in New York on August 12, but no trace of him has been found since. Following up on leads related to Osman's disappearance is made more complicated by the fact that New York City has seen some of the worst urban disturbances of this crisis.

The al-Jabbaris deposited their two children with Osman's brother, telling him they intended to go on a spiritual retreat sponsored by their local mosque. However, the mosque leadership informed law enforcement that no such retreat has been scheduled for several months. More significantly, we have discovered that Osman's cousin, Farouk al-Jabbari, a former Miami Gardens resident with suspected links to Islamist extremists in Pakistan, has been out of the country for several months and his whereabouts are unknown.

Considering this extensive circumstantial evidence, we have named the al-Jabbaris as persons of interest in this case. Additionally, two women from their mosque have not been heard from in several weeks, and other mosque attendees reported an unfamiliar man, who identified himself to one individual as a medical doctor, attending Friday prayers with Osman al-Jabbari. Attempts are being made to ascertain his identity.

Teams are also scouring security footage from Disney World in an attempt to determine if the al-Jabbaris visited the park during the time frame in question. This may indicate a plot by a larger terrorist organization to introduce smallpox into a well-traveled area either by setting off a device equipped to release the virus or by simply placing infected persons in contact with as many people as possible. Feasibility studies for these and other potential plots are currently under way.

★★★

Could It Really Happen?

The idea of something as timeless as a summer family vacation being targeted by terrorists is horrifying but certainly not unrealistic. The Magic Kingdom Park at Walt Disney World was the most-visited theme park in the world in 2014, with over 19 million people passing through its gates.[2] Those 19 million people came from all over the country and the world—and, if exposed to a deadly virus, they would likely be able to take it back to their communities even before the symptoms presented themselves.

The specific threat of weaponized smallpox is very real as well. The disease was one of the world's deadliest, and although it has been officially eradicated, it still exists in limited quantities for research purposes. It's possible that some smallpox material is in a compromised position that could result in it falling into the wrong hands.

If smallpox were released in the United States, how would the government respond? Thankfully, no such emergency has occurred, but we have been able to gain some insight through other crises, real and imagined. A 2001 war game exercise known as "Dark Winter" helped examine what might happen in the case of a smallpox outbreak in the United States. In addition, the 2014 outbreak of Ebola in West Africa and its subsequent limited emergence in this country helped showcase the government's response in the face of a real emergency.

"One of the Greatest Scourges of Mankind": The Smallpox Threat

Smallpox cast its deadly shadow over a wide swath of human history. In just the twentieth century, it was responsible for the deaths of some 300 million people.[3] It is known to have been a killer thousands of years before that: the body of the ancient Egyptian pharaoh Ramses V, who died in 1157 BC, showed signs of the disease's telltale rash.[4] That rash is what gives the disease its name: "pox" comes from the Latin root for "spotted."[5]

Unfortunately, by the time the rash appears, the victim is already in danger. The incubation period for smallpox can last up to seventeen days, followed by four days of initial symptoms, according to the Centers for Disease Control and Prevention.[6] These symptoms are usually nonspecific, including headaches, fever, and potentially vomiting.

Specific symptoms can begin up to twenty-one days after exposure and are usually internal, involving small bumps that develop inside the victim's mouth and on the tongue. Those lead to open sores in the mouth that, according to CDC, mark the period where the victim is most capable of spreading the disease to others.[7] Over about four days, the rash spreads from inside the mouth and crops up on the skin, typically covering the entire body in twenty-four hours, before turning into raised bumps, which then fill with fluid. These fluid-filled bumps are a "major distinguishing characteristic" that points specifically to smallpox.[8]

Over the next sixteen days, the bumps undergo a process of turning into hard pustules, which then crust over and scab, before the scabs finally fall off. The entire process can last up to forty-one days. The CDC notes that victims are "contagious to others until all of the scabs have fallen off."[9]

That is, if they make it that long. The most common form of the disease, called "variola major," ends up killing about 30 percent of those infected.[10] The figures in the fictional scenario above—3,321 infected and 1,022 killed—reflect that death rate.

Even those who survive smallpox will likely be unable to forget their experience. Once the scabs fall off, permanent scarring can remain, particularly on the face and extremities.[11] It can also cause its victims to go blind.[12]

This is the threat our world faces if smallpox is once again unleashed. Dr. Gregory Koblentz of George Mason University, who studies bioterrorism and how to defend against it, summed things up well when he told a British newspaper: "I hope to God we never see another case of smallpox." Dr. Koblentz noted that the virus had killed more people "than all of the wars of the 20th century combined." Before it was eradicated, he said, "smallpox was one of the greatest scourges of mankind."[13]

How Safe Are We from Smallpox Today?

As noted above, smallpox has been declared eradicated. It no longer occurs in nature, and the last time it did was in Somalia in 1977.[14] What eventually stopped smallpox from becoming a global killer was mass vaccination, a strategy adopted by a number of countries, which finally culminated in a program begun by the World Health Organization in 1966 that set out to stop the disease once and for all.[15] By using a strategy of "containment and surveillance," WHO was able to respond effectively to outbreaks as they occurred.[16] In 1977, after the case in Somalia was confirmed, WHO vaccinated nearly fifty-five thousand people in just two weeks.[17]

By 1980, the World Health Organization was able to declare that the disease had been eradicated.[18] Modern medicine had finally vanquished a killer that had menaced the world for centuries. But between the last natural case in 1977 and the formal declaration of eradication in 1980, an additional smallpox incident occurred that is still worth bearing in mind today.

In 1978, Janet Parker, who worked in a laboratory at the University of Birmingham in England that was conducting research on smallpox, was taken ill with what was originally thought to be a drug reaction. But she later developed pustules, was diagnosed with smallpox, and became the last known human to die of the disease.[19] According to the BBC, "the ensuing investigation never established exactly how the smallpox virus had escaped from the university's laboratory."[20]

Today, only two locations have been sanctioned to house samples of the smallpox virus for research purposes: the American CDC in Atlanta, and Russia's State Research Center of Virology and Biotechnology, also known as Vector.[21] The presence of smallpox in Russia has been a source of repeated concern, especially considering the chaos that surrounded the breakup of the Soviet Union.

Rumors persisted among the scientific community early in the twenty-first century about Soviet or Russian supplies of smallpox—or individuals with the expertise to turn it into a deadly weapon—that may have been exported. In 2002, Donald A. Henderson, who led the WHO smallpox eradication program, told *National Geographic* that there was "some evidence that smallpox may already have been transported out of Russia to the Middle East, possibly to Iran or Iraq, and maybe even North Korea."[22] The same report quoted Kanatjan Alibekov—a Soviet biological warfare expert who defected to the United States in 1992—as saying that some of his former colleagues may have ended up in Iran. "There may be a couple in Iran," said Alibekov, who changed his name to Ken Alibek upon his defection, "but if so, we're not talking big numbers. Very few." Alibek added, somewhat ominously, "A few is all it takes."[23]

The intelligence community caught wind of this as well. As far back as 1994, according to the *Wall Street Journal*, the Defense Intelligence Agency was aware "that both Iraq and North Korea sought and received smallpox technology from the Russians in the early 1990s."[24]

Unaccounted-for samples of the smallpox virus have even been known to show up closer to home. In July 2014, workers cleaning out some storage space at the National Institutes of Health in Bethesda, Maryland, discovered six vials of smallpox left over from the 1950s.[25] They were immediately taken via secure transport to Atlanta for testing at the CDC, where at least two were found to contain viable samples of smallpox.[26]

Rumors of foreign smallpox and the accidental discovery of forgotten samples in a U.S. government lab may not be clear indications that a bioterrorist attack featuring smallpox is imminent, but they continue to raise important questions. A few mislaid containers of the virus, and the expertise to properly weaponize them, could allow a small group to unleash a global calamity. The CDC maintains today that "there are concerns that the smallpox virus could be used for bioterrorism."[27]

At the moment, the United States possesses enough smallpox vaccine to inoculate the entire population if necessary.[28] The vaccine is most effective, however, the earlier it is administered. For most people, receiving the vaccine within three days of their initial exposure to smallpox "will completely prevent or significantly modify" the disease's progress, the CDC explains.[29] But after that, it could be less effective. If given four to seven days after exposure, the vaccine only "likely offers some protection or may modify the severity" of smallpox.[30] The issue, as faced in our fictional scenario, is getting people vaccinated in time.

"Dark Winter": Smallpox Comes to America

In December of 2002 the United States fell victim to a small-pox attack. If you missed this on the news, that's understandable: it didn't really happen. A simulated attack set in December 2002 was the subject of a "war game" held in June 2001, known as "Dark Winter."

For the Dark Winter exercise, fourteen participants portray-ing senior policy makers gamed out a two-week scenario resulting from the release of smallpox at three American shopping malls at a time of heightened international tension.[31] Among the participants were Sam Nunn, a former Democratic senator from Georgia, who played the president of the United States; and Frank Keating, then the Republican governor of Oklahoma, who played a fictionalized version of his state's chief executive.[32] The exercise was organized by several academic and nonprofit groups—including the Johns Hopkins Center for Civilian Biodefense Studies and the Center for Strategic and International Studies—and approximately fifty people in the bioterrorism policy field observed.[33]

THE Dark Winter scenario began with 20 cases of smallpox being reported in Oklahoma City on December 9, along with 7 in Philadelphia and 9 in Atlanta. That jumped to 2,000 cases, along with 300 deaths, by December 15, and the following week saw a further increase to 16,000 cases and 1,000 deaths, all while law and order was breaking down in the affected areas. By the end of the simulation, "health authorities" were predicting three million Americans stricken with smallpox and one million dead within a matter of weeks.[34]

As a contemporary report noted, Dark Winter was "a game, but no one involved was having any fun."[35] The findings after the exercise were not especially encouraging. They concluded that:[36]

> ➤ A bioterror attack could lead to far-reaching national secu-
> rity concerns for the United States, including "massive civilian

casualties, breakdown in essential institutions, violation of democratic processes, civil disorder, loss of confidence in government and reduced U.S. strategic flexibility abroad."

➤ Our response to such an attack would be further hampered by "major 'fault lines' [that] exist between different levels of government (federal, state, and local), between government and the private sector, among different institutions and agencies, and within the public and private sector."

➤ Our public health infrastructure suffered from an "institutionally limited surge capacity [that] could result in hospitals being overwhelmed and becoming inoperable, and it could impede public health agencies' analysis of the scope, source and progress of the epidemic, their ability to educate and reassure the public, and their capacity to limit causalties and the spread of disease."

➤ Effective communication strategies would be critical in the event of such a crisis, including "dealing with the press effectively, communication with citizens, [and] maintaining the information flows necessary for command and control at all institutional levels."

➤ Keeping order and stopping the spread of disease "will present significant ethical, political, cultural, operational, and legal challenges."

Progress has been made since these dour predictions were made in 2001. Significantly, as noted above, the United States now has enough smallpox vaccine available to cover our entire population in the event the disease is used as a weapon against us. But challenges still remain.

A blue-ribbon panel of experts, organized by the Hudson Institute and Inter-University Center for Terrorism Studies and chaired by former Connecticut senator Joe Lieberman and former secretary of homeland security Tom Ridge, concluded in June 2015 that, despite spending approximately $10 billion on biodefense every year since 2001, "the United States still isn't adequately prepared to protect its citizens from a major biological or chemical event."[37]

As a critical case study, they cited the Ebola outbreak of 2014, when four individuals were diagnosed with the deadly virus on American soil. This case bears particular attention as an example of the government's handling of a real-life infectious disease crisis.

Ebola in America

The massive Ebola outbreak that would eventually reach the United States began in Guinea in March 2014 and soon spread to Liberia and Sierra Leone. Infections spread to other countries over the next few months, and in August the World Health Organization officially announced "an international emergency."[38] The Centers for Disease Control eventually called it "the largest Ebola outbreak in history,"[39] and as of this writing it had claimed more than eleven thousand lives in six countries. Of those, two of the deaths occurred in the United States. One of these individuals was first diagnosed in Sierra Leone, and the other was diagnosed in Dallas, Texas.

The initial Dallas patient, Thomas Eric Duncan, a Liberian national, traveled to the United States while sick in order to visit some relatives. Duncan first visited a hospital on September 26, 2014, complaining of a fever, but despite telling a nurse of his time in Liberia, he was merely sent home with antibiotics and over-the-counter pain medication.[40] Two days later, he was back in the hospital, and on September 30 the CDC confirmed the first case of Ebola in the United States.[41]

Duncan died of Ebola on October 8, and in the next few weeks two nurses who treated Duncan at Texas Health Presbyterian Hospital Dallas would also be diagnosed with the virus. The nurses, Nina Pham and Amber Vinson, eventually recovered. Soon after they were diagnosed, however, the Obama administration took action in response to the crisis that left much to be desired.

For instance, President Obama remained staunchly against any sort of "travel ban" on citizens from Ebola-stricken countries entering the United States. "We can't just cut ourselves off from West Africa," the President said in his weekly radio address to the nation on October 18. "Trying to seal off an entire region of the world—if that were even possible—could actually make the situation worse." But paradoxically he also warned that "before this is over, we may see more isolated cases here in America."[42]

The day before President Obama defended his plan to maintain open travel between the United States and the region most affected by Ebola, the White House announced that Ron Klain would "coordinate the government's comprehensive response to Ebola."[43] Klain had no background in public health, but he did have an extensive background in politics. A longtime Democratic operative, he had served as chief of staff to Vice Presidents Gore and Biden. Klain was a prime example of what's known in Washington-speak as a "czar." He may have been politically connected, but he was the wrong man for the job. An individual with specific medical and public health expertise was needed for a dire situation.

Although the Ebola crisis eventually died down, the Obama administration's actions did not seem to signal a government ready to respond to a deliberate bioterrorism attack.

What Can We Do to Stop This?

The threats of diseases like smallpox being used in a bioterror attack demand prompt attention from our government. We have clearly not yet heeded all of the lessons of the Dark Winter exercise in 2001. Our biodefense efforts need to be stepped up, and it needs to happen soon. Some of the general policy suggestions below have been on a slow simmer behind the scenes, while others were brought into stark focus as part of the 2014 Ebola crisis.

APPOINT A PERMANENT WHITE HOUSE OFFICIAL RESPONSIBLE FOR BIOTERROR POLICY. Ron Klain was enlisted to temporarily run the White House Ebola response efforts despite having no background in medicine, public health, or defense. This kind of ad hoc appointment of a political operative would not serve the nation well in the event of a bioterror attack. The administrations of George W. Bush and Bill Clinton both boasted a special assistant to the president for biodefense policy, who could be responsible not only for man-made threats like weaponized smallpox but also for nature-made crises like the Ebola outbreak.[44] The Obama administration—or, barring that, their immediate successors—should reinstate this position and fill it with a qualified individual. This person should be a central point of contact for all of the various government agencies involved in biodefense. In addition, he or she should be invested with the budgetary authority to accomplish the mission of effecting biodefense measures quickly in the midst of a crisis.[45]

STREAMLINE CONGRESSIONAL OVERSIGHT OF BIODEFENSE PREPARATION AT DHS. The Department of Homeland Security (DHS) is responsible for much of our national efforts to combat bioterrorism. Unfortunately, ever since DHS was first created in the wake of 9/11, it has been difficult for the American people's representatives in Congress to make sure this critical agency is performing at its best. In 2008 a commission on weapons of mass destruction and terrorism chaired by former senators Bob Graham and Jim Talent—which warned about the dangers of bioterrorism—noted that sixteen full committees and forty subcommittees in the House of Representatives alone claimed some form of jurisdiction over DHS. Take it from me, it's still a mess. Congress should follow the recommendation made by the Commission on the Prevention of Weapons of Mass Destruction Proliferation and Terrorism (the Graham/Talent WMD Commission) back in 2008 and bring DHS oversight under the sole jurisdiction of the Committees on Homeland Security in the House and Senate.[46] That would simplify and strengthen the relationship between DHS and Congress as we collaborate on biodefense and many other critical issues.

Both of these improvements would go a long way toward keeping the different branches and agencies in government on the same page when it comes to coordinating a response to a biological threat, no matter its source. Establishing these clear lines of authority is the first step. Following on from that, further specific steps can be implemented, including:

REASSESSING—THEN REVAMPING OR REPLACING—DHS'S BIOWATCH PRO-GRAM. The BioWatch program is an example of a good idea left to die thanks to government inefficiency. It placed sensors in dozens of metropolitan areas designed to detect aerosolized biological agents in the air, like those that would be deployed in a bioterror attack. But BioWatch was fraught with problems. Systems in some cities produced faulty results, while others had to undergo constant repairs. Even at its best, the "Generation 2" BioWatch system—as far as development went—could "take up to 36 hours to detect and confirm the presence of biological pathogens," according to a GAO report.[47] Finally, in April 2014, DHS scrapped the program altogether, canceling BioWatch "Generation 3" after racking up a cost to the taxpayers of over $1.1 billion.[48] We need a functioning biological sensor program, and we should get a working product for our money. If BioWatch doesn't fit the bill, it needs to be replaced with a program that does.

FOLLOWING A COMMONSENSE VISA POLICY DURING BIOLOGICAL EMERGEN-CIES. President Obama's insistence on maintaining open lanes of travel from West Africa to the United States during the Ebola crisis was irresponsible and was pursued over the objections of members of Congress from both parties.[49] Visas should have been temporarily suspended for the hardest-hit countries—Liberia, Guinea, and Sierra Leone—until their own Ebola situations stabilized. Obviously, it was not the intent of Ebola sufferers to come to the United States to purposefully infect Americans. But what's to stop terrorists from taking advantage of some future foreign health crisis along the same scale and willfully dispatching infected individuals to American shores on a bioterror suicide mission? In any event, a commonsense temporary visa restriction policy should be part of our all-of-the-above biodefense strategy.

7
Final Approach
Terror in the Skies of Los Angeles on Oscar Night

KUALA LUMPUR INTERNATIONAL AIRPORT
KUALA LUMPUR, MALAYSIA
FEBRUARY 27, 2022
11:16 P.M.

Sulaiman puffed on his cigarette as he sat in his pickup. He was parked in the middle of an unused traffic circle, part of the ring road around the Kuala Lumpur airport. Behind him, the fuel storage facility was lit up like a small city, the giant white tanks gleaming like so many high-rises. In front of him, it was much darker: the weak streetlights along the ring road often flickered, and there was very little traffic to illuminate the stretch with headlights.

He had been mostly undisturbed, for which he counted himself lucky. His default state of boredom had been jolted into hyperawareness whenever a car passed by, but this had happened only twice. At least, he thought it had only happened twice: he might have dozed through a third. Sulaiman felt guilty about this. For what he was being paid, he ought to be able to stay awake.

He wasn't exactly sure who was paying him, but they had certainly been generous. Sulaiman was getting over 7,000 ringgit—nearly $2,000—just to sit here and wait in the dark. He would get another 7,000 when the job was done. At least, that's what he was told. He hadn't seen any of it yet. In any event, he knew he had to stay awake. If someone was willing to throw around that kind of money, Sulaiman figured he didn't want to get on their bad side.

Don't know, don't want to know, he thought.

Fourteen thousand ringgit. He wondered what he'd do first. Probably hit the clubs in downtown Kuala Lumpur at least once before sending a chunk to his mother, who still lived deep in the interior, in a small town in the state of Pahang, where Sulaiman had grown up. It would have taken him months to earn that much in his job as a baggage handler at the airport. It would have taken him over a year to earn it in his last job, picking tea on a massive plantation in the Pahang hills. He didn't even bother to calculate how long it would have taken at the job before that, at the timber company he'd worked at since he was twelve. Working with the loggers had been terrifying: at least once a day for eight years he had thought he was going to die, or at least lose a limb. But the work had been steady, until the president of the timber company emptied the safe and ran off one day.

Sulaiman had been lucky to get the job on the tea plantation, but soon realized it was going nowhere. So, at twenty-four, like many young men his age, he had headed for the big city. Working as a baggage handler was easy, safe, and paid fairly well. He had carved out a decent life for himself in Kuala Lumpur. But what really made it worthwhile were the occasional cash commissions he got for making "deliveries."

When he had first arrived he'd met up with a friend from Pahang who had made the trip to the city a few years before. This friend introduced him to some acquaintances in the local underworld who were happy to get to know someone on the inside at Kuala Lumpur International. As a result, Sulaiman was paid a few hundred ringgit here and there for dropping off or picking up certain packages on certain flights that probably would have had a hard time getting past the scanners. He had only one rule: Never look inside.

In his own mind, this helped him rationalize his illicit activity. When his normal contacts approached him, it was almost always drugs. He knew that and had made his peace with it: drugs were good business, and if someone was willing to pay to put that in their body, that was their problem. Sometimes, however, he took referrals—friends of his normal partners. There could have been anything in those packages. Sulaiman had heard bizarre stories of endangered reptiles, even human organs, coming in that way. But as long as he didn't know what he was transporting, he was content to do the occasional service for the local black market economy.

Don't know, don't want to know.

The people he was meeting tonight were just such a referral, some "friends of friends." He heard a low crunching sound and saw a car appear out of the gloom and pull up alongside his truck. They weren't using headlights and had pulled off the main road into the pothole-ridden lot without him even noticing. They rolled their window down. Sulaiman was about to throw away his cigarette, but then decided to hold on to it. He'd look tougher.

It was dark in the other car, but he could tell he'd never seen the men before. They both had heavy beards. Without speaking, the driver reached with both hands to pass Sulaiman a package slightly bigger than a shoe box. As Sulaiman grabbed it with his hands, he felt the weight of the box—as if it were filled with lead. It strained his biceps, which weren't weak, given how much he used them to load massive suitcases on and off carts. Next they handed over a piece of notepaper on which were written a number of details: an airline, a flight number, a terminal, and an aircraft tail number. Sulaiman flipped on his mobile phone light to read it; the cab light was too risky.

"Any problems?" asked man in the driver's seat.

"No problems," Sulaiman replied. Then he gathered his courage. "Except my money."

The man in the passenger seat fumbled around and eventually a clear plastic bag full of banded bills was tossed into Sulaiman's window.

"Seven thousand," the first man said. He passed another mobile phone through the window.

"That phone has one number in it. Take a picture of the package in the cargo hold and send it to that number. Then smash the phone. We'll send the other seven thousand through your friends."

Sulaiman shook his head. "No deal. I don't trust those guys. How do I know I'll ever see it?"

The man in the passenger seat leaned over and spoke in a flat voice: "That is hardly our problem. And don't get any ideas about taking the 7,000 without doing the job. If we do not receive a picture tonight of that package in the hold, we will go to Pahang. We will visit your mother, Maryam, and your sister, Puteri, and, if Allah wills it, we will kill them. And we will take pictures. We will come back here and show you the pictures and then, if Allah wills it, we will kill you too."

Sulaiman saw a look in the man's eyes that he recognized as pure evil. Without a word, trying to disguise his fear, he turned the key of his truck and drove back toward the airport with his delivery.

As he drove, he ran over the flight details on the piece of paper. He'd already committed them to memory. That aircraft was loading at Satellite Terminal A, the main international terminal. This worked out well. Sulaiman had originally been on duty at the Main Terminal tonight, but had faked a phone call to the luggage office, answered it himself, and then told his boss they needed an extra pair of hands over on the international side. That would explain his absence, and he could show up at the other terminal with enough time to load his package before anyone noticed he was out of place. Even if that happened, he could just plead confusion: guys went to the wrong workstations all the time. This plan hadn't failed yet.

He crisscrossed down the airport service roads, taking every shortcut he knew to get to Satellite Terminal A. He parked the truck behind some hangars and switched to a luggage cart, in which he cruised past a dozen parking bays until he found the one he needed.

The drop-off was actually the easiest part: over in a few minutes after all that waiting. Sulaiman pulled the luggage cart over and joined the crew loading up the Boeing 747's cargo hold, announcing that he was relief sent over from the Main Terminal. The other men shrugged and paid him little notice. He tossed in a few suitcases, then smoothly picked up his package and tucked it in among the others. As he took a photo, making his movements as surreptitious as he could, the glow of his phone attracted the attention of another baggage handler. Sulaiman quickly looked down at the phone, then smiled at the other worker. "The wife," he muttered. The other man smiled back and shook his head. Sulaiman checked again: the text had gone through.

He loaded a few more suitcases and then pulled the reverse of his previous strategy. He ducked into the international terminal's baggage office, faked a phone call, and then told the crew he had to head back across the airport. After some shared words of complaint, he hopped in the luggage cart and departed. He headed back to his original workstation to finish his shift, his mind stopping briefly to consider that before long the 747 would depart and his package—whatever it was—would be on the way to its destination—wherever that was.

Don't know, don't want to know.

DOLBY THEATRE
HOLLYWOOD AVENUE AND HIGHLAND BOULEVARD
LOS ANGELES, CALIFORNIA
FEBRUARY 27, 2022
3:22 P.M.

How do you say "Back off" to a two-time Oscar winner? Amy Prescott had been prepared to encounter all manner of strange situations when she first came out to L.A. as an aimless intern looking for a job—any job—in show business, but this, she could safely say, was a question that had never occurred to her.

She recognized the tall man with the salt-and-pepper hair and beard standing on the famous red carpet at the ninety-fourth annual Academy Awards. He was a screenwriter, once considered the best of his generation—a generation from which Amy's own was at least two removed. Still, he'd adapted everything from Shakespeare to vampire fiction for the screen, and had earned two of the coveted gold statuettes in the process. He was someone, Amy knew, who could be expected to throw his weight around.

The young woman standing with him, however, was unknown to Amy. She was also apparently unknown to the two hulking security men, nearly bulging out of their tuxedos, who had positioned themselves on either side of her.

"She is a legal permanent resident of the United States," the screenwriter was explaining haughtily in a clipped, probably assumed voice. "My people submitted her residency documents for prescreening weeks ago and we were assured there were no problems whatsoever."

As far as Amy was concerned, he could have been describing competing theories of particle physics. Security was not her department; she was a production manager. Technically speaking, she was an assistant production manager—titles meant a lot in Hollywood—but today, on Oscar Day, she was filling the boss's shoes. The red carpet production manager was home with a debilitating case of flu, and Amy, at twenty-five, had been handed her big break.

She stood there in her evening dress, tablet computer in hand and earpiece with mic firmly affixed to her head, and attempted to tell this Hollywood legend that there was nothing she could do to get his companion into the ceremony. She tried not to feel guilty: it wasn't her fault he had dragged her into this. He had clearly sought out anyone with a head mic who looked like they were involved in the production, and proceeded to complain.

"I'm sorry sir," she said as diplomatically as possible. "You'll need to discuss it with the head of security. These gentlemen can take you to him. But if she hasn't been precleared, I'm not sure even he will be able to help."

"We'll see about that," the screenwriter sniffed, and stomped off with his embarrassed girlfriend in tow, flanked by the two security guards.

Amy felt bad for him. Security procedures this year were no joke: multiple checkpoints, thorough limousine searches, even retinal scans to access some areas. She has been vaguely aware of threats against the Oscars before, but it was something she assumed happened every year.

Right now she had her own problems to attend to. Some journalists had strayed from their assigned interview space, and it was time to politely remind them to move back. Traffic on the carpet had to be kept moving. Meanwhile the director of the telecast had e-mailed her twice since she'd been chatting with the screenwriter, and it looked like the second message contained lots of exclamation points. The chatter and noise of Hollywood's ultimate celebration of itself swelled all around her, but before diving back into the fray she took a moment to look up into the unusually clear late-winter sky. She had made it.

MIRABEL HOTEL
HILL STREET AND SECOND STREET
LOS ANGELES, CALIFORNIA
FEBRUARY 27, 2022
3:51 P.M.

The sky that greeted Saif when he awoke had been so astoundingly clear, far better than the reports had suggested, that he had said a prayer then and there that this weather would hold all day. It had. He could not believe his good fortune. He had come very close to e-mailing his colleagues to inform them of how well everything was proceeding, but the orders from the Khorasan Group had been very specific: no communication until the job was done or unless something went wrong.

So far, nothing had. The plan was already half-completed by now. He had received confirmation several hours ago that Preparation Phase One had gone successfully in Kuala Lumpur. This morning, completion of Preparation Phase Two, at the Loews Hollywood Hotel just a short distance away, was confirmed as well. Now all that remained were Execution Phases One and Two, and he calculated that those were only a few minutes away. Very soon he would fulfill his mission and complete the journey that had begun many years ago in a suburban Southern California basement with a boy they then called Allen Cunningham.

Recalling that name made Saif shudder. His mind and body recoiled alike at the infidel label he had once carried. But that was behind him now. Soon he would bring honor to his new family: his *ustadh* and his brothers in the jihad.

When he had spent so much time scrolling through Twitter those many years ago, bored in the basement late one night, he had not been looking for the jihad. The jihad had found him. The tweets caught his attention, then the tweets led to direct messages, and that led to further interaction over secure communication apps.

In that online world he found a sense of purpose that had eluded him his entire life. Growing up, all through school, most everything had eluded him: friends, girlfriends, academic achievement. Even his parents had pulled away, skipping his high school graduation and dropping what cursory interest they'd had in his attending college.

In these online forums, however, he was accepted. In fact, he was courted. His zeal for learning distinguished him from most of the rabble of posters. Bit by bit, he had learned the ways of Allah, the Prophet Muhammad, and the lesser prophets like Bin Laden and al-Zawahiri. He did take one college course, an Arabic class at the community college in the next town. That was where he had picked up his new moniker: Saif, or "sword."

Saif became closer and closer with his friends overseas, chatting for hours on end, sharing in their victories and defeats as their empire spread mile by bloody mile in war-torn Iraq and lawless Syria. As they grew to trust him, more and more senior Al Qaeda figures introduced themselves to him online, until one day he received an instant message that changed everything.

He was incredulous at first. Surely one of the top Khorasan Group operatives had not deigned to contact someone so unworthy as Saif directly. As they chatted over several weeks, it became clear: his newest online acquaintance was a member of that elite inner circle of Al Qaeda planners and leaders. To Saif, formerly known as Allen Cunningham, this new contact was known simply as *Ustadh:* "Teacher."

Over the course of a year, in weekly sessions, he was shown the brilliance of the Khorasan plans and was tutored in the skills he would need to carry out his part in them. At one point he drew up the courage to ask his *ustadh:* "Why me?"

"Because," his mentor had replied, "you are a righteous American. You will be the one to spread the true faith among your people. You will be a prophet unto the depths of evil itself."

NOW Saif stood ready to carry out the mission. This would be one of Khorasan's first operations outside the Middle East in some time. They had been lying low for several years, replenishing their ranks, planning and strategizing. The initial goal had been broad: a major attack on the West. Of course, they had to pick a target. Saif remembered doing the research for more senior members as they discussed options in online chats long into the night. When the answer came to them, it had seemed so simple.

For too long they and their brothers in the global jihad had focused on military and political targets. But it was more than America's invading armies and power-mad government they hated. The culture of filth that America exported alongside its monstrous political ideology—with which it attempted to corrupt the minds of young Muslims the world over—was equally if not more abhorrent. Why not, they reasoned, strike at the heart of that culture: Hollywood?

About eight miles away from Saif's low-rise hotel, degenerates from all over the world were being disgorged from limousines and traipsing down a red carpet, preparing to spend a few hours clapping for themselves. They were congratulating one another for perpetuating their monopoly on world culture for another year, and handing out awards to the most licentious of their number. The Khorasan Group, Al Qaeda's best and brightest, was about to show them that Allah's war was against them too.

Saif looked at the clock on his computer and felt his heart jump briefly. It was almost time. He activated his state-of-the-art GPS tracking software and rejoiced at what it showed. The target was right where it was supposed to be, right on time. It was just about to make landfall over L.A. after a long, long flight across the Pacific.

DOLBY THEATRE
HOLLYWOOD AVENUE AND HIGHLAND BOULEVARD
LOS ANGELES, CALIFORNIA
FEBRUARY 27, 2022
4:12 P.M.

Amy Prescott finally had a moment to breathe. The live feed playing in the corner of her tablet told her the opening monologue was nearing completion, and it would be a while before winners started filing back out into her area to appear before the press and wave their small statuettes next to a giant version of it that had already been set up for photo calls. They would stand there, look good, and maybe answer two or three softball questions before it was Amy's job to hustle them off. But the first winners wouldn't be there for a few minutes yet.

"How's it look out there?" Ron, the director, squawked nervously in her ear.

"Just fine, Ron," she answered, for the third time in ten minutes.

She took a discreet look around to make sure none of the bored reporters—or, more importantly, photographers—happened to be watching her, then bent her knees slightly to reach down and fix a heel strap that had been bothering her for some time.

That was when she heard it. Later, she would misremember this first sound as louder than it was, but really it was just a dull boom, like the roll of distant thunder. She stood up and looked, expecting to see a rain cloud intruding on this gorgeous day.

Instead, she saw a fireball in the sky. Flaming streaks could be seen falling toward the earth. An airplane had blown apart in front of her eyes. She heard a scream beside her, and then more as others turned to look. She could only stand still. She heard shutters begin to snap madly. Her hand went to her ear: she had to tell Ron, had to tell the people inside.

The world shook. Another deep rumble, this time much, much closer. Light fixtures set up along the red carpet toppled over, and a number of photographers tumbled to the ground. The giant Oscar statue swayed back and forth for a moment and then fell forward with a hollow thud. Amy managed to stay on her feet but stumbled out into the street. She was dazed, disoriented. Her tablet lay shattered on the pavement. She walked unsteadily a few feet toward the entrance to the shopping complex next door, but then she stopped still. She could see the Loews Hollywood Hotel, just behind the Dolby Theatre. The Loews was on fire.

After-Action Report to the President
on the Los Angeles Bombings

EYES ONLY

February 28, 2022

LOCATION: White House Situation Room
Washington, D.C.

KILLED: 372 passengers and crew of Boeing 747; 16 killed by aircraft debris; 6 guests and 1 housekeeper at the Loews Hollywood Hotel. Total: 395.

WOUNDED: 46 injured by aircraft debris; 17 injured at Loews Hollywood Hotel; 12 injured in surrounding area; 22 injured during evacuations. Total: 97

AFTERMATH: All air traffic over American airspace grounded.

Academy Awards ceremony evacuated.

Loews Hollywood Hotel and surrounding buildings evacuated.

Downtown Los Angeles sealed off.

Estimated millions of dollars in damage to property caused by aircraft debris.

Surge in Al Qaeda propaganda traffic due to interruption of Academy Awards broadcast.

SUMMARY: Yesterday afternoon Pacific Time, approximately 20 minutes into the Academy Awards ceremony, a Boeing 747 was brought down over downtown Los Angeles. Approximately 60 seconds later, an explosion ripped through three guest rooms on the sixth floor of the Loews Hollywood Hotel, adjacent to the Dolby Theatre, where the award ceremony was under way. Al Qaeda claimed responsibility immediately, with a statement and video message issued to mainstream news outlets and social media Web sites simultaneously. They are not mentioned in the official statement, but due to the sophistication of the plot and the materials involved we can conclude with reasonable certainty that it was planned and carried out by elite Khorasan Group operatives.

The aircraft involved had departed Kuala Lumpur International Airport (KUL) approximately 19 hours before. Malaysian intelligence has reviewed all baggage scans and reports that there were no hazardous or potentially hazardous materials detected on the flight. A U.S. team is en route to KUL to independently confirm this assessment. The aircraft proceeded to Narita International Airport in Tokyo (NRT), where it stopped briefly and took on more passengers, fuel, and cargo. Japanese intelligence also reports that there was no loading or attempted loading of suspicious materials onto the aircraft at this time, and a U.S. asset in Tokyo has been able to confirm this.

The flight crossed the Pacific Ocean without incident, made landfall over Los Angeles, and proceeded to follow the standard flight path to land at Los Angeles International Airport (LAX). This involves flying over the downtown area of the city in a gradual descent before banking to the south and eventually assuming a westward heading to approach the airport. At the time of the explosion, the aircraft was traveling at about 5,300 feet.

The aircraft broke apart immediately due to the force of the blast. Those victims near the blast were killed instantly. Due to the low altitude, most of the victims were likely alive until they reached the ground. The tail section, the engines, and some portions of the wings were the largest pieces to fall to the ground intact, and therefore caused the most damage. The fuselage broke into a number of smaller pieces. Damage to homes and businesses on the ground was extensive, though it will be some time before a solid estimate can be made. A number of pieces of debris crashed on a busy freeway, and the resulting pileups were responsible for a number of fatalities.

Investigation and recovery efforts are ongoing on the ground, and the crash site has been sealed off by local and federal law enforcement to the extent possible. The exact parameters of the debris distribution area, however, have not been firmly fixed, as debris continues to be discovered further and further from the crash epicenter. All efforts are being taken to prevent the public from tampering with debris before it can be reported to law enforcement.

There were 351 passengers and 21 crew listed on the manifest—from 11 countries—and so far only 17 bodies have been positively identified. Recovery of human remains has proven difficult. All countries have been asked to run background checks on their citizens present on board, and U.S. intelligence is running our own checks concurrently.

Both the flight data recorder and the cockpit voice recorder have been successfully recovered. The former landed on the roof of a Ford Explorer—the driver of which escaped with only minor injuries—and the latter was discovered in the kitchen of a destroyed restaurant. A detailed analysis of their contents is under way, but preliminary findings indicate no suspicious activity aboard the aircraft at any point during the flight. In addition, our own preliminary survey of passengers has come up with no individuals with suspected terror links. We have, however, received reports of at least one piece of wreckage which may be contaminated with pentaerythritol tetranitrate (PETN) explosive residue.

At this time, we are led to conclude that there was no hijacker or suicide bomber aboard the aircraft, but that a bomb was placed which either avoided or was not detected by airport security and was subsequently detonated—likely by remote—once the aircraft was over Los Angeles.

Approximately one minute after the detonation of the bomb aboard the aircraft, another explosive was detonated eight miles to the north at the Loews Hollywood Hotel, next door to the Dolby Theatre. The bomb went off on the sixth floor, destroying the guest room in which it had been placed and the two on either side. Other rooms and the hallway sustained minor damage. The room in which the bomb was located was unoccupied. Two guests were killed in each of the adjoining rooms. One additional guest and a member of the hotel staff were killed in the hallway. Fire alarms were sounded, and the building was evacuated immediately.

The blast produced a significant shock wave felt by bystanders outside and on the nearby red carpet area outside the Dolby. The vibrations were also felt inside the theater. In the live broadcast footage, the host appears visibly shaken and looks offstage, and members of the audience can be seen standing up and looking around. Due to a network delay, most viewers saw only a few seconds of this commotion before the broadcast cut to a commercial.

The ceremony was stopped, and as event organizers received reports of the two bombings, the decision was made to evacuate the Dolby Theatre. The evacuation, by all accounts, did not go smoothly. Though all exits were utilized effectively, conflicts between law enforcement, event security, and various celebrities' private security teams contributed to an atmosphere of confusion and panic. Some injuries were reported during the evacuation, but no panic. Engineers are currently analyzing the Dolby Theatre to determine if the building is in structural danger.

Within minutes of the bombs' detonation, as the evacuation of the Loews, Dolby, and surrounding buildings was under way, social media postings began to appear from accounts known to be linked to Al Qaeda. Many used a screenshot apparently captured moments before, showing the Academy Awards host with a look of terror on his face. The Arabic text on a number of these postings read: "The fear is just beginning."

Longer statements followed, in which Al Qaeda claimed full responsibility for both the airplane and hotel bombings. These appeared first on social media, and were e-mailed to major mainstream news outlets around the world shortly thereafter. They linked to a video which shows a marked advancement in Al Qaeda's production values, with clips of Western feature films showing violence against Muslims intercut with actual footage of hostage murder, suicide bombing, and other Al Qaeda attacks. A voice-over delivers a message chastising Hollywood for being "a cesspool of sin and filth which you think will overflow onto the entire world, but without considering the strength of the millions in the army of Allah, who you cannot corrupt." The film industry is accused of being a tool of American "imperialism." A number of lines are anti-Semitic and anti-Israel.

We have no reason to disbelieve Al Qaeda's claim of responsibility for both incidents. Preliminary evidence from the Loews Hotel has also turned up potential evidence of PETN residue, in addition to fragments of what is believed to be a mobile phone, which likely acted as a detonator. It is our belief that the hotel bomb, like the airliner bomb, was detonated remotely, likely by the same individual.

The individual responsible for detonating both bombs likely served as a U.S.-based coordinator for the attack, working in collaboration with Al Qaeda operatives overseas. This would indicate a previously unknown Al Qaeda presence in the Los Angeles area, and given how well concealed their operations have been, we suspect the involvement of radicalized United States citizens. We are working to determine their identities and current status.

Aside from the Dolby-Loews complex and the areas specifically affected by aircraft debris, virtually the entire city of Los Angeles has been shut down. Transport has ground to a halt, as new areas are continually sealed off in order to investigate potential and confirmed evidence. This has affected traffic and commerce across the West Coast and internationally, as a major transport hub has been put out of commission.

All air traffic in the United States was grounded immediately once the midair explosion had been confirmed. In a few cases, fighter jet escorts were deployed, but there were no further incidents in the air. Air operations can be expected to recommence tomorrow.

★★★

Could This Really Happen?

Terrorists have been able to cause the greatest amount of airborne devastation by hijacking aircraft and crashing them, as they did on 9/11. However, that was only one of a number of plots by Al Qaeda and other jihadists targeting aircraft. Many of these involved simply blowing the plane up in midair. Even after 9/11, Al Qaeda returned to the simple idea of planting a bomb aboard an aircraft. By examining pre- and post-9/11 terrorist plots against airliners, we can see the potential for them to learn from their mistakes and build on numerous failed plots to one day, perhaps, successfully achieve their goal.

In addition, we often think of terrorists as targeting symbols of America's power establishment: politics, finance, the military. But our cultural exports are a form of "soft power" as well, and terrorists are far from unaware of that. That kind of outside-the-box thinking, along with aggregating technical expertise, is the purview of Al Qaeda's elite Khorasan Group, whose members would likely have the wherewithal to plan and execute an attack along the lines that this scenario describes. Finally, the disturbing rise of homegrown violent extremists suggest that Al Qaeda or other terror groups might easily find willing accomplices among the U.S. population, like our fictional bomb triggerman.

The Khorasan Group

The name "Khorasan" sprang into American public consciousness seemingly from out of nowhere in September 2014, but it is laden with meaning and symbolism for the jihadist movement and for Al Qaeda in particular. In antiquity, "Khorasan" referred to a Muslim-ruled territory which included parts of modern-day Afghanistan, Iran, and Turkmenistan. The name has been applied to various geographic designations in that area, and modern Iran had a province called Khorasan until 2004.[1]

The name was given new meaning by none other than Osama bin Laden himself. Lawrence Wright, in his detailed study of the lead-up to 9/11, *The Looming Tower*, points out that when Bin Laden first set up shop in the caves of Afghanistan in 1996, he rechristened his new home Khorasan. This was no accident. According to Wright, one of the more dubious of the *hadith*s (purported teachings of the Prophet Muhammad) "states that in the last days the armies of Islam will unfold black banners . . . and come out of Khorasan."[2]

In January of 2015, the head of Britain's MI5 was likely referring to the Khorasan Group when he said, "We still face more complex and ambitious plots that follow the now sadly well established approach of al Qaeda and its imitators—attempts to cause large scale loss of life, often by attacking transport systems or iconic targets. We know, for example, that a group of core al Qaeda terrorists in Syria is planning mass casualty attacks against the west."[3]

Today, the Khorasan Group consists of about fifty of Al Qaeda's most seasoned, vicious, and dangerous terrorists.[4] This cell was formed in 2012, when Bin Laden's successor, Ayman al-Zawahiri, ordered Muhsin al-Fadhli and other operatives to join an Al Qaeda branch, known as al-Nusra, that had carved out a safe haven in war-torn Syria.

The ongoing civil war there created space for Khorasan to build, according to the Department of Defense, "training camps, an explosives and munitions production facility, a communication building and command and control facilities."[5]

Like his predecessor, Zawahiri began dreaming of attacking the United States and its western allies more than twenty years ago. Today, while Zawahiri hides in Pakistan, his organization's best hope for attacking the American homeland is its small but deadly division. As U.S. director of national intelligence James R. Clapper said last year, "in terms of threat to the homeland, Khorasan may pose as much of a danger as the Islamic State."[6]

U.S. air strikes did eliminate Muhsin al-Fadhli, Khorasan's first leader and a former Bin Laden protégé, in July 2015. But one man's death is not enough to destroy the group. Government officials have concluded that it remains a threat to the West.[7]

What makes the Khorasan Group so dangerous to the United States?

For one thing, it is the worst of Al Qaeda's worst. It was formed by veterans of Al Qaeda's battles in Afghanistan and Pakistan. Its terrorists were smart enough, tough enough, and lucky enough to survive a war that lasted longer than a decade, cost the United States *trillions* of dollars, and was waged by the best-trained and -equipped soldiers, sailors, airmen, and marines in the history of human conflict. And Khorasan's primary mission is to murder Westerners in the West, especially Americans in America.[8]

Khorasan is particularly dangerous because it is recruiting American and European citizens who can travel freely on their U.S. and European passports. In particular, it is trying to find Westerners who are already fighting for Islamist extremist groups in Syria, and it is attempting to return them to their home countries. The Department of Defense has referred to such plans as "imminent attack plotting."[9] According to James Phillips of the Heritage Foundation, the "Khorasan group hopes to train and deploy these recruits, who hold American and European passports, for attacks against Western targets."[10] Before American air strikes in Syria in 2014, the Joint Chiefs' director of operations said, "The intelligence reports indicated that the Khorasan Group was in the final stages of plans to execute major attacks against Western targets and potentially the U.S. homeland."[11]

Particularly dangerous is Khorasan's work with Ibrahim al-Asiri, a talented bomb maker. His bombs are notoriously difficult to detect. According to Phillips, the "innovative" al-Asiri "has developed sophisticated explosive devices that have been placed on at least three aircraft bound for the United States."[12] Al-Asiri and other high-ranking Al Qaeda veterans give the group "greater experience in transnational terrorist operations and access to more sophisticated bombs" than its rivals.

Al Qaeda's Obsession with Airplanes

According to the 9/11 Commission, when Al Qaeda leaders were planning the attacks of September 11, they referred to the plot as "the planes operation." Perhaps the only surprising thing about the banal title is that Bin Laden and his associates didn't find it confusing. After all, there had been multiple operations involving airplanes before 9/11. And there would be more after 9/11. Almost since its inception, Al Qaeda has been obsessed with airplanes. And as we try to anticipate and prevent future terrorist attacks, we should expect and combat future attempts by Al Qaeda to bomb airplanes and use them as weapons.

1995: Bojinka

On December 11, 1994, an engineer with a degree from Britain's Swansea University boarded Philippine Airlines Flight 434 in Manila. Once on board, he attached a small bomb below one of the plane's seats. It was not the first time he had planted a bomb built to kill as many civilians as possible. Not long before, he had bombed a theater in Manila. The previous year, he had planted a bomb in the garage of the World Trade Center, which killed six people and injured more than a thousand more. The engineer's name was Ramzi Yousef.[13]

When Yousef's plane landed in Cebu before continuing on to Tokyo, he disembarked. Only after Flight 434 was airborne over the Pacific did it become clear why Yousef had boarded the plane—and why he had disembarked. Shortly before noon, the bomb exploded, killing the passenger sitting directly above it. Ten more passengers were wounded, but, amazingly, the plane was not damaged enough to cause a crash. Its heroic pilot made an emergency landing in Guam shortly before Yousef made an anonymous call to the Associated Press claiming credit for the attack in the name of an Al Qaeda–funded terrorist organization in the Philippines called Abu Sayyaf.

Authorities did not know it at the time, but Yousef's bombing of Flight 434 was a practice run. Yousef's plan was for a much grander and deadlier terrorist attack. He planned for five terrorists to plant bombs on jumbo jets, get off the planes at layovers, and then board new planes, where the process would be repeated. Some bombers would change planes four times in one day before all eleven bombs in Yousef's plan were hidden on eleven different planes. Then, through a timing device, all eleven bombs would go off at roughly the same time on planes flying from Asia to the United States. He called the project "Bojinka," which means "the big bang."

The *Los Angeles Times* later referred to Bojinka as "devastating in its complexity and technical brilliance," and after Yousef's largely successful test run in late 1994, the plan was on the cusp of becoming a reality. With his chief coconspirator, Abdul Hakim Murad, Yousef had begun mixing the chemicals—undetectable by even advanced bomb-screening machines—they would carry on the planes in ordinary containers like the bottles used for contact lens solution. They had also outlined the details of the plan on their computers, including the names of airports, the chosen flight numbers, and the settings for the timers.

As U.S. attorney Mary Jo White later said, "It was frightening. There were people wandering the globe able to do this." Of course, we now know that the Bojinka plot failed, but it wasn't due to any reason we can count on to save us with any frequency. In early 1995, just a few weeks before Bojinka was scheduled to launch, Yousef and Murad's apartment in Manila caught fire. When police investigated, they found dolls wearing clothes that contained flammable chemicals. They also found a file called "Bojinka" on a laptop. And with that—a stroke of luck caused by an apartment fire—Bojinka was uncovered, Murad was arrested, and Yousef fled to Pakistan, where he was eventually caught and extradited to the United States.

In 1997, Yousef was tried in federal court for the Bojinka

conspiracy and for the 1993 World Trade Center bombing. He will spend the rest of his life in jail. But he made clear during his questioning that other terrorists were knowledgeable about his techniques. Many of them were—and are—all too willing to try to succeed where Yousef failed. And many of them remain at large.

The Shoe Bomber

Everyone who has flown on a commercial airplane in the past fourteen years knows that you have to take your shoes off before you pass through the TSA's security checkpoint. The practice began a little more than two months after the September 11 attacks, in response to an Al Qaeda terrorist's attempt to bring down an airplane with a bomb hidden in his shoe.

Richard Reid was the son of a Jamaican father and a British mother. He converted to Islam during a prison sentence, and he learned the tricks of the terrorism trade at an Al Qaeda training camp in Afghanistan. After returning to Europe, he likely linked up with a bomb maker for Al Qaeda who built a bomb into the rubber sole of a high-top tennis shoe.[14]

On December 22, 2001, Reid walked in his high-tops right through the security checkpoint at Charles de Gaulle Airport. He boarded American Airlines Flight 63 and settled into Seat 29A. The plane was airborne on its way from Paris to Miami when a flight attendant smelled sulfur.

The smell of sulfur was coming from the matches Reid was using to ignite his shoe bomb. Another flight attendant, a five-foot-two-inch woman of tremendous courage, lunged over Reid's seat and wrestled with the six-foot-four terrorist. Reid bit her through her skin, but no amount of barbarity or ferocity could save his foiled plan. Passengers and other crew members took control of him, and he was injected with sedatives by two doctors on the flight.

At Reid's sentencing hearing in a federal court in Boston, he proclaimed, "I am at war with your country." He added, "I further admit my allegiance to Sheik Osama bin Laden, to Islam, and to the religion of Allah."

The Parcel Bombs

By 2010, Al Qaeda's Ibrahim al-Asiri, the innovative bomb maker discussed above, was fresh from his involvement in an associate's failed attempt to explode a bomb smuggled onto a plane in his underwear. Then, in the fall of 2010, al-Asiri made two bombs that airport security technology was incapable of identifying. For an explosive material, he used PETN, a white powder made all across the world and frequently used in quarrying. The PETN was packed into two desktop printer cartridges, which provided ideal disguises for the chemical. In the words of explosives expert Roland Alford, "In this case they used the fact that it was a powder in a compartment, within a device (a printer) in which you would expect to find powder."[15]

Al-Asiri's bombs were made in Yemen and packed in two parcels addressed for Chicago, one traveling via UPS and the other via Federal Express. In a show of dark humor showing that the packages were likely never intended to reach Chicago—and that Islamist fundamentalists hold grudges for a *really* long time—one parcel was addressed to a notorious French knight who mistreated Muslims in the Crusades, and the other was addressed to Torquemada's successor in the Spanish Inquisition. Another indication of Al Qaeda's intent was that the bombs were designed so that pressing a button on a cell phone would cause them to explode.

Fortunately, on October 29, the Saudi government was tipped off to the plot, and the two parcels were found on their way to the United States, having made it as far as Dubai (in one case) and Great Britain (in the other). When one of them was defused, it was just seventeen minutes from exploding.

Shortly after the plot was foiled, Al Qaeda in the Arabian Peninsula released a statement claiming responsibility and saying that they "intend to spread the idea [of parcel bombs on planes] to our mujahedeen brothers in the world and enlarge the circle of its application to include civilian aircraft in the West as well as cargo aircraft."

If Al Qaeda's history of bringing terrorism to air travel is any indication—and it *is* an indication—the group's warning of their "intent to spread the idea" should be taken quite seriously. And the threat is only expanding. In October 2015, ISIS entered the ranks of airborne terror by bringing down a Russian passenger jet carrying 224 people over the Sinai Peninsula—the worst terror attack against an airliner since 9/11. Intelligence assessments determined that ISIS or an affiliated group was able to place a bomb aboard the Airbus jet likely due to inadequate airport security, or possibly even with the help of someone on the inside. And if ISIS is already targeting Russian airliners, American aircraft could be next.

Homegrown Help

The fictional terrorist we describe, a disaffected young American radicalized online, is a representation of an increasingly disturbing trend. Given terror groups' ubiquitous presence online, it should hardly be surprising that we are seeing more and more recruits not only join up but actually set in motion plans to perpetrate violent acts on behalf of these groups on American soil. And they're able to do this without ever meeting their jihadist comrades, except online.

Online radicalization has contributed to a shocking influx of homegrown terror operatives. This is not just a matter of one or two sick individuals. In a one-year period in 2014–15, more than sixty supporters of ISIS alone had been arrested or indicted—more than one per week.[16] By February 2015, FBI director James Comey could report that his agency was investigating ISIS supporters "in various stages of radicalizing" in every single state in the nation.[17]

The plots uncovered so far have varied in their methods but were consistent in their depravity. Celebrations of the 2015 Fourth of July holiday were targeted specifically, as were law enforcement officers. Mass shootings were planned, including one on a college campus. One extremist from Ohio intended to detonate pipe bombs at the U.S. Capitol.[18] In the shootings at two Chattanooga military offices, we saw what happens when these homegrown threats are not detected in time.

The would-be pipe bomber from Ohio was inspired by ISIS, and the Chattanooga shooter preferred the writings of an Al Qaeda cleric. Whichever group inspires violent American extremists, the effects could be devastating.

What Can We Do to Stop This?

Preventing a scenario like this would require action on two fronts: countermeasures against the specific tactics that a terrorist group might employ, as well as a concerted effort to work against the strategies they use to attract American adherents online who could help them carry out the plot. Currently, our ability to detect threats at foreign airports is being strengthened but could be bolstered even further. But more broadly, our efforts to counter violent extremism here in the United States are shockingly inadequate.

The guidelines below could help bolster our defenses at home and abroad:

ENFORCE STRICTER SECURITY STANDARDS AT FOREIGN AIRPORTS. The explosive device that destroyed the jetliner in this scenario went undetected at two major airports: Kuala Lumpur and Tokyo. Unfortunately, aviation security measures are only as strong as their weakest link. A misstep at one airport can lead to terrible consequences half a world away. Standard protocols must be in place to make sure that (a) nothing gets aboard an airplane that hasn't been scanned, and (b) explosive detection capabilities are maximized. In July 2014, the Transportation Security Administration announced extra inspection procedures on U.S.-bound flights at foreign airports for passengers' electronic devices. However, only certain airports were required to put the new restrictions in place.[19] In addition, TSA—an agency with plenty of flaws of its own—depends on foreign airport and airline staff to actually implement these procedures.[20] TSA and its parent agency, the Department of Homeland Security, must ensure buy-in from (and oversight of) foreign screening entities, including the airlines themselves, and expand these enhanced screening procedures to as many airports as they can. The goal, after all, is to have as few weak links in international aviation security as possible.

ORGANIZE AND ENHANCE OUR FIGHT AGAINST VIOLENT EXTREMISM IN THE UNITED STATES. Earlier I described how more than sixty ISIS supporters had been apprehended over the course of a year, an average of more than one every week. What if I told you that there were only about two dozen full-time counterterrorism staff members working to stop the radicalization of Americans by terrorist groups? In one year we have had to arrest twice as many homegrown radicals as there are people who work full-time to counter violent extremism. Bureaucratic complications muddy the waters further. At least half a dozen government entities within the Department of Homeland Security have some responsibility for this issue. What's more, all of their efforts are woefully underfunded. Only about $15 million is devoted to keeping American citizens from falling under the spell of our enemies—a tiny fraction of our total counterterrorism spending. This is an issue of bipartisan concern. As my top Democratic colleague on the House Committee on Homeland Security, ranking member Bennie Thompson of Mississippi, has pointed out: "Prevention is likely to be more cost effective than surveillance, trials, or wars."[21] It's a basic concept, but it doesn't seem to have caught on. We spend billions to stop the threat of committed extremists, but comparatively little to counter violent extremist ideology in the first place. If the Obama administration will not make it a priority to ramp up the fight against violent extremism on our shores, the next one must do so on day one. Bureaucratic red tape must not be allowed to get in the way of decisive action, and the men and women fighting this battle should receive sufficient levels of staffing and funding to get the job done.

EMPOWER LOCAL COMMUNITIES TO COUNTER VIOLENT EXTREMISM. This is not a battle that can be fought entirely from Washington, and it cannot be fought by law enforcement alone. We need the input of the members of our local communities, who would often be among the first to spot signs of radicalization in a friend, neighbor, or classmate. In most cases of radicalization, there are usually flags and warning signs. Unfortunately, these are too often identified only after the fact once a terrorist attack has been perpetrated. For instance, 2013 Boston Marathon bomber Tamerlan Tsarnaev was kicked out of his mosque following radical rantings, yet authorities were not aware.[22] Communities should be educated about what they should look for in a potentially radicalized person, how to guide that person away from a dangerous path, and how to report radical activities to law enforcement. Part of this involves developing a strategy to show that extremism is not an outlet of one's faith but an outlet of violence, and sharing this with community leaders. Communities should encourage the development of "off-ramps" from the path of radicalization to stop potentially violent individuals before they set in motion a chain of events that could bring harm to many.

8

North Atlantic Storm

Russia Launches a New Cold War

SOUTHERN LITHUANIA
MAY 6, 2018
5:25 A.M.

Those driving east on Route 128 would probably not have noticed—or thought anything of—the two vans pulled over to the side of the road at the junction of Route 4704 and the A4 highway.

In the lead van, Feliks Dobroslaw checked his wristwatch. They had a few more minutes yet, though not long enough to catch any more shut-eye. Feliks didn't quite trust himself. If he fell asleep and missed the jumping-off time, he would never hear the end of it from Dmitry and his boys in the van behind him.

Feliks's squad was made up mostly of ethnic Poles, while Dmitry's was mostly ethnic Russians. Neither group wanted to see the current Lithuanian government stay in power, and both felt they would be much better off under Russian protection, but their common cause had not managed to stamp out every rivalry among them. Fights had broken out occasionally among the groups at their training camps, especially after the vodka was brought out in the evenings, and Feliks and Dmitry had regularly been called upon to restore order. But sometimes those things happen when men spend their days running obstacle courses and shooting targets deep in the woods, with several hours of indoctrination training thrown in for good measure. Feliks had plenty of confidence that they were ready.

Still, he wanted the Lithuanian Polish contingent to be the first to spring into action. He would not have admitted it to himself, but he felt he had to show off for Dmitry. Because Dmitry was Russian himself, he enjoyed greater favor with Sergey, the mysterious man from Moscow who had first brought Dmitry and Feliks together in the first place. Over drinks in a Vilnius café, Sergey had told both men that he'd seen how committed they were to the Russian and Polish political youth movements in Lithuania, and asked how truly dedicated they were to the cause of change for their people.

Now Feliks was ready to prove his dedication. He checked his watch again: 5:45 exactly. Without a word he turned the key in the van's ignition, and the sound of the engine coming to life startled awake any men in the van who had been dozing. He pulled the van off the shoulder and into the middle of the road, then cut the engine.

"All right, boys," he said, "time to get to work."

The men filed out of the van and took up defensive positions around it. Two of them opened the trunk and brought out some sandbags, on which they began to assemble a PK machine gun.

With no small measure of pride, Feliks noticed that Dmitry's van full of Russian Lithuanians took a few extra minutes to come to life before driving some distance down the road to set up their own roadblock on the other side of the junction.

Feliks's radio, clipped to his shoulder, squawked something at him. It was Dmitry, asking if Feliks's squad was in position. Feliks replied that they were, and Dmitry said he would make the report to Sergey. *Of course*, thought Feliks, *you get to talk to Sergey*.

Their job, and the job of several other teams like theirs made up of Lithuanian Poles and Russians, would be to hold a critical east–west route across southern Lithuania between the Russian territory of Kaliningrad on the Baltic Sea and the staunchly pro-Russian nation of Belarus.

Feliks hadn't been told much—and he suspected Dmitry knew more than he was letting on—but he did know that Russia, out of concern for its people in Kaliningrad as well as ethnic Lithuanian Russians, was preparing to invade. This morning, armored columns would enter Lithuania from two directions, from

Kaliningrad in the east and from Russian bases in Belarus in the west. A lifeline to Kaliningrad had to be maintained, and teams of loyal civilians like Feliks, Dmitry, and their men had been mobilized to help keep the land route open until the soldiers arrived.

As it began to grow light around them, Feliks lit a cigarette. There was still no traffic on the road. All over the country, Lithuanians would soon be waking up to a brand-new day.

THE first two hours at the checkpoint passed with minimal disturbances. Traffic was beginning to pick up, but the majority of drivers were wisely deciding to turn around as soon as Feliks' men and their weapons came into view. The few cars that did come all the way up to their barricade were usually allowed to proceed, but they were warned politely to be on the lookout for military maneuvers on the road. When they stopped the occasional truck, it was suggested to the driver that he might be better off getting off the road altogether. There was no sense in adding to the civilians' alarm. Most of them seemed obliging enough.

There was a brief moment of excitement when a police car, apparently from the town of Naujieji Valkininkai, decided to approach. As it stopped and one door began to open, one of Feliks's men, acting without orders, took it upon himself to fire a few rounds in the general direction of—but well above—the car. Before the policeman could even close his door, his partner in the driver's seat threw the car into reverse and spun around. Feliks knew he should discipline the errant shooter, but they all had such a good laugh about it that he didn't want to puncture morale. It was critical to keep everyone together.

One of the men in the machine-gun nest had switched on a battery-powered radio some time ago, and it was from there they had learned that their little checkpoint was clearly part of something much larger.

The news stations were abuzz with reports from all over the Baltic states. In Lithuania, it had been confirmed that military vehicles had been seen crossing the border from Kaliningrad and from Belarus, though none had yet reached Feliks's checkpoint.

In Latvia, there had been an uprising of ethnic Russians in the eastern Latgale region. A "People's Republic of Latgale" had been declared and separatists had taken over the town hall in the region's largest city, Daugavpils. Estonia was reeling from two separate attacks on the Russian border: several explosions of unknown origin had been reported in the northern border city of Narva; in the south, armed men in green uniforms with no insignia had disembarked from a train to seize the Koidula railway border station.

The men were energized by this news, and Feliks admonished them to stay alert. They still hadn't seen any signs of the soldiers yet, which meant their mission was far from over. Regular radio contact with Dmitry reported that they hadn't had any word, either.

Suddenly, one of Feliks's men shouted and pointed down the road: "There they are!"

Feliks ran to retrieve his binoculars from the van and, looking down the stretch of highway, saw a convoy of armored vehicles approaching. He recognized the T-14 Armata tanks, along with T-15 and Bumerang armored personnel carriers. He turned and ran back to the van, shouting commands at his men, who scrambled to clear away the machine-gun nest. Feliks moved the van out of the way and jumped out as the column drew up to their position.

He and his men cheered and waved as the vehicles rumbled past. They bore no identifying marks of any kind. Nor, as far as Feliks could see, were there any insignia on the uniforms of the men in the turrets who waved back and returned their salutes.

But Feliks didn't have to see insignia to know what was going on: Russia was finally on the move.

EMBASSY OF THE UNITED STATES OF AMERICA
VILNIUS, LITHUANIA
MAY 6, 2018
9:49 A.M.

Marilyn Woodner saw the bright flash of orange out of the corner of her eye and immediately rushed to the window. Just inside the embassy gate, a fresh black patch was still smoldering on the ground. Someone in the crowd of demonstrators on the other side of the gate had thrown a Molotov cocktail. This was getting serious.

As Marilyn watched, a jeep pulled up in front of the gate and several Marines climbed out. Already, most of the embassy's contingent of Marine guards had been deployed around the perimeter. So far, trouble had come only at the front gate. There were chants of "Yankee dogs go home!" and signs bearing slogans against "U.S. Imperialism"—uncommon sights in Vilnius but not inherently dangerous. But the crowd seemed to be growing larger, and when they started throwing Molotov cocktails, Marilyn understood the game might soon change.

The ambassador and some staff had already been moved to the embassy's safe room—mostly as a precaution, as there were no plans to evacuate at the moment—but Marilyn refused to leave her office. They were hunkering down, but they weren't running. As deputy chief of mission, she was now the acting head of the official American presence in Lithuania. A career foreign service officer, Marilyn had been in some tough spots. Her early years as an FSO had been spent in the Middle East, where she'd endured plenty of these kinds of demonstrations before, and worse. She hadn't come to Europe only to be chased out by an unruly crowd.

She remained at her desk for practical reasons too. The disturbance at the embassy in Vilnius had begun only about an hour earlier, but more serious incidents had been erupting all across the region. Border clashes had been reported in Estonia and separatists had seized local government buildings in eastern Latvia. Most disturbingly, just forty miles south of Vilnius, columns of armored vehicles had been reported but not yet identified. The Russians did occasionally move military hardware to and from Kaliningrad, but so far the Kremlin had not responded to American or any other diplomatic requests for clarification. Moscow was silent.

Shouting and the sound of trampling feet tore Marilyn away from her screen.

Randy Orbach, the embassy's political officer, appeared in Marilyn's doorway.

"It looks like they're coming up to the north fence too," he said with a level of concern that Marilyn was quick to notice in her fellow veteran of the foreign service. The northern side of the embassy compound was across the street from a park, where a separate, smaller demonstration had been reported earlier in the morning. But if they were moving across to the embassy, it could mean a larger coordinated effort.

Marilyn got up from her desk. "Let's go and see," she said calmly. She did, however, take care to grab her mobile phone, her tablet, and the folder she'd gathered of her most important papers and take them with her.

As they made their way down to the lobby, past other embassy staffers and Marine guards dashing up and down carrying document boxes, Randy asked: "Have you heard anything from D.C.?"

Marilyn shook her head. "Not since we moved the Ambassador. No cables, no e-mails, nothing." Randy nodded, and Marilyn could see him beginning to sweat.

"What about Norm?" Randy asked. "What's he saying?" Norman Prescott was the embassy's regional security officer, who'd expressed concern about security at the compound just weeks ago to Marilyn and the ambassador. In the face of heated Kremlin rhetoric, they had agreed with his assessment. They had seen an uptick in disturbances around the compound: someone had even lobbed a Molotov cocktail over the wall a few months before, although nobody was injured. The senior staff had decided to cable the State Department in Washington to let them know that, if trouble came, the embassy might not be able to defend itself.

"Norm says as long as they stay outside the gates, we've got nothing to worry about," Marilyn told Randy, trying to sound as upbeat as she could. "I sent him to the radio room to try to update Washington."

They walked down the stairs into the lobby, where that morning the consular section had opened for business as usual only to be shut down once the demonstration began in force. Papers littered the floor now. A few Marine guards armed with shotguns stood nervously at the main doors, where the gate and the agitated crowd could be seen across a parking lot. One of the Marines, Gunnery Sergeant Jacobson, was looking out the doors as well, talking into his radio.

"Gunny," Marilyn called, to get Jacobson's attention, "is it true they're on the north side too?"

"Yes, ma'am," said the Marine quickly. "They're massing on the north fence and we're seeing groups come up from the east and west too."

My God, thought Marilyn. *We're being encircled.* This was what she and Norm had feared most. This wasn't a demonstration; it was an attack. The open park to the north and west of the compound could be used to land helicopters in the event of an evacuation, but if crowds were massing in those areas, their escape routes would be cut off.

Marilyn had to think quickly. She might not have much time, maybe not even time to call Washington. She prayed Norman had been able to get in touch. Randy grabbed her arm and pointed to the television mounted on the wall. It was muted, but Marilyn could see the Russian president was speaking. Randy ran over and manually turned up the volume. As she watched along with Randy and Gunnery Sergeant Jacobson, Marilyn, a fluent Russian speaker, translated in her head:

"To the international community, I want to make clear," the president was saying, "Russia will not stand by while Russian territory and Russian people are threatened by other states. Russian people living in states with questionable legitimacy of their own have a right to exercise self-determination, to demand their autonomy or, if they wish, to join under the banner of a new united Russia. If these people have chosen to rise up, as they have now done in Lithuania, Latvia, and Estonia, Russia will answer the call to defend their rights."

So it was true, Marilyn thought. The intelligence from Moscow had hinted at this for months, but now she was hearing it for herself. The Russian president really was calling the Baltic states "illegitimate."

The president continued: "And I will say to any other nation, or any group of nations, that thinks it can interfere with questions of Russian territorial sovereignty, or hinder the self-determination of Russian people to unite themselves with the motherland: We will defend against your aggression. Russia will fight, and we will fight until we have won."

As she turned to face her colleagues, an explosion shook the building. It was close. A voice crackled over Jacobson's radio: "They're over the north wall! Repeat, the crowd has breached the north wall!"

"Bar the doors!" Jacobson ordered, and he and the other Marines began moving chairs, desks, trash cans, and anything else they could lift in front of the main doors. Marilyn looked at Randy.

"Grab anyone you can find and start destroying the computers. Start with my office. Throw them down the stairs if you have to." Randy nodded. Marilyn could hardly believe what she heard herself say next:

"I'm going to go send the emergency codes."

NORTH ATLANTIC COUNCIL CHAMBER
NORTH ATLANTIC TREATY ORGANIZATION HEADQUARTERS
BRUSSELS, BELGIUM
MAY 6, 2018
10:38 A.M.

This was exactly the kind of day that Jonas Palecki had trained for, but he hardly had enough time to stop and think about that. He had been a freelance translator for NATO for just under a year, and while he'd handled his share of tense meetings, this was his first full-fledged crisis.

The emergency meeting of the North Atlantic Council had been called for 10:30, and members were still filing in. Jonas had arrived several hours earlier; his phone had gone off shortly after news of the crisis in Lithuania broke. The NATO staff, short on Lithuanian speakers even on its best days, needed all hands on deck.

In the cab on the way to NATO headquarters, Jonas had said a prayer of thanks to his Lithuanian grandmother, from whom he had learned his ancestral language while growing up in Chicago. It had opened up a whole new world to him after college, and a whole new life as a freelance editor, English teacher, and translator in Brussels—a truly international city. As breaking-news updates flashed across his phone during the drive, Jonas knew he could very well be on his way to witness history.

The secretary-general, from Sweden, was attempting to call the meeting to order. Jonas made sure his headset was secure, and listened.

"Ladies and gentlemen," the secretary-general said in English, "as events continue to move very fast, I suggest we get this meeting under way as quickly as possible. To that end, the Permanent Representative from Lithuania is recognized."

A hush went over the room as Andrius Gedvilas, a tall, gray-haired man whose carriage had always suggested to Jonas a diplomat of centuries ago rather than the typical international bureaucrat one often encountered in Brussels, rose to his feet and removed his glasses.

"My fellow permanent representatives, it is my intention to be brief," Gedvilas began in English. That would make Jonas's job easier, but he could still be called upon to help with translating into French, NATO's other official language.

"I must be brief," Gedvilas continued, "because I believe we have very little time in which to make decisions which could very well alter the history of free peoples around the world. This morning, as you all know, Russian regular army forces and separatist militias backed by Russia have launched multiple attacks against the sovereignty of the Baltic states. I have been monitoring the situation with the permanent representatives from Latvia and Estonia, and they can confirm reports of attacks in their countries. But the greatest threat appears to have shown itself in Lithuania."

Gedvilas took a breath and removed a handkerchief to wipe some sweat from his brow.

"Columns of tanks and troop carriers have been sighted on roads in southern Lithuania. We believe they crossed into the country early in the morning from Kaliningrad and from Belarus. Meanwhile, civil disturbances continue in Vilnius. The Presidential Palace has been surrounded by demonstrators shouting pro-Russian slogans. Just a moment ago I informed the permanent representative from the United States that his country's embassy has been reported under attack."

An excited murmur went through the entire room. Jonas felt a lump form in his throat.

Gedvilas straightened himself up. "Ladies and gentlemen, the only statement from the president of the Russian Federation is a claim that they are only protecting the territorial integrity of Kaliningrad and the freedom of Russians in Lithuania. I would say to this body that whatever pretext the Kremlin has imagined, we are now faced with a definitive challenge under Article Five of the Washington Treaty. A NATO member has been subjected to an unprovoked attack."

Jonas, who had been listening to Gedvilas speak for months, had never before detected a quiver in his voice as he was hearing now.

"As a student of history, I learned how the nations of Western Europe stood together shoulder to shoulder to stop totalitarian forces time and again. Saving civilization like that is no small accomplishment, but we cannot forget the burden that our shared history has laid at our feet. Ladies and gentlemen, history has caught up with us once again. Once again a totalitarian regime has taken advantage of Western complacency to threaten the entire continent."

Jonas could see that Gedvilas was looking directly across the council table at the permanent representative of the United States.

"If we do not agree to take up the burden of mutual defense now—if we do not stand together—then the Atlantic alliance that our countries have worked to build for generations will crumble and fall in an afternoon."

The room was totally silent. Jonas looked at the American representative. He had not been able to meet the eyes of his Lithuanian counterpart; he was looking down at his notes.

"I implore you to come to our aid," he said, his eyes trained on the American. "My family has been taken. Hundreds are missing. Many are dead. If you will not stand by my people, if you will not keep your promise, then we have no hope. The NATO alliance is dead."

Turning to the other representatives and noting their impassive faces, his head dropped. "I yield back my time."

NAVAL OCEAN PROCESSING FACILITY DAM NECK
MAY 6, 2018
HAMPTON ROADS, VIRGINIA
1:08 A.M.

Linda Mays was already on her second cup of coffee. She had told herself she ought to be cutting back, but the way she figured, those rules went out the window when she got stuck with the night shift. Still, two cups after barely an hour on duty . . . Maybe, she thought, it's best to hold off on number three.

It beat sea duty, Mays told herself. At the Naval Ocean Processing Facility (NOPF) Dam Neck, part of the sprawling network of naval bases in the southeast corner of Virginia, she could just walk down the hall from her station and get a cup whenever she needed one. And there was no pitching and rolling.

As a civilian working for the Office of Naval Intelligence, Mays had been to sea occasionally, usually for short times on classified missions. Technically on loan from the Central Intelligence Agency, Mays was an oceanographer by training. She could understand why ONI had specifically requested her for this particular mission. The unclassified version of her job description—the version she told people she met at parties—was that she was very good at spotting things in the ocean: things that were supposed to be there as well as things that weren't.

Strictly speaking, Mays might as well have been at sea at that very moment. She and the navy crew to which she was assigned may have been situated comfortably on shore, steps away from pristine Virginia beachfront, but the ship under their command was a few hundred miles east, chugging around the Atlantic.

Mays and the sailors who sat in front of several control panels in the darkened room were conducting sea trials of the *Sea Stalker*, the Navy's latest generation of Anti-Submarine Warfare (ASW) Continuous Trail Unmanned Vessel, or ACTUV. The civilian press usually called it a "floating drone." It was unarmed, remotely controlled, and could spend upwards of ninety days at sea, trawling up and down wide swaths of ocean, looking for submarines. This newest prototype could look farther and deeper than its predecessors, and—though nobody besides the developers and Linda Mays's team knew it—it was the first ACTUV capable of detecting nuclear-powered submarines.[1]

This project was supposed to be the "future" of U.S. anti-submarine warfare, and Mays certainly hoped the Pentagon had been right to bet it all on this program. Of course, they hadn't had much choice. Budget cuts had seen other technological development programs wither and die; this one had only survived through clever congressional wrangling. Even then, they could only afford to bring a few civilian consultants onto the project, which meant extra shifts for her. The Navy was stretched thin around the world, forced to do more with less—to do more with expensive floating robots.

Mays stood at the back of the room and sipped her coffee. She followed the journey of the *Sea Stalker* as it was played out on the screen arrays in front of her, watching over the heads of the dozen naval technicians seated at the controls. Live feed was beamed onto some screens, lines of data streamed across others. Here in Mays's world, it was quiet. The *Sea Stalker* was simply moving along its predetermined test route, with no problems to report. She had woken up shortly before her shift to skim the news and had seen that things were getting bad in Europe. Some elements of the fleet were probably on alert—or would be soon—but she still had her job to do here.

"Ma'am?" one of the young naval technicians called out to her timidly, raising his hand like a student in a class. He couldn't have been more than nineteen. Mays walked over to his station.

"What is it?"

"I think I've picked up something."

Linda's eyes flashed up and down his screen, taking in the underwater mapping data coming from the *Sea Stalker*'s sonar array. The lines were definitely showing an anomaly.

"What have we got on video?" Linda called out to the room. Another sailor, a young woman, raised her hand.

"I think I've got something here, ma'am."

As Linda stared at the live feed, a shape slowly began to materialize.

"Pilot, all stop!" Linda commanded. Another sailor flipped a few switches, and hundreds of miles away the *Sea Stalker*'s engines halted.

"Tighten up on the bogey," Linda directed the lead sonar operator. "Do a 180-degree scan and see if you can draw me a picture."

"Yes, ma'am."

Under the ocean's surface, the *Sea Stalker*'s multiple sonar arrays went to work, forming an outline of the moving shape they'd come across. A few seconds later the green outline was displayed on the sonar operator's screen.

Linda went cold. It was a Russian *Borei*-class. And it was very far from home.

"Save that image and upload it to the Net," Linda commanded calmly. She walked over to her own computer terminal. She would have to send this image in over the secure network immediately. As she reached for the phone to call the Pentagon to let them know what was coming, she noticed her hand was shaking—and it wasn't the coffee.

USS *RONALD REAGAN* (CVN-76)
THE BALTIC SEA
MAY 6, 2018
10:52 A.M.

Captain Edward Carnes could hardly believe the information that his communications center had been relaying all morning. Borders crumbling in Latvia and Estonia . . . Lithuania invaded outright by soldiers with no insignia on their uniforms or vehicles . . . the U.S. embassy in Vilnius surrounded.

Carnes had contacted the Navy's European command in Naples several times to inquire about plans for a rescue mission, but the response had been the same every time: "Stand by." It was as if the Pentagon had been caught totally off guard, the same as the Europeans.

Carnes had decided against his executive officer's suggestion to sound the call to general quarters, at least for the moment. Telling the men to man their battle stations might only serve to heighten tension. He had grounded all flight sorties for the moment, until the situation on the ground became clearer or orders directed otherwise. There was no sense inviting trouble.

Picking up his binoculars, Carnes scanned the sea shimmering icily out in front of the *Reagan*. There was nothing on the horizon. Carnes was not exactly sure what he had expected to see.

He directed a friendly smile toward Boatswain's Mate Alvarez, the boatswain's mate of the watch and one of the *Reagan's* top enlisted sailors. "Well, no Russkies swimming towards us," Carnes said, and Boatswain's Mate Alvarez politely acknowledged her commanding officer's poor attempt at humor.

He thought the coast might be clear enough to get the breakfast he'd been putting off, until the bridge telephone rang. Alvarez answered. She listened for a moment, then turned toward Carnes.

"Sir," she said, "radar reports a contact coming from the northeast, and closing fast."

Carnes went back to his seat and raised his binoculars. "Bearing?" he asked.

Alvarez asked for the bearing and repeated it for Carnes. "Contact still closing," she added.

There it was, just a speck in the sky, but heading straight toward them unmistakably. As it drew nearer, Carnes could clearly tell what he was looking at: a Russian Sukhoi Su-27, a Flanker fighter jet.

They picked a hell of a time to buzz us, Carnes thought. Still, the Russians who showed up like this tended to fly by "clean"— without carrying missiles. This guy would probably make a quick pass and then bug out for home.

But as he looked through his binoculars, Carnes began to get a sinking feeling. Something wasn't right here: every instinct he had told him that. As the Flanker finally passed along the *Reagan*'s port side and every head turned to watch him through the bridge windows, Carnes saw what he'd been dreading: this Russian wasn't flying "clean"; he was fully armed.

"General quarters," announced Captain Carnes matter-of-factly to the bridge.

Behind him, his executive officer moved over to the intercom and switched on the general quarters alarm. Carnes looked up and saw the Russian coming around for another pass as his XO intoned in a voice that was now carrying across the entire ship:

"General quarters, General quarters. All hands man your battle stations. This is not a drill. Repeat, this is not a drill."

OUTER BANKS OF NORTH CAROLINA
MAY 6, 2018
8:07 A.M.

The four-man crew of the Coast Guard MH-60 Jayhawk helicopter scanned the expanse of the ocean beneath them, but the copilot, Lieutenant Al Nguyen, was finding it slightly difficult to concentrate. He imagined the rest of the crew was, too—at least, everyone except Lieutenant Snell, the pilot. But Nguyen knew the other two—Ravitch the flight mechanic and Nelson the rescue swimmer—had the same things on their minds as he did. They'd been talking about it at breakfast, before the call had come in about the stranded fishermen they were now on their way to find.

While America had been sleeping, Eastern Europe was falling apart. There was fighting in all three of the Baltic states; that was all they knew for sure. Most of the troops who had crossed their borders bore no insignia, but all signs pointed to Russia. NATO had yet to make a final decision about taking action. The rumor at breakfast was that the Germans were holding up the plans, but the news out of Brussels was constantly changing. The White House would only say that the President had been on the phone with European leaders and that conversations were ongoing. The Kremlin, apparently, was not answering.

Meanwhile, in a comparatively smaller crisis, a charter boat out of Manteo had run out of gas and been stranded without a working radio all night. Once the men on board finally got in touch with the Elizabeth City Coast Guard station, they seemed in fine spirits: they appeared to have brought along an extra cooler of beer in case of just such an emergency. They'd been able to report their position, which the chopper was quickly approaching. The four men in the helicopter wanted to find the stricken vessel as soon as possible—to make sure everyone was safe, of course, but also so they could get back to their station in Elizabeth City and catch up on the news from Europe.

"Contact!" Lieutenant Snell announced in his flat baritone.

Sure enough, there was the fishing boat, a forty-three-footer that looked to Nguyen like she had a fair amount of pickup—when she was gassed up. And there were the three fishermen—two without shirts—standing on the deck, all waving enthusiastically.

"Contact confirmed," Snell reported in. "All passengers and crew accounted for. You can send the boat out to pick them up." He gave the coordinates, circled the stricken boat once more, and headed for home.

"Looks like you won't be getting wet today, Nelson!" Nguyen shouted over his shoulder.

"That's just fine," the rescue swimmer replied. "I already had a shower."

"Check this out, guys!" exclaimed Ravitch, the flight mechanic, who was situated at the open starboard side door. "We got a little Sea World action out here!"

Seeing whales breaching or pods of dolphins scampering in and out of the waves was an extra perk of the job and, Nguyen had to admit, one of his favorites. He craned his neck to starboard and caught a disturbance on the water as a dark shape began to rise to the surface.

But it kept rising. And rising.

Within seconds, the men found themselves looking at a surfaced submarine. For a moment nobody said anything. Then Snell got back on the radio.

"Elizabeth City, please confirm: Are there any naval exercises scheduled in our sector today?"

The reply came back: "Stand by."

As they waited, Snell brought the chopper around for another pass. Nguyen took another look at the shape and felt his heart nearly stop.

"Elizabeth City, please confirm—" Snell was saying again.

"Don't bother," said Nguyen quietly. His pilot turned to look at him.

"It's not ours. It's Russian."

GULF SHORES PUBLIC BEACH
GULF SHORES, ALABAMA
MAY 6, 2018
8:32 A.M.

Lissette Guerrero's heart raced for a moment as she scanned the water for her children through her binoculars. Max and Amy weren't where they had been a minute ago. But she found them soon enough, and her heart rate went back to normal.

She set the binoculars down in her lap and eased back into her chair. "Try to relax," her husband had said. Easy for him to say. Frank was back in Pensacola, just over the Florida line, doing what he loved. He'd just been promoted to lieutenant at his fire station, and that meant longer hours, but they'd both been so proud when he got the news that it hardly mattered. He was due to join them the following day, and then the Guerrero family vacation could really get started in earnest.

But for now it was just Lissette and their kids, six-year-old Max and four-year-old Amy. The kids who'd insisted on heading straight to the beach as soon as they woke up. Lissette had seen something on TV about sharks' preferred feeding time, but she couldn't remember now if it was early in the morning or later in the evening. She resisted the temptation to look it up on her phone. For a firefighter's wife, she still had a terrible nervous streak.

There were only a few other families down this early, and some college kids who looked like they hadn't left since the day before—or longer. Lissette hardly needed the binoculars. Still, Max was starting to swim out farther than she would have liked, and Amy would, of course, try to follow him, so she kept them handy just in case.

She raised them to her eyes once more, checked the kids, and was getting ready to put them down when she noticed something else, far beyond the kids. There was some kind of disturbance farther out to sea. As Lissette watched, a giant shape crashed through the waves and disappeared again in a cloud of its own spray. Immediately she thought it must have been a whale, but as the spray died away and this shape reappeared, she saw it was a submarine calmly sitting on the surface.

The other people on the beach had noticed too. Many were pointing; some waved. One of the college kids was waking the others up. Lissette walked down to the surf, where Max and Amy had seen the submarine and were waving at it excitedly.

"Look at the boat, Mommy!" Max exclaimed. Anything water-related fascinated him these days.

"I know!" Lissette replied, genuinely sharing her kids' enthusiasm. This wasn't something you saw at the Gulf Shores beach every day. She passed the binoculars down to Max. She'd shown him how to use them the day before.

He stared for a minute, then Amy began to clamor for her turn. Lissette took the binoculars from her son to pass them to her daughter, but she couldn't resist one more quick look for herself.

There was some activity on the low conning tower, in the forward section of the submarine. Something was rising up from it. In a moment, Lissette realized it was a flag being raised, which was then followed by another. The lower flag was white with a blue X. Above that, Lissette caught a flash of red, white, and blue, but quickly realized it wasn't the Stars and Stripes. This flag had only three large horizontal stripes: white, then blue, then red.

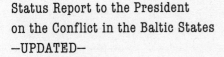

Status Report to the President
on the Conflict in the Baltic States
—UPDATED—

EYES ONLY

May 6, 2018

LOCATION: The White House

KILLED: Unknown

WOUNDED: Unknown

ONGOING EFFECTS:
*** FLASH: Coast Guard Air Station Elizabeth City (NC) reports sighting a Russian *Borei*-class ballistic missile submarine off the coast of North
Carolina. Unconfirmed reports also received of a possible *Borei* sighting off
Georgia in the vicinity of King's Bay ***
*** FLASH II: Local law enforcement agencies report multiple sightings of
a submarine flying the Russian national flag and naval ensign in the Gulf
of Mexico in the vicinity of Gulf Shores, AL, and Pensacola, FL. No military
confirmation as yet. ***

Pro-Russian militias and uniformed troops without insignia—all but certainly Russian regulars—have established a presence in all three Baltic
states and are in position to potentially capture one capital city.

Estonia: The northern city of Narva has seen several hours of bombing
and rioting as armed groups fight running gun battles in the streets.
The southern railway station at Koidula on the Russian border has been
seized by what appear to be highly trained special operations forces,
likely Spetsnaz. Rail traffic between Estonia and Russia has been cut off.
The capital, Tallinn, appears relatively quiet.

Latvia: Militants in the eastern region of Latgale have proclaimed a
breakaway state, the "People's Republic of Latgale," and have formally
announced their intention to ally themselves with the Russian Federation. The center of the uprising appears to be the city of Daugavpils, the
second-largest city in Latvia, where the town hall has been seized by
armed men. No major disturbances have been reported in Riga.

Lithuania: Regular army personnel with sophisticated vehicles and equipment have crossed into Lithuanian territory from Kaliningrad and Belarus in what appears to be a coordinated assault. The armored columns, assisted by local militia, have succeeded in holding a supply line between Russian positions in Kaliningrad and Belarus.

Significant disturbances continue in Vilnius. A number of buildings have been surrounded by demonstrators who appear to be aligned with the country's Russian and Polish minority movements. The Presidential Palace has been surrounded, but President Veselka has been removed to a secure location.

According to the U.S. Embassy, Vilnius remains under siege by demonstrators who have breached the perimeter walls and are now surrounding the building itself. Ambassador Parker remains in the compound's secure shelter. The embassy's Marine guards and some local police are providing security, and despite throwing some incendiary devices the crowd has not yet made any move to attack the building itself. Options for potential evacuation of embassy staff will be submitted under separate cover.

Outside of the Baltic States, increasingly aggressive Russian military activity has been reported, sometimes directed against American assets.

Russian fighter jets have flown at least three sorties in the last few hours over the USS *Ronald Reagan*'s carrier battle group in the Baltic Sea. The jets appear to be fully armed, and while they have not attacked the *Reagan* or any other ship in the group, they appear to be actively attempting to provoke an American vessel into firing first.

A Russian military buildup is reportedly under way in the Crimean Peninsula. Troops and vehicles are being flown and ferried in from the Russian mainland, and additional ships are known to be under way to join the Russian Black Sea Fleet.

Russian activity in the Arctic region increased within the last 12 hours. Elmendorf Air Force Base in Alaska has twice had to scramble fighters to intercept Tupolev Tu-95 Bear nuclear-capable bomber sorties. In one instance, the bombers were accompanied by Su-27 Flanker fighter escorts. Additionally, Canadian and Russian icebreaking vessels were involved in a temporary standoff in a disputed territory.

The Russian government has so far only addressed the incursion into Lithuania, which they have defended as a means of protecting Russian people and territory in Kaliningrad. They insist there is no connection with the other attacks in the Baltics.

The Baltic States' representatives to NATO contend that the action in Lithuania alone—if not the entire series of attacks taken together—certainly constitutes a challenge to the mutual defense clause in Article 5 of the NATO charter. Our own experts agree with this, yet NATO has not issued a formal statement confirming that Article 5 has been invoked.

Politically, the situation remains extremely fragile. The NATO Council has been in almost continuous session, but no consensus has emerged regarding a response. At the moment, the German government seems to be the most staunchly opposed to the use of force, while the French foreign minister has indicated that his government is on the fence.

SUMMARY: In the early morning hours of May 6 (Eastern European time), paramilitary and regular forces—which our intelligence links with Russia—began a series of attacks against the Baltic States. The choice of this particular date appears significant in itself: today is St. George's Day in Russia, and the black-and-orange ribbon of St. George has been a popular badge of pro-Russian separatists.[2]

A crucial rail link to Estonia has been cut off, and pro-Russian militia units are wreaking havoc in a northern border city, but they have not yet declared any political objectives. A clear political declaration has been made in Latvia, however, where the eastern, heavily ethnic Russian region of Latgale has declared itself an independent republic, with its capital at Daugavpils, Latvia's "second city," which is now itself in rebel hands.

The most serious confrontations have occurred in Lithuania, where unidentified military equipment, including T-14 tanks and T-15 and Bumerang armored personnel carriers known to be Russian in origin, has established a heavy presence along roadways in the south of the country linking the Russian enclave of Kaliningrad with Russia's ally, Belarus.

Early reports suggest that various strategic junctions of southern Lithuanian roads were seized by plainclothes militia members and blocked off early in the morning, before the armored columns entered Lithuanian territory. This would indicate coordination between the Kremlin invasion planners and the militia forces on the ground, but such a connection will likely be difficult to conclusively prove.

Meanwhile, political agitators touched off a number of demonstrations in Vilnius, which have caused the evacuation of the President after the Presidential Palace was surrounded and placed the American embassy in a state of siege. Scattered demonstrations were reported at the British,

French, German, and other western embassies, but the anti-U.S. protests have been the most sustained and the most violent. Communication with embassy staff inside suggests they can survive two to four more days on the supplies they have left, but they continue to request immediate evacuation. The Lithuanian military reports it is currently unable to assist in that effort.

The armored columns to the south of Vilnius have made no move toward the capital, nor do they appear to have fired on any Lithuanian or international targets. Their movements are being closely monitored.

Brussels is in a state of confusion. Discussions are being conducted at multiple levels, between NATO representatives, foreign ministers, and heads of state. While most parties privately agree that this situation justifies mounting a mutual defense under Article 5 of the North Atlantic charter, NATO has not issued a formal statement declaring this.

Europe's potential for collective action appears to have ground to a standstill. There is no consensus naturally forming among NATO allies on a potential method of response, and in this leadership vacuum, the German position of avoiding war with Russia is only gaining more adherents. The United States is being looked at to lead the NATO and world response, but has yet to act.

Meanwhile, Russian *Borei*-class submarines appear to be taking up strategic positions along our Atlantic and Gulf coasts. Not all sightings have been confirmed and there appears to be no clear intent shown, but analysts have suggested their positions are close enough to sea-lanes that they may be planning to impose an ad hoc blockade. A modern naval blockade against the United States would be unprecedented and would almost certainly require action.

★★★

Could It Really Happen?

Elsewhere in this book, we've considered attacks that America's enemies might launch on our own shores. The specter of terror in our homeland is always threatening, and, sadly, we have become used to seeing stories of conflict in well-known global hot spots like the Middle East. But crises that threaten to upend global stability can erupt anywhere in the world—and have a direct impact on our homeland.

For many decades, the United States and its allies fought a "cold war" against Russia and Eastern European nations under its control through the Warsaw Pact. The conflict cost billions of dollars, put many lives at risk, and on more than one occasion drifted dangerously close to a full-scale nuclear conflict. There is growing concern that Russia is determined to reassemble its Soviet-era empire and stoke a second Cold War.

The United States' involvement with the North Atlantic Treaty Organization (NATO) is one of our most important defense commitments, and I believe that alliance will only prove more critical in the face of mounting Russian aggression. Article 5 of the North Atlantic Treaty, which created NATO, states in part:

> The Parties agree that an armed attack against one or more of them in Europe or North America shall be considered an attack against them all and consequently they agree that, if such an armed attack occurs, each of them, in exercise of the right of individual or collective self-defence recognised by Article 51 of the Charter of the United Nations, will assist the Party or Parties so attacked by taking forthwith, individually and in concert with the other Parties, such action as it deems necessary, including the use of armed force, to restore and maintain the security of the North Atlantic area.

This is very clear: it means an attack on one is an attack on all. I feel that we are approaching a time when Russia will seek to test NATO's resolve in enforcing this provision. Russian president Vladimir Putin has imperial ambitions and has embarked on a campaign to expand his country's sphere of influence bit by bit, all while testing the resolve of his Western rivals.

Putin: The Man and His Rhetoric

Vladimir Putin has held significant power in Russia effectively since 1999 and from the beginning has presented a challenge to the West. When he first took office, the Clinton administration felt Putin to be a "modernizer" who could build on Boris Yeltsin's democratic reforms in Russia.[3] Yet, even in his first term, Putin appealed to Russian nationalism by bringing back symbols of previous Soviet glory. For instance, Russia readopted the melody of the old Soviet national anthem, albeit with new lyrics.[4]

Putin's first two terms as president overlapped mostly with those of U.S. president George W. Bush, who famously remarked after their first meeting that he "looked [Putin] in the eye" and "found him to be very straightforward and trustworthy," and said he was "able to get a sense of his soul."[5] Vice President Dick Cheney, for his part, was unable to shake the specter of Putin's past. When he thought of the Russian leader, Cheney said, "I think K.G.B., K.G.B., K.G.B."[6] By 2006, however, even President Bush had revised his judgment and dubbed Putin a "czar."[7]

Shortly thereafter, Putin gave a startling glimpse of his worldview as his second term drew to a close in 2007. That February, speaking at a conference in Munich—the same city where Hitler's Germany challenged democratic Europe and British prime minister Neville Chamberlain blinked—Putin delivered rhetoric that seemed to directly castigate the United States.[8]

Putin claimed the United States was trying to set itself up at the center of a "unipolar world," with "one single center of power, one single center of force and one single master." "The United States has overstepped its borders in all spheres—economic, political and humanitarian," Putin said, as then–secretary of defense Robert Gates and other American delegates listened in the audience, "and has imposed itself on other states." Obviously referring to the ongoing conflicts in Iraq and Afghanistan, Putin accused America of a "hyper-inflated use of force," arguing that the U.S. lurched "from one conflict to another without achieving a fully-fledged solution to any of them."[9] One British correspondent remarked that "afterwards in the corridors there were dark mutterings by some about a new Cold War."[10]

Reading between the lines, and given his subsequent actions, it is not difficult to see that President Putin was not merely lamenting that the United States had become, in his view, a "hyper-inflated" power. He may have also been tacitly signaling that a balance was needed against the U.S. Putin's speech in Munich may have intended to set Russia up for working as a counterweight to the United States once again, to reassert itself in its former spheres of influence. Two later conflicts, one the very next year, have proven Russia's willingness to do just that.

2008: The Russian Invasion of Georgia

On August 8, 2009, a significant Russian force entered the Republic of Georgia to intervene in Georgian efforts to assert control over the breakaway territories of Abkhazia and South Ossetia. Russian-backed separatists had been effectively controlling those territories for years, seeking independence for them along with closer ties with Russia. In a total of five days of fighting, Russian forces pushed Georgian troops out of the disputed areas. About a thousand died in the conflict, while tens of thousands more found themselves displaced.[11]

While disagreements over the status of South Ossetia and Abkhazia had been going on for some time, the Russian decision to invade may have been brought about by two goals asserted by Georgia in 2008: a renewed commitment to reintegrate territory controlled by pro-Russian separatists, and increased movement toward NATO membership.

Mikheil Saakashvili, known for a pro-Western stance, was reelected president of Georgia in January of 2008, partly on the promise of unifying the country, which included the breakaway republics.[12] Later, at a NATO summit in April, President Bush made efforts to advance both Georgia's and Ukraine's efforts to join the organization, and hoped to start the two nations on NATO's Membership Action Plan. France and Germany firmly opposed the effort, however, in order to avoid offending Russia.[13] Putin himself, who had initially threatened to boycott the summit if NATO embraced Ukraine and Georgia,[14] told reporters once he arrived that "a powerful military bloc on our borders will be taken by Russia as a direct threat to the security of our country."[15]

Dmitry Medvedev was due to replace Putin as president in

May, but Putin made sure to assert Russian influence over Georgia before he left that office and switched over to prime minister. On April 16 he opened formal relations between Russia and the separatist governments in Abkhazia and South Ossetia.[16] Tensions mounted until Georgian troops attacked South Ossetia's separatist capital, Tskhinvali, in August, at which point Russia invaded. As the tanks rolled in, President Medvedev said he intended to "protect the lives and dignity of Russian citizens wherever they are located."[17]

Before they stopped their advance on August 12, Russian forces had moved out of the disputed regions and into recognized Georgian territory. They eventually pulled back, and a peace agreement negotiated by President Nicolas Sarkozy of France ended the brief war. But the decision to push forward outside the initial conflict zone was a defining aspect of this conflict. Michael Emerson of the Centre for European Policy Studies called that tactic "a throwback to earlier times, and totally incompatible with the political and moral principles of modern Europe."[18]

In addition to being one of very few nations to recognize the "independence" of Abkhazia and South Ossetia, Russia left behind troops at the conflict's end that continue to control approximately 20 percent of Georgian territory.[19]

The coordination with separatists, the pretext of defending Russian citizens, and the militarization of invaded territory are all strategies that would be employed by Russia yet again in a more recent conflict.

2014: The Invasion of Crimea

In February 2014, Russian troops once again entered the sovereign territory of another state as a result of a domestic situation that was not to Vladimir Putin's liking. On February 22, after months of massive street protests calling for closer alignment with the European Union, Ukraine's pro-Russian president Viktor Yanukovych fled the capital city of Kiev, allowing a more pro-Western interim government to take over.[20] With Yanukovych on the run, Putin held a secret meeting where he declared to his advisors his intention not to let this crisis go to waste: "We must start working on returning Crimea to Russia," he said.[21]

Just days later, the first "little green men"—well-equipped and well-armed troops in green uniforms without insignia, widely believed to be Russian—began appearing around strategic sites on the Crimean Peninsula, such as airports.[22] At the same time, other unidentified "masked men with guns" took over Crimean local government offices and raised the Russian flag.[23]

On March 1, Russia produced its pretext for a full-blown invasion of Crimea. Russia's ambassador to the United Nations, Vitaly Churkin, produced a letter reportedly written by Yanukovych, the Ukrainian president in absentia, that formally asked for Russian military intervention "given the extraordinary situation in Ukraine, this threat and the threat to our compatriots, Russian citizens and the Black Sea Fleet."[24]

Despite turning over the Crimean Peninsula to Ukraine in 1954, Russia did maintain a heavy presence there, including the headquarters of the Russian Navy's Black Sea Fleet at the port of Sevastopol.[25] It was easy, therefore, to move in extra troops in order to quickly assume control of the entire peninsula.

Once the troops were in place and an interim government set up with a new Crimean prime minister—fringe pro-Russian politician Sergei Aksyonov—a vote was held in an attempt to legitimize the Russian takeover. Just before the vote was taken, the Russian foreign ministry issued a statement once again affirming that "Russia is aware of its responsibility for the lives of compatriots and fellow citizens in Ukraine and reserves the right to take people under its protection."[26]

On March 16, Crimea held a referendum—in violation of the Ukrainian constitution—on the question of whether to join Russia. The reported outcome was 96.7 percent in favor, but subsequent analysis citing the Russian government's own figures has shown that only a maximum of 30 percent of Crimeans could have voted for accession to Russia.[27] The United States and the European Union imposed sanctions against Russia in protest, but that didn't stop Putin: two days after the vote, he signed legislation that formally made Crimea part of Russia once again.[28]

At first, Putin and his government denied Russian military involvement in the Ukraine takeover. In March, he claimed the "little green men" stationed around the peninsula were not regulars but simply local militia, all of whom had apparently decided to buy matching uniforms from a "local shop."[29] He revealed a glimmer of the truth in April when he admitted on Russian television that "Crimean self-defense forces were of course backed by Russian servicemen."[30] In the same interview, however, he stated that "nothing [about the invasion] was prepared in advance. Everything was done on the spur of the moment, so to speak."[31]

Putin, of course, has no problem changing his narrative. In March of 2015, he told an entirely different story as part of a flashy documentary entitled *Crimea: Path to the Homeland* that was produced for the one-year anniversary of Crimea's "homecoming." It was here that Putin revealed his late-night meeting to decide the fate of Crimea. He also admitted that once President Yanukovych left his post, Russia sent special forces operatives into Crimea, where they were instrumental in the early stages of the takeover. Troops were brought in "under the guise of reinforcing our military facilities in Crimea," and strikingly, according to Putin, it was all legal. The agreements governing Russia's existing bases in Crimea allowed up to twenty thousand Russian troops on the peninsula, and Putin said they never went over that threshold.[32]

Despite international protests and little recognition of its change in status from other countries, Crimea today remains a de facto part of Russia. Putin took over the territory by force of arms, despite the political theater of the sham referendum.

Russia's long-term plans for Crimea have already become a matter of concern for NATO. Early in 2015, U.S. Air Force general Philip M. Breedlove, supreme allied commander of NATO and head of the U.S. European Command, noted the increased militarization of the peninsula since the Russian takeover. "What we have seen is that Crimea has been transformed in some fairly significant ways as far as weapon systems in the Crimea," said Breedlove. He described the weapons systems as ranging "from air defense systems that reach nearly half of the Black Sea to surface attack systems that reach almost all of the Black Sea area." These new assets are turning Crimea into "a great platform for power projection into this area."[33]

Crimea is, of course, not the only flashpoint in the Ukraine conflict. The ongoing violence in the eastern Donbass region bears similar hallmarks. In April 2014, pro-Russian protesters took over government offices in the cities of Donetsk and Luhansk; both of these areas declared themselves independent states after illegitimate referendums the following month.[34] Evidence has consistently surfaced of Russian troops assisting separatists in the east—with a recent Ukrainian estimate suggesting as many as 9,000 Russian troops were involved—but the Kremlin continues to deny this.[35]

We have already seen how this conflict can affect those beyond the borders of Ukraine. In September 2014, 298 civilians were killed when Malaysian Airlines Flight 17 was shot out of the sky over Ukraine, reportedly by a Russian Buk missile launcher operated by pro-Russian forces, or even Russians themselves.[36]

Russian action in Georgia and Ukraine paints a stark picture of Putin's idea of international diplomacy. The question is: Where does he stop?

Imperial Ambitions: Are the Baltic States Next?

Russia's interests in Ukraine are not guided by a goal of simply annexing any territory they can. Putin has expressed a desire to bring previously Russian-held areas back into the fold once again. In April 2014, in the wake of the Crimean takeover, he discussed the concept of "Novorossiya" on Russian television:

> I would like to remind you that what was called Novorossiya back in the tsarist days—Kharkov, Lugansk, Donetsk, Kherson, Nikolayev and Odessa—were not part of Ukraine back then. The center of that territory was Novorossiysk, so the region is called Novorossiya. Russia lost these territories for various reasons, but the people remained.[37]

The historical region Putin is describing is located in the south-eastern portion of Ukraine, including the part of the Ukrainian mainland from which the Crimean Peninsula juts out. So far, the conflict in Ukraine has not enveloped all of what was once "Novo-rossiya," but Putin's comments show the sense of history at the root of his expansionist thinking.

For this reason, recent signals sent from Russia toward the Baltic states have become a cause for concern.

In March 2015, a group of Russian generals reportedly made very specific threats against the Baltic states in the event of increased NATO military activity in any of the three nations. The threats came as an American armored column made its way across Eastern Europe that same month.[38]

Disturbing reports from Moscow in late June 2015 indicated that the Russia prosecutor general's office, known as the Genprocuratura, is in the process of formally investigating whether the Baltic states are, in fact, sovereign nations.[39] Two members of the Russian parliament from Putin's United Russia Party have requested that the Genprocuratura look into whether the former Soviet Union acted legally when it recognized the independence of the three Baltic states in 1991.[40]

The rehashing of Soviet-era territorial decisions appears to be in vogue in Russia at the moment. Shortly before investigating the Baltics, the Genprocuratura ruled that the 1954 transfer of Crimea between the Russian and Ukrainian Soviet Socialist Republics had, in fact, been illegal, thereby providing a tidy ex post facto justification for the return of Crimea to Russian control in 2014. "Most likely," according to a source in the prosecutor's office quoted in Russian media, "the Baltic States' independence will be found to be equally illegal."[41]

What Can We Do to Stop This?

We have a pretty good idea of what Vladimir Putin is trying to do. He wants to throw a new Iron Curtain up across Europe, but this time it's not about an ideological divide between communism and democracy. Putin wants to seal off Russia's sphere of influence, to secure his country's dominance over its neighbors. The question is: How far will he go? Where will this new Iron Curtain finally spring up?

I believe Putin will go as far as he can until the West decides to stand up and stop him. NATO will be key to checking Russian aggression, and the United States will need to lead our allies to stiffen Western resolve. Unfortunately, the Obama administration hasn't placed a priority on doing that. Because of recent foreign policy failures, the United States and our European allies are at greater risk from an increasingly belligerent Russia.

We need to change course now, before Putin gets so aggressive that he feels he can threaten our homeland. We can counter his efforts by taking these decisive actions:

RECOGNIZE THE THREAT. It's time to acknowledge that Russia and the United States are, once again, competing for influence in world affairs. And as a direct threat to the United States, Russia's arsenals of nuclear and conventional weapons remain forces to be reckoned with. Governor Mitt Romney was widely ridiculed during the 2012 election for suggesting that Russia was our greatest geopolitical foe. The Ukraine crisis should have been enough to prove him right, and even more recently, in July 2015, President Obama's own nominee for chairman of the Joint Chiefs of Staff, Marine general Joseph Dunford, told Congress that "Russia presents the greatest threat to our national security." He called Putin's actions "nothing short of alarming."[42] The Obama administration has consistently gotten Russia wrong, first during the misguided attempt at a "reset" in relations, and later in 2012 when President Obama meekly asked Russia's then-president Medvedev for "space" in discussing issues like missile defense until after election, when Obama said he would "have more flexibility." Russia only takes advantage of American "flexibility."[43] And we don't need to "reset," we need to *reassert*.

PRACTICE TOUGHER DIPLOMACY. The administration has talked a big game and made sure to condemn Russia's actions, but words can only go so far. Sometimes the words themselves don't even go as far as they should. At one House Committee on Foreign Affairs hearing during the Ukraine crisis, I asked an administration official about whether Russia's actions constituted an act of war—and, of course, he couldn't give a straight answer.[44] We need to call Russia's modern-day imperialism as we see it, and not be afraid to back up strong words with actions.

SUPPORT RUSSIA'S PRESENT—AND POTENTIALLY FUTURE—TARGETS. We have not done nearly enough to support the Ukrainians as they fight an unbalanced war against separatists backed by Russian equipment and personnel. The Obama administration has provided some limited military equipment, but we need to go a step further and provide the Ukrainians what they really need: defensive weapons, equipment, and expertise. There are signs that this situation is escalating: a small number of American troops have been sent to train Ukrainian forces.[45] But they would be even more effective if they were equipped with defensive arms and equipment. This should include Humvees, lethal weaponry such as armor-piercing missiles to counter Russian tanks, as well as unmanned aerial vehicles and medical supplies.[46]

PROJECT FORCE TO REASSURE OUR EUROPEAN ALLIES. The administration has continued with planned drawdowns and realignments of American military forces in Europe that make it more difficult to counter Russian aggression. By some estimates, only eighty-one American armored combat vehicles remain permanently stationed in Europe, as opposed to more than one thousand Russian vehicles massed just on the Ukrainian border.[47] Recently, the military sent convoys rolling on a thousand-mile journey through Eastern Europe as a show of strength.[48] That's a step in the right direction, but Putin needs to know there's more where that came from, especially if he intends to make moves on the Baltic states. As this scenario shows, Russia presents a threat not only on the ground but at sea as well. This is a bad time for the United States to have its smallest navy since 1916. Retired admiral James Stavridis, a former NATO supreme commander, estimated that defense spending had been cut by 30 percent over the last ten years, in the face of a Russia whose actions are, in the admiral's words, "not appropriate behavior in the 21st century."[49] Certainly there remains no excuse for President Obama's decision to cancel missile defense projects in Poland and the Czech Republic.[50] There was no excuse when he made the decision in 2009, and with Russia still on the move, there is certainly no excuse now. Missile defense in Europe is essential to our own security and that of our allies.

STRIKE AN ECONOMIC BLOW WITH ENERGY EXPORTS. Russia is currently the largest single supplier of crude oil and natural gas to Europe, accounting for about one-third of the continent's total imports of each. The countries closest to Russia—including the Baltic states—are among the most dependent, receiving almost all of their energy by the grace of Vladimir Putin.[51] This is a key weapon in Russia's arsenal. The threat of Putin turning off the gas valve is enough to make any nation think twice before taking a firm stand against his other aggressive actions. But what if Russia had some competition? According to data released by BP in June 2015, the United States has already surpassed Russia to become the world's largest producer of oil and natural gas combined.[52] Unfortunately, President Obama has not seen fit to lift the ban on American crude oil exports that has somehow remained on the books since the 1970s.[53] Lifting this ban and allowing American oil to flow into the European market would show Putin that he's not the only energy game in town, and it would give our allies some much-needed relief from dependence on Russia.

MAKE SURE OUR DIPLOMATIC FACILITIES ARE PROPERLY PROTECTED. American embassies and consulates are some of our nation's most prominent symbols overseas, and consequently targets for anti-American violence. We have seen this around the world, notably the 1979 seizure of our embassy in Tehran, and more recently the September 11, 2012, attack on the consulate in Benghazi, Libya. In our fictional scenario, the Vilnius embassy's regional security officer (RSO) evaluated the security situation of his compound and reported to the ambassador and deputy chief of mission that they could be in danger in the event of an attack. These concerns were submitted to the State Department but received no response. Less than a month before they were attacked, the diplomatic staff in Benghazi sent the State Department a classified cable which read, in part:

> RSO (Regional Security Officer) expressed concerns with the ability to defend Post in the event of a coordinated attack due to limited manpower, security measures, weapons capabilities, host nation support, and the overall size of the compound.[54]

I asked then–secretary of state Hillary Clinton about that cable at a congressional hearing months later, and she replied: "That cable did not come to my attention." She further explained that nobody in her office had seen the cable, either, and proceeded to remind the committee that "1.43 million cables a year come to the State Department" and that they were "reported through the bureaucracy." This is not an excuse. The result of the assault on the Benghazi compound was four Americans dead, including Ambassador Christopher Stevens. That should not be blamed on "bureaucracy."[55] The State Department should respond to these concerns quickly and make sure embassies and consulates are properly protected. As we have seen, delays could cost lives.

AFTERWORD

This book has outlined some of the scenarios that in the not-too-distant future could bring our nation to an unprecedented crisis, so that we can counter them before they happen. But equally important are the scenarios I haven't envisioned—that none of us have. These unknowns lurk just beyond our imaginations. Because we cannot know every threat, cannot predict every danger, we need to be a nation vigilant against threats from all comers and all corners. Unfortunately, as these pages have shown, we haven't been doing that job well enough over the past few years.

Former secretary of state Dean Rusk once said: "At any moment of the day or night, two-thirds of the world's people are awake, and some of them are up to no good." Rusk, who served in the administrations of John F. Kennedy and Lyndon B. Johnson and died in 1994, could hardly have imagined the tools available to those who are "up to no good" at this point in the twenty-first century.

Our world is increasingly connected, thanks to a myriad of technological advances. Very few inhabited places left on earth remain out of reach of some form of instantaneous communication. This has led to astonishing breakthroughs. But, as Thomas Friedman among many others points out, this literal and figurative connectivity can have its downsides as well. In *The World Is Flat: A Brief History of the Twenty-First Century*, Friedman notes that "Al Qaeda has learned to use many of the same instruments for global collaboration [that a major international corporation would] but instead of producing products and profits with them, it has produced murder and mayhem." This expertise, of course, is not confined to Al Qaeda. Any terrorist organization is able to use the Internet for more efficient fund-raising, recruitment, training, and issuing of orders—as ISIS continues to show. It is also an invaluable tool for spreading the propaganda that is any terror group's lifeblood.

We cannot afford to pretend, as some on both the left and right appear eager to do, that these dangers are not real and that the threats do not continue to evolve. They are very real, and our enemies are not easily curtailed or eliminated. In 2010, the U.S. military was reported to have killed or captured 80 percent of the leadership of the "Al Qaeda in Iraq" terrorist group. Just five years later this group has rebuilt itself into the Islamic State and rules wide swaths of Syrian and Iraqi territory as their own caliphate.

Rogue nation-states such as Iran and North Korea are under the control of regimes that cannot be counted on to act rationally on the world stage. They can, however, be counted on to regularly make bellicose statements calling for the destruction of their neighbors—and, of course, the United States. They also have well-known nuclear ambitions, and histories of clandestine research toward achieving that goal.

Russia, an established nuclear power, was once a very predictable rival. Now, with Vladimir Putin in power in some form or other since 1999, Russia's national motivations and movements have changed. Anti-American sentiment is political red meat to much of Putin's power base, and his exploitation of that to retain control could embolden fringe elements to take actions against the United States that even the Russian government would never (officially) sanction themselves.

China has its own global ambitions. And the communist-led power has shown an increasing willingness to challenge the United States. It is building a stronger military and working on new, subversive technologies to circumvent America's economic and military might.

As noted, it's not just other countries and so-called caliphates we have to worry about. Other elements not confined to any particular part of the world—drug cartels and criminal organizations—can cause havoc on their own or acting in collaboration with another enemy. Common cause against the United States can be a powerful force in uniting different groups: it brought Boko Haram under the ISIS banner, and may yet bring ISIS and Al Qaeda closer together. We must be prepared for more of these terrorist "super-group" alliances in the future.

Nearly every day we encounter reminders that such catastrophic attacks do not and will not occur in a vacuum. Events in motion around the world inform and inspire the actions and reactions of individuals and groups, which sometimes converge into plots against American lives and interests. A previously unknown terror recruit lured into radicalism over social media can, out of nowhere, become a household name and achieve martyrdom, taking innocents with him and in turn inspiring others to launch attacks.

What American leaders say and do is watched, listened to, noted, and catalogued by those who would do our nation harm. They probe our weaknesses and gauge how we respond to provocations. When the President of the United States announces that the fight against terrorism is winding down, or refers to a well-armed, well-organized terrorist army as a "J.V. team," our enemies notice. When we leave an American consulate in a volatile part of the world inadequately defended, leading to the murder of an ambassador and other U.S. personnel, our enemies notice. When our government defines a mass shooting by an avowed jihadist on a U.S. military base as "workplace violence," our enemies notice. When our politicians fail to grasp the nature of the threats we face and instead try to distort them to suit a political agenda, our enemies applaud.

Someday, perhaps in the not-too-distant future, our leaders will be brought to account for another spectacular terror attack against the United States. The litany of questions that they will face is already grimly familiar: Why couldn't we connect the dots? How did our imaginations fail to conceive the threat?

But what if we could avoid the need for some—maybe all—of these questions? What if we could prevent them from being asked in the first place?

I have made it my mission—in my work, my life, and in this book—to make sure we consider future threats in order to thwart them. Because I've seen the consequences of waiting until it's too late to take action.

On a recent visit to Iraq, I met again with the men and women who have spent the years since the attacks of September 11 helping to fight America's enemies. These young Americans have carried out their duties in the deserts of Iraq, in the mountains of Afghanistan, and in dangerous zones that dot nearly every continent of the globe. Always with the hope of peace in their hearts.

When I made my way to a city in the southern part of Iraq, a soldier pointed out a recent archaeological discovery just on the horizon: the remains of what many believe to be the house of Abraham, the prophet recognized by three of the world's major religions. I was amazed as I looked upon this four-thousand-year-old structure from which Judaism, Christianity, and Islam might well have sprung.

I thought then, as I hope now, that perhaps one day the

followers of those three faiths will be able to coexist in peace—
that we could find a way to live in a world where future generations don't have to imagine the worst-case scenarios. Such is the
hope that inspired me to write this book. And I feel ever grateful
to the men and women who work every day and every night to
make the dream a reality.

ACKNOWLEDGMENTS

Writing my first book has been a challenging and rewarding experience, and I am grateful to a number of people who played a part in the process. Keith Urbahn, Matt Latimer, Dylan Colligan, and the team at Javelin helped conceive this project and shepherd it from the very beginning. Tina Constable, Campbell Wharton, and Mary Choteborsky at Crown provided thoughtful guidance every step of the way. I especially appreciate the assistance from those who offered their expertise on the various threats covered in this book, including Richard Clarke, Mike Doran, Arthur Herman, I. Lewis Libby, Bill Luti, Dan McKivergan, and Nick Palarino.

The staff in my congressional office and the House Committee on Homeland Security deserve recognition for the hard work they do every day to protect the American people.

Finally, I remain mindful that the freedom to write and publish any book is guaranteed by the men and women of the United States military, and the civilian employees who support our armed services and intelligence operations. That is why every dollar I earn from the proceeds of this book will go to charities that serve the needs of veterans and their families.

NOTES

Introduction

1. Frank Furedi, "Book of the Week: *Our Nation Unhinged*," *Times Higher Education*, May 28, 2009, https://www.timeshighereducation.com/books/book-of-the-week-our-nation-unhinged/406707.article

Chapter 1: Unfinished Business

1. *The 9/11 Commission Report: Final Report of the National Commission on Terrorist Attacks Upon the United States*, official government edition (Washington, DC: U.S. Government Printing Office, 2004), 155, http://www.9-11commission.gov/report/911Report.pdf

2. "Al Qaeda Associates Charged in Attack on USS Cole, Attempted Attack on Another U.S. Naval Vessel," press release, *U.S. Department of Justice*, May 15, 2003, http://www.justice.gov/archive/opa/pr/2003/May/03_crm_298.htm

3. Phil Hirschkorn, "Who Was Fahd al-Quso?" *CBS News*, May 7, 2012, http://www.cbsnews.com/news/who-was-fahd-al-quso/

4. "Jordan: Al Qaeda Killed U.S. Diplomat," *CNN*, December 14, 2002, http://www.cnn.com/2002/WORLD/meast/12/14/jordan.killing/

5. *The 9/11 Commission Report: Final Report of the National Commission on Terrorist Attacks Upon the United States*, 73.

6. "Al-Qaida Timeline: Plots and Attacks," *NBC News*, accessed August 25, 2015, http://www.nbcnews.com/id/4677978/ns/world_news-hunt_for_al_qaida/t/al-qaida-timeline-plots-attacks/#.VUvZ3a1VhHw

7. *The 9/11 Commission Report: Final Report of the National Commission on Terrorist Attacks Upon the United States*, 72.

8. *The 9/11 Commission Report: Final Report of the National Commission on Terrorist Attacks Upon the United States*, 155.

9. *The 9/11 Commission Report: Final Report of the National Commission on Terrorist Attacks Upon the United States*, 248.

10. Daniel Byman and Jennifer Williams, "Al-Qaeda vs. ISIS: The Battle for the Soul of Jihad," *Newsweek*, March 27, 2015, http://www .newsweek.com/al-qaeda-vs-isis-battle-soul-jihad-317414

11. Daveed Gartenstein-Ross and Bridget Moreng, "Al Qaeda Is Beating the Islamic State," *Politico*, April 14, 2015, http://www.politico.com/ magazine/story/2015/04/al-qaeda-is-beating-the-islamic-state-116954 .html#.VUvhFqlVhHw

12. "ISIS, Al Qaeda Affiliate Reportedly Unite to Fight US-Backed Rebels in Syria," *Fox News*, November 13, 2014, http://www.foxnews .com/world/2014/11/13/isis-al-qaeda-reportedly-reach-accord-in -syria/

13. Rukmini Callimachi, "Boko Haram Generates Uncertainty with Pledge of Allegiance to Islamic State," *New York Times*, March 7, 2015, http://www.nytimes.com/2015/03/08/world/africa/boko-haram-is-said -to-pledge-allegiance-to-islamic-state.html?_r=0

14. Nima Elbagir, Paul Cruickshank, and Mohammed Tawfeeq, "Boko Haram Purportedly Pledges Allegiance to ISIS," *CNN*, March 9, 2015, http://www.cnn.com/2015/03/07/africa/nigeria-boko-haram-isis/index .html

15. Hamdi Alkhshali and Steve Almasy, "ISIS Leader Purportedly Accepts Boko Haram's Pledge of Allegiance," *CNN*, March 12, 2015, http:// www.cnn.com/2015/03/12/middleeast/isis-boko-haram/

16. Ibid.

17. Janice Cheryl Beaver, "U.S. International Borders: Brief Facts" (Report No. RS21729), Congressional Research Service, November 9, 2006, https://www.fas.org/sgp/crs/misc/RS21729.pdf

18. Gavin John, "Sheer Size of US-Canada Border Stokes Terrorism Fears," *Fox News*, November 17, 2014, http://www.foxnews.com/us/2014/ 11/17/sheer-size-us-canada-border-stokes-terrorism-fears/

19. Deborah Hastings, "Man Walking in Maine Is Arrested, Accused of Being Rwandan War Crimes Fugitive," *New York Daily News*, August 7, 2014, http://www.nydailynews.com/news/national/rwandan-war-crimes -fugitive-nabbed-maine-article-1.1895764

20. Nancy Youssef, "Is ISIS Building a Drone Army?" *Daily Beast*,

March 18, 2015, http://www.thedailybeast.com/articles/2015/03/18/is
-isis-building-a-drone-army.html

21. Ibid.

22. "Man, 26, Charged in Plot to Bomb Pentagon Using Model Airplane," *CNN*, September 29, 2011, http://www.cnn.com/2011/09/28/us/
massachusetts-pentagon-plot-arrest/

23. Brian Ballou, "Rezwan Ferdaus of Ashland Sentenced to
17 Years in Terror Plot; Plotted to Blow Up Pentagon, Capitol," *Boston Globe*, November 1, 2012, http://www.boston.com/metrodesk/
2012/11/01/rezwan-ferdaus-ashland-sentenced-years-terror-plot/
KKvy6D6n2PfXfbEfA4iMwJ/story.html

24. "Man Sentenced in Boston for Plotting Attack on Pentagon and U.S.
Capitol and Attempting to Provide Detonation Devices to Terrorists,"
Federal Bureau of Investigation press release, November 1, 2012, http://
www.fbi.gov/boston/press-releases/2012/man-sentenced-in-boston-for
-plotting-attack-on-pentagon-and-u.s.-capitol-and-attempting-to-provide
-detonation-devices-to-terrorists

25. Jack Date and Mike Levine, "Gyrocopter Was Detected by Radar
Before Landing at Capitol, Pilot Deserves Stiffer Penalty, Officials Say,"
ABC News, April 29, 2015, http://abcnews.go.com/US/florida-mans
-gyrocopter-detected-radar-landing-capitol-lawn/story?id=30660032

26. "How Terrorists Are Using Social Media," *The Telegraph*, November 4, 2014, http://www.telegraph.co.uk/news/worldnews/islamic-state/
11207681/How-terrorists-are-using-social-media.html

27. Jenny Awford, "The Shocking Movie Made by Jihadi John's Sister: A
Dead Schoolgirl, Bloodied Footsteps and a Hooded Maniac Brandishing a
Knife," *Daily Mail*, February 27, 2015, http://www.dailymail.co.uk/news/
article-2971727/Jihadi-John-s-younger-sister-film-hooded-serial-killer
-chasing-schoolgirl-says-Revenge-NEVER-right-answer.html

28. "Massachusetts Man Charged with Plotting Attack on Pentagon
and U.S. Capitol and Attempting to Provide Material Support to Foreign
Terrorist Organization," Federal Bureau of Investigation press release,
September 28, 2011, https://www.fbi.gov/boston/press-releases/2011/
massachusetts-man-charged-with-plotting-attack-on-pentagon-and
-u.s.-capitol-and-attempting-to-provide-material-support-to-a-foreign
-terrorist-organization

29. "Mumbai Terror Attacks Fast Facts," *CNN*, April 13, 2015, http://
www.cnn.com/2013/09/18/world/asia/mumbai-terror-attacks/

30. "Fort Hood Shootings: The Meaning of 'Allahu Akbar,'" *The*

Telegraph, November 6, 2009, http://www.telegraph.co.uk/news/
worldnews/northamerica/usa/6516570/Fort-Hood-shootings-the
-meaning-of-Allahu-Akbar.html

31. Jeremy Schwartz, "Witnesses in Fort Hood Shooting Hearing Say
Hasan Returned to Shoot Same Victims Over and Over," *Austin American-
Statesman*, October 15, 2010, http://www.statesman.com/news/news/
state-regional/witnesses-in-fort-hood-shooting-hearing-say-hasan-/nRykN/

32. Rick Jervis and Doug Stanglin, "Nidal Hasan Found Guilty in Fort
Hood Killings," *USA Today*, August 23, 2013, http://www.usatoday.com/
story/news/nation/2013/08/23/nidal-hasan-guilty-fort-hood-shooting
-unanimous/2690899/

33. "Manhunt After Deadly Attack on Paris Newspaper," *CBS News*,
January 7, 2015, http://www.cbsnews.com/news/charlie-hebdo-french
-satirical-magazine-paris-office-attack-leaves-casualties/

34. Holly Watt, "Terrorists Shouted They Were from al-Qaeda in the
Yemen Before Charlie Hebdo Attack," *The Telegraph*, January 7, 2015,
http://www.telegraph.co.uk/news/worldnews/europe/france/11330636/
Terrorists-shouted-they-were-from-al-Qaeda-in-the-Yemen-before
-Charlie-Hebdo-attack.html

35. "Charlie Hebdo Attack: 3 Suspects, 4 Hostages Killed in Separate
Attacks near Paris," The Associated Press, January 9, 2015, http://www
.cbc.ca/news/world/charlie-hebdo-attack-3-suspects-4-hostages-killed-in
-separate-attacks-near-paris-1.2894956

36. "2015 Paris Terror Attacks Fast Facts," *CNN*. January 21, 2015,
http://www.cnn.com/2015/01/21/europe/2015-paris-terror-attacks-fast
-facts/

37. Brian Ross, Rhonda Schwartz, and James Gordon Meek, "Chattanooga Shooter Mohammod Abdulazeez Followed Al Qaeda Cleric
Online in 2013," *ABC News*, July 21, 2015, http://abcnews.go.com/US/
chattanooga-shooter-mohammod-abdulazeez-al-qaeda-cleric-online/story
?id=32585636

38. Jonathan Dienst and Miguel Almaguer, "Mohammad Youssef
Abdulazeez Downloaded Recordings from Radical Cleric, Officials
Say," *NBC News*, July 21, 2015, http://www.nbcnews.com/storyline/
chattanooga-shooting/mohammad-youssef-abdulazeez-downloaded
-recordings-radical-cleric-officials-say-n395986

39. Ross, Schwartz, and Meek, "Chattanooga Shooter Mohammod Abdulazeez Followed Al Qaeda Cleric Online in 2013."

40. Shelly Bradbury, "Minute by Minute: A Timeline of the Chattanooga Attack Revealed," *Chattanooga Times-Free Press*, July 23, 2015,

http://www.timesfreepress.com/news/local/story/2015/jul/23/minute
-minute-timeline-abdulazeezs-attack/316028/

41. "An American Strategy for Victory in the War Against Islamist
Terror," Video, posted by *Committee on Homeland Security*, February 12,
2015, http://homeland.house.gov/document/aei-global-fight-defeat
-islamist-terrorism

42. "An American Strategy for Victory in the War Against Islamist Terror," *Committee on Homeland Security*.

43. Ibid.

44. Erin McClam, "Tracing the Rise of ISIS into a Menace of Terror,"
NBC News, September 29, 2014, http://www.nbcnews.com/storyline/isis
-terror/tracing-rise-isis-menace-terror-n214266

45. Paul D. Shinkman, "Obama: 'Global War on Terror' Is Over," *U.S.
News & World Report*, May 23, 2013, http://www.usnews.com/news/
articles/2013/05/23/obama-global-war-on-terror-is-over

46. Glenn Kessler, "Spinning Obama's Reference to Islamic State
as a 'JV' team," *Washington Post*, September 3, 2014, http://www
.washingtonpost.com/blogs/fact-checker/wp/2014/09/03/spinning
-obamas-reference-to-isis-as-a-jv-team/

47. "An American Strategy for Victory in the War Against Islamist Terror," *Committee on Homeland Security*.

48. Michael McCaul, "Why National Security Matters More Than Ever
in 2016 Election," *Fox News*, August 7, 2015, http://www.foxnews.com/
opinion/2015/08/07/national-security-election.html

49. Emma-Jo Morris, "McCaul: Overthrow Assad to Attack the Islamic
State," *Washington Free Beacon*, July 23, 2013, http://freebeacon.com/
national-security/mccaul-overthrow-assad-to-attack-the-islamic-state/

50. "An American Strategy for Victory in the War Against Islamist Terror," *Committee on Homeland Security*.

51. Ibid.

52. Ibid.

Chapter 2: The Venezuelan Connection

1. "Former Argentine President on Trial over Jewish Center Terrorist
Attack," *The Associated Press*, August 6, 2015, http://www.theguardian
.com/world/2015/aug/06/former-argentine-president-carlos-menem
-charges-terrorist-attack

2. "Overview," *Port of Houston Authority*, accessed August 26, 2015,
http://www.portofhouston.com/about-us/overview/

3. "The Complete Transcript of Netanyahu's address to Congress," *Washington Post*, March 3, 2015, http://www.washingtonpost.com/blogs/ post-politics/wp/2015/03/03/full-text-netanyahus-address-to-congress/

4. Roger F. Noriega and Jose R. Cardenas, "The Mounting Hezbollah Threat in Latin America," *American Enterprise Institute*, October 2011, http://www.aei.org/wp-content/uploads/2011/10/Updated -No3LatinAmerican%202011g.pdf

5. Jeffrey Goldberg, "In the Party of God," *The New Yorker*, October 28, 2002, http://www.newyorker.com/magazine/2002/10/28/in-the-party-of -god-2

6. Sara A. Carter, "Exclusive: Hezbollah Uses Mexican Drug Routes into U.S.," *The Washington Times*, March 27, 2009, http://www .washingtontimes.com/news/2009/mar/27/hezbollah-uses-mexican-drug -routes-into-us/?page=all

7. Goldberg, "In the Party of God."

8. Jim Michaels, "Recalling the Deadly 1983 Attack on the Marine Barracks," *USA Today*, October 23, 2013, http://www.usatoday.com/story/ nation/2013/10/23/marines-beirut-lebanon-hezbollah/3171593/

9. Noriega and Cardenas, "The Mounting Hezbollah Threat in Latin America."

10. Ibid.

11. Ibid.

12. Ibid.

13. Ibid.

14. "Iran Helping Venezuela Look for Uranium," *Reuters*, September 25, 2009, http://www.reuters.com/article/2009/09/26/us-nuclear-iran -venezuela-sb-idUSTRE58P03T20090926

15. Catherine Herridge, "New Photos Reveal Expanding Reach of Iran in Venezuela and Other Parts of Latin America," *Fox News Latino*, March 17, 2015, http://latino.foxnews.com/latino/politics/2015/03/17/ new-photos-reveal-expanding-reach-iran-in-venezuela-and-other-parts -latin/

16. Ibid.

17. Ibid.

18. Ibid.

19. Noriega and Cardenas, "The Mounting Hezbollah Threat in Latin America."

20. Ibid.

21. Ibid.

22. Linette Lopez, "Aeroterror: A Regular Flight from Caracas to Tehran Carried More Drugs and Money Than People," *Business Insider,* March 25, 2015. http://www.businessinsider.com/aeroterror-venezuela -iran-and-latin-america-2015-3

23. Ed Barnes, "Exclusive: Venezuela Cancels Round-Trip 'Terror Flight' to Syria and Iran," *Fox News,* September 14, 2010. http://www .foxnews.com/us/2010/09/14/terror-flight-venezuela-iran-illicit-arms -hezbollah-hamas-protest/

24. Lopez, "Aeroterror: A Regular Flight from Caracas to Tehran."

25. Ibid.

26. Barnes, "Exclusive: Venezuela Cancels Round-Trip 'Terror Flight' to Syria and Iran."

27. Ibid.

28. Ibid.

29. *Testimony of Ambassador Roger F. Noriega, United States Senate Committee on Foreign Relations Subcommittee on the Western Hemisphere, Peace Corps, and Global Narcotics Affairs,* 112th Congress, February 16, 2012, http://www.foreign.senate.gov/imo/media/doc/Roger_Noriega _Testimony1.pdf

30. Ibid.

31. Carter, "Exclusive: Hezbollah Uses Mexican Drug Routes into U.S."

32. Noriega and Cardenas, "The Mounting Hezbollah Threat in Latin America."

33. Ibid.

34. Jonathan Medalia, " 'Dirty Bombs': Technical Background, Attack Prevention and Response, Issues for Congress" (Report No. R41890), Congressional Research Service, June 24, 2011, https://www.fas.org/sgp/ crs/nuke/R41890.pdf

35. Samuel Brenner, "Protecting America's Colleges and Universities," in *Homeland Security: Public Spaces and Social Institutions,* ed. James J. F. Forest (Westport, CT: Praeger Security International, 2006), 143.

36. "Radiological Attack—Dirty Bombs and Other Devices," *National Academy of Sciences,* 2004, http://www.dhs.gov/xlibrary/assets/prep _radiological_fact_sheet.pdf

37. "Source Trafficking," *BBC News,* accessed August 26, 2015, http:// news.bbc.co.uk/2/shared/spl/hi/in_depth/dirty_bomb/html/4.stm

38. Ibid.

39. Medalia, "'Dirty Bombs': Technical Background, Attack Prevention and Response, Issues for Congress."

40. "Research Reactor," *Nuclear Threat Initiative*, accessed August 26, 2015, http://www.nti.org/glossary/#research-reactor

41. Brenner, "Protecting America's Colleges and Universities," 143.

42. Charles D. Ferguson and William C. Potter, *The Four Faces of Nuclear Terrorism* (New York: Routledge, 2005), 261-262.

43. "Isfahan (Esfahan) Nuclear Technology Center (INTC)," *Nuclear Threat Initiative*, accessed August 26, 2015, http://www.nti.org/facilities/237/

44. Carter, "Exclusive: Hezbollah Uses Mexican Drug Routes into U.S."

45. Noriega and Cardenas, "The Mounting Hezbollah Threat in Latin America."

46. Ibid.

47. Michael McCaul, "McCaul: It's Time to Secure America's Border Once and For All," *Austin American-Statesman*, January 25, 2015, http://www.statesman.com/news/news/opinion/mccaul-its-time-to-secure-americas-border-once-and/njtMm/

48. "Article in Issue IX of ISIS Magazine 'Dabiq' Discusses How Pakistani Nuclear Weapons Can Be Purchased, Transported to U.S. Through Smugglers," *Jihad and Terrorism Threat Monitor*, Middle East Media Research Institute, May 26, 2015, http://www.memrijttm.org/article-in-issue-ix-of-isis-magazine-dabiq-discusses-how-pakistani-nuclear-weapons-can-be-purchased-transported-to-us-through-smugglers.html

49. Desmond Butler and Vadim Ghidra, "AP Investigation: Nuclear Black Market Seeks IS Extremists," Associated Press, October 7, 2015, http://bigstory.ap.org/article/9f77a17c001f4cf3baeb28990b0d92eb/ap-investigation-nuclear-smugglers-sought-terrorist-buyers

50. "Article in Issue IX of ISIS Magazine 'Dabiq' Discusses How Pakistani Nuclear Weapons Can Be Purchased, Transported to U.S. Through Smugglers," *Jihad and Terrorism Threat Monitor*, Middle East Media Research Institute, May 26, 2015, http://www.memrijttm.org/article-in-issue-ix-of-isis-magazine-dabiq-discusses-how-pakistani-nuclear-weapons-can-be-purchased-transported-to-us-through-smugglers.html

51. "Don't Let Them Have Their Yellowcake and Eat It Too," *CBS News*, July 15, 2015, http://www.cbsnews.com/news/benjamin-netanyahu-mighty-military-israel-lobby-congress-iran-nuclear/

52. Ibid.

53. Ibid.

54. Ibid.

55. "Thousands of Iranian Long-Range Missiles Await Enemies: Iran Cmdr.," *PressTV*, March 1, 2013, http://www.presstv.com/detail/2013/03/01/291356/iran-missiles-ready-to-counter-enemies/

56. Maria Khan, "Iran's President Rouhani: Sanctions Will Be Lifted," *International Business Times*, November 24, 2014, http://www.ibtimes.co.uk/irans-president-rouhani-sanctions-will-be-lifted-1476395

57. "Full Text of Netanyahu's Response to Nuke Deal: It Will Fuel Iran's Efforts to Destroy Israel," *The Times of Israel*, July 14, 2015, http://www.timesofisrael.com/full-text-of-netanyahus-response-to-nuke-deal-it-will-fuel-irans-efforts-to-destroy-israel/

58. Daniel Wiser, "Expert: U.S. Must Rely on Russia to Preserve Arms Embargo on Iran," *Washington Free Beacon*, July 15, 2015, http://freebeacon.com/national-security/expert-u-s-must-rely-on-russia-to-preserve-arms-embargo-on-iran/

59. "Russia Confirms Sale of S-300 Missile Systems to Iran," AFP, May 26, 2015, http://news.yahoo.com/russia-confirms-sale-300-missile-systems-iran-182047663.html

60. Wiser, "Expert: U.S. Must Rely on Russia to Preserve Arms Embargo on Iran."

61. Greg Botelho, "Iran Nuclear Deal Full of Complex Issues and Moving Parts," CNN, July 14, 2015, http://www.cnn.com/2015/07/14/politics/iran-nuclear-deal-highlights/

62. Ibid.

63. McCaul, "McCaul: It's Time to Secure America's Border Once and For All."

64. Ibid.

65. "McCaul Hearing Finds Bipartisan Agreement: DHS Mismanagement Affects Mission Performance," Office of U.S. Representative Michael McCaul press release, March 1, 2012, http://mccaul.house.gov/media-center/press-releases/mccaul-hearing-finds-bipartisan-agreement-dhs-mismanagement-affects

66. Marc A. Thiessen, "Obama's Secret Iran Deals Exposed," *Washington Post*, July 27, 2015, https://www.washingtonpost.com/opinions/obamas-secret-iran-deals-exposed/2015/07/27/26d14dbc-3460-11e5-8e66-07b4603ec92a_story.html

Chapter 3: The Manchurian Campaign

1. Min Zeng and Lingling Wei, "Japan Overtakes China As Largest U.S. Bondholder," *Wall Street Journal*, April 15, 2015, http://www.wsj.com/articles/japan-overtakes-china-as-largest-u-s-bondholder-1429129765

2. Alan C. Miller, "Democrats Return Illegal Contribution; Politics: South Korean Subsidiary's $250,000 Donation Violated Ban on Money from Foreign Nationals," *Los Angeles Times*, September 21, 1996, http://pqasb.pqarchiver.com/latimes/doc/293383626.html?FMT=ABS&FMTS=ABS:FT&type=current&date=Sep 21, 1996&author=ALAN C. MILLER&pub=Los Angeles Times (pre-1997 Fulltext)&edition=&startpage=16&desc=Democrats Return Illegal Contributio%23http://pqasb

3. Bob Woodward and Brian Duffy, "Chinese Embassy Role in Contributions Probed," *Washington Post*, February 13, 1997, http://www.washingtonpost.com/wp-srv/politics/special/campfin/stories/china1.htm

4. Roberto Suro and Bob Woodward, "Chung Ties Funds to DNC," *Washington Post*, May 16, 1998, http://www.washingtonpost.com/wp-srv/politics/special/campfin/stories/cf051698.htm

5. Wolf Blitzer, "Johnny Chung Says Chinese Official Gave Him $300,000 for Clinton Campaign," *CNN*, April 4, 1999, http://www.cnn.com/ALLPOLITICS/stories/1999/04/04/china.clinton.money/

6. David Jackson and Lena H. Sun, "Liu's Deals with Chung: An Intercontinental Puzzle," *Washington Post*, May 23, 1998, http://www.washingtonpost.com/wp-srv/politics/special/campfin/stories/liu052498.htm

7. Ibid.

8. Suro and Woodward, "Chung Ties Funds to DNC."

9. Jackson and Sun, "Liu's Deals with Chung: An Intercontinental Puzzle."

10. William C. Rempel and Alan C. Miller, "Donor Contradicts White House," *Washington Post*, July 27, 1997, http://www.washingtonpost.com/wp-srv/politics/special/campfin/stories/cf072797.htm

11. Ibid.

12. Michael Moore, "Chinese Army Still Haunted by the Ghosts of Tiananmen Square," *The Telegraph*, June 3, 2014, http://www.telegraph.co.uk/news/worldnews/asia/china/10871334/Chinese-army-still-haunted-by-the-ghosts-of-Tiananmen-Square.html

13. Jackson and Sun, "Liu's Deals with Chung: An Intercontinental Puzzle."

14. Ibid.

15. Ibid.

16. Suro and Woodward, "Chung Ties Funds to DNC."

17. David Johnston, "Committee Told of Beijing Cash for Democrats," *Washington Post*, May 12, 1999, http://www.nytimes.com/1999/05/12/us/committee-told-of-beijing-cash-for-democrats.html

18. Jackson and Sun, "Liu's Deals with Chung: An Intercontinental Puzzle."

19. John Pomfret, "China Denies Contribution Charges," *Washington Post*, May 20, 1998, http://www.washingtonpost.com/wp-srv/politics/special/campfin/stories/cf052098b.htm

20. Rene Sanchez, "Agent in Spy Saga 'Was One of Us,' " *Washington Post*, April 20, 2003, http://www.udel.edu/globalagenda/2003/student/readings/fbichinaspy.html

21. William C. Rempel, Henry Weinstein, and Alan C. Miller, "Testimony Links Top China Official, Funds for Clinton," *Los Angeles Times*, April 4, 1999, http://articles.latimes.com/print/1999/apr/04/news/mn-24189

22. Ibid.

23. Ibid.

24. Rempel, Weinstein, and Miller, "Testimony Links Top China Official, Funds for Clinton."

25. Ibid.

26. Ibid.

27. Jeff Gerth, David Johnston, and Don Van Natta Jr., "Evidence of Broad Plan by China to Buy Entrée to U.S. Technology," *New York Times*, December 15, 1998, http://www.nytimes.com/1998/12/15/us/evidence-of-broad-plan-by-china-to-buy-entree-to-us-technology.html?pagewanted=1&pagewanted=all

28. Terry Frieden, "Fund-Raiser Charlie Trie Pleads Guilty Under Plea Agreement," *CNN*, May 21, 1999, http://web.archive.org/web/20060805092557/http://www.cnn.com/ALLPOLITICS/stories/1999/05/21/trie/

29. The *Washington Post* Staff, "Campaign Finance Key Player: John Huang," *Washington Post*, July 24, 1997, http://www.washingtonpost.com/wp-srv/politics/special/campfin/players/huang.htm

30. Jeff Gerth, David Johnston, and Don Van Natta Jr., "Evidence of Broad Plan by China to Buy Entrée to U.S. Technology."

31. Lewis A. Neil, "Freeh Says Reno Clearly Misread Prosecutor Law," *New York Times*, July 16, 1998, http://www.nytimes.com/1998/07/16/us/freeh-says-reno-clearly-misread-prosecutor-law.html

32. Chris Mondics, "Panel: Fund-Raising Rules Ignored the Report Condemns How the Democratic Party Got Campaign Money," *Inquirer Washington Bureau*, March 5, 1998, http://articles.philly.com/1998-03-05/news/25744755_1_fund-raising-campaign-money-democratic-party

33. Michael Pillsbury, *The Hundred-Year Marathon* (New York: Henry Holt and Co., 2014), 90.

34. Pillsbury, "Mr. White and Ms. Green," 90–91.

35. Ibid., 91.

36. Ibid.

37. Ibid.

38. Pierre Thomas, "Justice May Probe Links Between China Policy, Campaign Cash," *CNN*, May 17, 1998, http://www.cnn.com/ALLPOLITICS/1998/05/17/satellite.review/

39. Gerth, Johnston, and Van Natta Jr., "Evidence of Broad Plan by China to Buy Entree to U.S. Technology."

40. Ibid.

41. Ben Brumfield, "U.S. Defense Chief to China: End South China Sea Expansion," *CNN*, May 30, 2015, http://www.cnn.com/2015/05/30/politics/singapore-south-china-sea-ash-carter/

42. *Remarks by the President in Town Hall with YSEALI Initiative Fellows*, June 2, 2015 (Washington, D.C.: The White House, Office of the Press Secretary), https://www.whitehouse.gov/the-press-office/2015/06/02/remarks-president-town-hall-yseali-initiative-fellows

43. Josh Rogin, "Ash Carter Talks Tough on China, But It's Just Talk," *Bloomberg View*, May 30, 2015, http://www.bloombergview.com/articles/2015-05-30/ash-carter-talks-tough-on-china-but-it-s-just-talk

44. Stephanie Condon, "As China Flexes Its Muscles, America Looks for the Right Response," *CBS News*, June 3, 2015, http://www.cbsnews.com/news/as-china-flexes-its-muscles-america-looks-for-the-right-response/

45. Gina Chon, "US Accuses Chinese Professors of Spying," *CNBC Politics*, May 19, 2015, http://www.cnbc.com/2015/05/19/us-accuses-chinese-professors-of-spying.html

46. Del Quentin Wilber, "Economic Spying by China Spurs New Tactics From U.S. Prosecutors," *Bloomberg Business*, May 21, 2015, http://www.bloomberg.com/news/articles/2015-05-21/economic-spying-by-china-spurs-new-tactics-from-u-s-prosecutors

47. Robert Windrem, "China Read Emails of Top U.S. Officials," *NBC News*, August 10, 2015, http://www.nbcnews.com/news/us-news/china-read-emails-top-us-officials-n406046

48. Mark Honsenball and Patricia Zengerle, "U.S. Unlikely to Blame China Publicly Over OPM Data Breach: Officials," *Reuters*, July 22, 2015, http://www.reuters.com/article/2015/07/22/us-cybersecurity-usa-china-idUSKCN0PW2AA20150722

49. Daniel W. Drezner, "Anatomy of a Whole-of-Government Foreign Policy Failure," *Washington Post*, March 17, 2015, http://www.washingtonpost.com/posteverything/wp/2015/03/27/anatomy-of-a-whole-of-government-foreign-policy-failure/

50. Lingling Wei, "China Moves to Devalue Yuan," *Wall Street Journal*, August 11, 2015, http://www.wsj.com/articles/china-moves-to-devalue-the-yuan-1439258401

51. "Free Trade Must Not Be a Casualty of the Currency Wars," *Washington Post*, August 30, 2011, http://www.washingtonpost.com/opinions/free-trade-must-not-be-a-casualty-of-the-currency-wars/2011/08/29/gIQAtvzbqJ_story.html

52. *Foreign Nationals*, July 2003 (Washington, D.C.: *Federal Election Commission*), http://www.fec.gov/pages/brochures/foreign.shtml

53. Alexander Marlow, "Chinese Government Paid Bill Clinton Lucrative Speaking Fee as Sec. State Hillary Made 'Asia Pivot,'" *Breitbart*, May 11, 2015, http://www.breitbart.com/national-security/2015/05/11/chinese-govt-paid-bill-clinton-lucrative-speaking-fee-as-sec-state-hillary-made-asia-pivot/

54. Julianna Goldman, "Chinese Company Pledged $2 Million to Clinton Foundation in 2013," *CBS This Morning*, March 16, 2015, http://www.cbsnews.com/news/chinese-company-pledged-2-million-to-clinton-foundation-in-2013/

55. Marlow, "Chinese Government Paid Bill Clinton Lucrative Speaking Fee as Sec. State Hillary Made 'Asia Pivot.'"

56. "Chinese Billionaire Clinton Fan Sees 'Friendly' Presidency," *Bloomberg Politics*, June 22, 2015, http://www.bloomberg.com/politics/articles/2015-06-22/chinese-billionaire-fan-of-clinton-sees-friendly-presidency

57. Ibid.

Chapter 4: Black Friday

1. Lev Grossman and Jay Newton-Small, "The Secret Web: Where Drugs, Porn and Murder Live Online," *Time*, November 11, 2013, http://time.com/630/the-secret-web-where-drugs-porn-and-murder-live-online/; "Going Dark: The Internet Behind the Internet," *All Tech Considered*, NPR, May 25, 2014, http://www.npr.org/sections/alltechconsidered/2014/05/25/315821415/going-dark-the-internet-behind-the-internet

2. Grossman and Newton-Small, "The Secret Web: Where Drugs, Porn and Murder Live Online," 2.

3. See, e.g., *Brigham City v. Stuart*, 547 U. S. 398, 403 (2006).

4. Jeffrey Gettleman, "Somalia's Insurgents Embrace Twitter as a Weapon," *New York Times*, December 14, 2011, http://www.nytimes.com/2011/12/15/world/africa/somalias-rebels-embrace-twitter-as-a-weapon.html?_r=0; Lauren Ploch, "Countering Terrorism in East Africa: The U.S. Response," (Report No. R41473), Congressional Research Service, Nov. 3, 2010, https://www.fas.org/sgp/crs/terror/R41473.pdf

5. Ploch, "Countering Terrorism in East Africa: The U.S. Response," 8.

6. Jeremy Pelofsky, "Al Shabaab Recruited Dozens of Americans: U.S. Report," *Reuters*, July 27, 2011, http://www.reuters.com/article/2011/07/27/us-usa-security-somalia-idUSTRE76Q58M20110727, at 2.

7. Ploch, "Countering Terrorism in East Africa: The U.S. Response"; Feisal Omar and Abdi Sheikh, "Somalia Hotel Siege Ends, 14 Dead: Government," *Reuters*, Mar. 28, 2015, http://in.reuters.com/article/2015/03/28/somalia-attacks-idINKBN0MO07820150328; Hamza Mohamed, "Al-Shabaab Stages Deadly Attack on Somalia Luxury Hotel: At Least 25 People Killed in an Attack on the Central Hotel in Mogadishu, Somali Police Say," *Al Jazeera*, Feb. 21, 2015, http://www.aljazeera.com/news/2015/02/deaths-attack-luxury-hotel-somalia-capital-mogadishu-150220103959237.html

8. Ploch, "Countering Terrorism in East Africa: The U.S. Response," 4.

9. Fox News, "Al Shabaab Calls for Attack on Mall of America in New Video," *Fox News*, February 25, 2015, http://www.foxnews.com/world/2015/02/23/al-shabaab-reportedly-calls-for-attack-on-mall-america-in-new-video/

10. Ibid.

11. David Francis, "Al-Shabab Threat Against Mall of America Could Be a Call to Action," *Foreign Policy*, February 23, 2015, http://foreignpolicy.com/2015/02/23/al-shabab-threat-against-mall-of-america-could-be-a-call-to-action/

12. David Howden, "Terror in Nairobi: The Full Story Behind Al-Shabaab's Mall Attack," *The Guardian*, October 4, 2013, http://www .theguardian.com/world/2013/oct/04/westgate-mall-attacks-kenya

13. *The Terrorist Threat from Al Shabaab, United States House of Repre-sentatives*, 113th Cong., October 3, 2013 (Washington, D.C.: House For-eign Affairs Committee), http://www.rand.org/content/dam/rand/pubs/ testimonies/CT400/CT400/RAND_CT400.pdf

14. Howden, "Terror in Nairobi: The Full Story Behind Al-Shabaab's Mall Attack."

15. *The Terrorist Threat from Al Shabaab, United States House of Representatives*.

16. Howden, "Terror in Nairobi: The Full Story Behind Al-Shabaab's Mall Attack."

17. Francis, "Al-Shabab Threat Against Mall of America Could Be a Call to Action."

18. *Investigative Report on Al Shabaab, United States House of Representa-tives*, Report, July 27, 2011 (Washington, D.C.: U.S. House of Representa-tives Committee on Homeland Security), https://homeland.house.gov/ document/investigative-report-al-shabaab, 2.

19. *The Terrorist Threat from Al Shabaab, United States House of Representatives*.

20. Jay Newton-Small, "An Alleged Terrorist's Family Waits in Hope and Fear," *Time*, September 27, 2013, http://nation.time.com/2013/09/ 27/a-terrorists-family-waits-in-hope-and-fear/

21. Ploch, "Countering Terrorism in East Africa: The U.S. Response," 16.

22. *Investigative Report on Al Shabaab, United States House of Represen-tatives*; Todd B. Jones, "Operation Rhino," *Offices of the United States At-torneys*, December 8, 2014, http://www.justice.gov/usao/priority-areas/ national-security/operation-rhino

23. Raya Jalabi, "Six Minnesota Men Charged with Conspiring to Support ISIS in Syria," *The Guardian*, April 20, 2015, http://www .theguardian.com/us-news/2015/apr/20/six-minnesota-men-islamic-state -syria-somali-american

24. "UN Says '25,000 Foreign Fighters' Joined Islamist Militants," *BBC News*, April 2, 2015, http://www.bbc.com/news/world-middle-east -32156541

25. Jeff Seldin, "Progress Seen in Stemming Flow of Foreign Fighters to IS," *Voice of America*, July 17, 2015, http://www.voanews.com/content/

progress-seen-stemming-flow-foreign-fighters-islamic-state/2867432
.html

26. "Visa Waiver Program," *U.S. Department of State,* accessed September 8, 2015, http://travel.state.gov/content/visas/english/visit/visa-waiver -program.html

27. Gettleman, "Somalia's Insurgents Embrace Twitter as a Weapon," 2.

28. Ibid., 1.

29. Ibid., 2.

30. Ibid.

31. Ibid., 3.

32. Ploch, "Countering Terrorism in East Africa: The U.S. Response," 9.

33. Gettleman, "Somalia's Insurgents Embrace Twitter as a Weapon," 2.

34. Bill Hudson Francis, "FBI: Al-Shabaab Released Video to Recruit Minn. Men for Jihad," WCCO, August 8, 2013, http://minnesota.cbslocal .com/2013/08/08/fbi-al-shabaab-released-violent-video-to-recruit-minn -men-for-jihad/

35. Gettleman, "Somalia's Insurgents Embrace Twitter as a Weapon"; Ploch, "Countering Terrorism in East Africa: The U.S. Response."

36. Ploch, "Countering Terrorism in East Africa: The U.S. Response," 4–5.

37. *Investigative Report on Al Shabaab, United States House of Representatives,* 6.

38. Ploch, "Countering Terrorism in East Africa: The U.S. Response," 1.

39. *Investigative Report on Al Shabaab, United States House of Representatives,* 6.

40. Grossman and Newton-Small, "The Secret Web: Where Drugs, Porn and Murder Live Online," 2.

41. Ibid., 1.

42. Ibid., 2.

43. Ibid., 3.

44. Michael McCaul, "Keep America Safe, Plug European Security Gaps That Allow ISIS and Al Qaeda Supporters to Travel with Ease," *Fox News Opinions,* April 21, 2015, http://www.foxnews.com/opinion/2015/ 04/21/keep-america-safe-plug-european-security-gaps-that-allow-isis-and -al-qaeda.html

45. "Chairman McCaul to Deliver Speech at Heritage Foundation on Terror Gone Viral," Committee on Homeland Security press release,

July 22, 2015, http://homeland.house.gov/press-release/chairman-mccaul
-deliver-speech-heritage-foundation-terror-gone-viral

46. "Chairman McCaul to Deliver Speech at Heritage Foundation on
Terror Gone Viral," Committee on Homeland Security press release.

Chapter 5: Going Dark

1. Vivek Wadhwa, "Quantum Computing Is About to Overturn Cybersecurity's Balance of Power," *Washington Post*, May 11, 2015, http://
www.washingtonpost.com/blogs/innovations/wp/2015/05/11/quantum
-computing-is-about-to-overturn-cybersecuritys-balance-of-power/

2. "Watch High-Speed Trading in Action," *CNN Money*, July 5, 2013,
https://www.youtube.com/watch?v=2u007Msq1qo

3. Matt Egan, "Flash Crash: Could It Happen Again?" *CNN Money*,
May 6, 2014, http://money.cnn.com/2014/05/06/investing/flash-crash
-anniversary/

4. Lloyd's, "Emerging Risks Report: Business Blackout," *Cambridge
Centre for Risk Studies*, May 2015, p. 12, http://www.lloyds.com/~/media
/files/news%20and%20insight/risk%20insight/2015/business%20blackout
/business%20blackout20150708.pdf

5. Lloyd's, "Emerging Risks Report: Business Blackout," 16.

6. Ibid., 16.

7. Ibid., 17.

8. Ibid., 16–17.

9. Ibid., 18.

10. Ibid., 12.

11. Ibid., 17.

12. Ibid.

13. Ibid., 4, 15.

14. Cory Bennett, "Interior Scrambles to Patch Security after OPM
Hack," *The Hill*, July 15, 2015, http://thehill.com/policy/cybersecurity
/248091-doi-scrambles-to-patch-security-holes-after-opm-hack

15. Ellen Nakashima, "Hacks of OPM Databases Compromised 22.1
Million People, Federal Authorities Say," *Washington Post*, July 9, 2015,
http://www.washingtonpost.com/blogs/federal-eye/wp/2015/07/09/
hack-of-security-clearance-system-affected-21-5-million-people-federal
-authorities-say/

16. Ibid.

17. Ibid.

18. Ibid.

19. Glenn Thrush and Gabriel Debenedetti, "Clinton: I Used Private Email Account for 'Convenience,'" *Politico*, March 10, 2015, http://www .politico.com/story/2015/03/hillary-clinton-email-press-conference -115947.html

20. Byron Tau, "Hillary Clinton's Email Dispute: An Updated Guide," *Wall Street Journal*, July 27, 2015, http://blogs.wsj.com/washwire/2015 /07/27/hillary-clintons-email-dispute-an-updated-guide/

21. Alana Wise, "Clinton: I Did Not Send or Get Classified Emails on Private Account," *Reuters*, July 25, 2015, http://www.reuters.com/article /2015/07/26/us-usa-election-clinton-idUSKCN0PZ0S920150726

22. Ibid.

23. Ibid.

24. Tau, "Hillary Clinton's Email Dispute: An Updated Guide."

25. Heather Brooke, "Inside the Secret World of Hackers," *The Guardian*, August 24, 2011, http://www.theguardian.com/technology/2011 /aug/24/inside-secret-world-of-hackers

26. Ibid.

27. Ibid.

28. David Gordon Smith and Kristen Allen, "The World from Berlin: Electronic Surveillance Scandal Hits Germany," *Spiegel*, October 10, 2011, http://www.spiegel.de/international/germany/the-world-from-berlin -electronic-surveillance-scandal-hits-germany-a-790944.html

29. Richard Clarke interview.

30. Jack Millner, "The Weyl Fermion Is Finally Discovered: Massless Particle First Theorised in 1929 Could Pave Way for Next-Generation Quantum Computing," *The Daily Mail*, July 23, 2015, http://www.dailymail.co .uk/sciencetech/article-3172007/Weyl-fermion-finally-discovered-Massless -particle-theorised-1929-pave-way-generation-quantum-computing.html

31. Wadhwa, "Quantum Computing Is About to Overturn Cybersecurity's Balance of Power."

32. Ibid.

33. Ibid.

34. Mark Ritter, "We're Entering a Golden Era of Quantum Computing Research," *A Smarter Planet*, April 29, 2015, http://asmarterplanet.com /blog/2015/04/golden-era-quantum-computing.html

35. Wadhwa, "Quantum Computing Is About to Overturn Cybersecurity's Balance of Power."

36. "D-Wave Lab Tour Part 1 (of 3) — The Infrastructure of the D-Wave Quantum Computer," YouTube video, posted by D-Wave Systems, May 6, 2015, https://www.youtube.com/watch?v=zDotDiK2UuY

37. "Approaching a Quantum Leap in Computing," *Stratfor Enterprises*, July 24, 2015, https://www.stratfor.com/analysis/approaching-quantum -leap-computing

38. Ibid.

39. Xie Tingting, "Chinese Physicists Show How Quantum Computers Can Boost Machine Learning," *CRJ English News*, April 2, 2015, http:// english.cri.cn/12394/2015/04/02/1261s872650.htm

40. Richard Clarke interview.

41. Jordan Malter, "Secrets of a Former High Speed Trader," *CNN*, August 12, 2013, http://money.cnn.com/video/investing/2013/08/12 /investing-former-high-speed-trader-secrets-hft.cnnmoney/

42. Ben Rooney, "UK Trader Arrested for Causing 2010 Stock Market 'Flash Crash,'" *CNN Money*, April 22, 2015, http://money.cnn.com/2015 /04/21/investing/flash-crash-uk-trader-arrested/

43. Matt Egan, "Flash Crash: Could It Happen Again?"

44. Lloyd's, "Emerging Risks Report: Business Blackout," 7.

45. "What Is a Zero-Day Vulnerability?" *Symantec*, http://www.pctools .com/security-news/zero-day-vulnerability/

46. Lloyd's, "Emerging Risks Report: Business Blackout," 10.

47. Ibid., 11.

48. Ibid.

49. Ibid., 53.

50. https://www.washingtonpost.com/local/trafficandcommuting/faa -airlines-still-working-to-resume-normal-air-traffic-after-major-glitch /2015/08/16/2f973a48-442c-11e5-846d-02792f854297_story.html

51. Lloyd's, "Emerging Risks Report: Business Blackout," 15.

52. Ibid., 4.

53. Ibid., 15.

54. Ibid., 4.

55. Brian Wingfield and Jeff Bliss, "Thousands Seen Dying If Terrorists Attack U.S. Power Grid," *Bloomberg Business*, November 14, 2012, http:// www.bloomberg.com/news/articles/2012-11-14/thousands-seen-dying-if -terrorists-attack-vulnerable-u-s-grid

56. Richard Clarke interview.

57. Richard Clarke, *Cyber War* (New York: Ecco Press 2011), 27.

58. Ibid.

59. Flora Drury, "North Korea's 'Ruthless Magic Weapon': The Cyber Warrior Factory 'Behind Sony Hack' Which Handpicks Genius Children to Target Enemies of Kim Jong un," *Daily Mail*, December 18, 2014, http://www.dailymail.co.uk/news/article-2877589/North-Korea-s-Bureau-21-cyber-warriors-trained-secretive-hacking-unit.html

60. Ju-Min Park and James Pearson, "In North Korea, Hackers Are a Handpicked, Pampered Elite," *Reuters*, December 5, 2014, http://www.reuters.com/article/2014/12/05/us-sony-cybersecurity-northkorea-idUSKCN0JJ08B20141205

61. "Profiling an Enigma: The Mystery of North Korea's Cyber Threat Landscape," *Hewlett-Packard Development Company, L.P.*, August 2014, http://h30499.www3.hp.com/hpeb/attachments/hpeb/off-by-on-software-security-blog/388/2/HPSR%20SecurityBriefing_Episode16_NorthKorea.pdf

62. Drury, "North Korea's 'Ruthless Magic Weapon.'"

63. Park and Pearson, "In North Korea, Hackers Are A Handpicked, Pampered Elite."

64. Drury, "North Korea's 'Ruthless Magic Weapon': The Cyber Warrior Factory 'Behind Sony Hack' Which Handpicks Genius Children to Target Enemies of Kim Jong un."

65. Clarke, *Cyber War*, 28.

66. Park and Pearson, "In North Korea, Hackers Are A Handpicked, Pampered Elite."

67. Clarke, *Cyber War*, 24.

68. Drury, "North Korea's 'Ruthless Magic Weapon': The Cyber Warrior Factory 'Behind Sony Hack' Which Handpicks Genius Children to Target Enemies of Kim Jong un."

69. Ibid.

70. Ryan Faughnder, "Sony Says Studio Hack Cost It $15 Million in Fiscal Third Quarter," *Los Angeles Times*, August 31, 2015, http://www.latimes.com/entertainment/envelope/cotown/la-et-ct-sony-hack-cost-20150204-story.html

71. Clarke, *Cyber War*, 24.

72. Ibid., 25–29.

73. Ibid., 29.

74. Ibid., 28.

75. Jae-soon Chang, "Cyberattacks Traced to North Korea," *Huffington Post*, May 25, 2011, http://www.huffingtonpost.com/2009/10/30 /cyberattacks-traced-to-no_n_339701.html

76. Gordon G. Chang, "Does Iran Have Secret Nukes in North Korea?" *The Daily Beast*, March 29, 2015, http://www.thedailybeast.com/articles /2015/03/29/does-iran-have-secret-nukes-in-north-korea.html

77. Wadhwa, "Quantum Computing Is About to Overturn Cybersecurity's Balance of Power."

78. Maria Farrell, "The Internet of Things—Who Wins, Who Loses?" *The Guardian*, August 14, 2015, http://www.theguardian.com /technology/2015/aug/14/internet-of-things-winners-and-losers-privacy -autonomy-capitalism

79. Clarke, *Cyber War*, 168–69.

Chapter 6: The Threat We Can't See

1. Noorhan Abbas and Dr. Eric Atwell, "The University of Leeds: Qurany Tool," http://www.comp.leeds.ac.uk/nora/html/2-59.html

2. Katia Hetter, "The World's Most Popular Amusement Park Is . . ." *CNN*, June 23, 2015, http://www.cnn.com/2015/06/03/travel/feat-most -popular-theme-parks-world-2014/

3. Colette Flight, "Smallpox: Eradicating the Scourge," *BBC*, February 17, 2011, http://www.bbc.co.uk/history/british/empire_seapower /smallpox_01.shtml

4. Flight, "Smallpox: Eradicating the Scourge."

5. "Smallpox Disease Overview," *Centers for Disease Control and Prevention*, February 6, 2007, http://www.bt.cdc.gov/agent/smallpox/overview /disease-facts.asp

6. Ibid.

7. Ibid.

8. Ibid.

9. Ibid.

10. Ibid.

11. "Diseases and Conditions: Smallpox," *Mayo Clinic*, August 16, 2014, http://www.mayoclinic.org/diseases-conditions/smallpox/basics /complications/con-20022769

12. Ibid.

13. Tamara Hinson, "Could Smallpox Really Be Turned into a Biological Weapon by Terrorists?" *Metro UK*, April 8, 2013, http://metro.co.uk /2013/04/08/could-smallpox-really-be-turned-into-a-biological-weapon -by-terrorists-3585028/

14. "Smallpox Disease Overview," *Centers for Disease Control and Prevention*.

15. Flight, "Smallpox: Eradicating the Scourge."

16. Ibid.

17. Ibid.

18. Ibid.

19. Esther Inglis-Arkell, "The Horrifying Story of the Last Death by Smallpox," *Ios9*, August 18, 2013, http://io9.com/the-horrifying-story-of -the-last-death-by-smallpox-1161664590

20. Flight, "Smallpox: Eradicating the Scourge."

21. Ibid.

22. Lewis M. Simons, "Weapons of Mass Destruction," *National Geographic*, November 2012, http://ngm.nationalgeographic.com/ngm/0211 /feature1/fulltext.html

23. Simons, "Weapons of Mass Destruction."

24. David Could and Nicholas Kulish, "Iraq and North Korea Possess Smallpox, Intelligence Indicates," *Wall Street Journal*, November 6, 2002, http://www.wsj.com/articles/SB1036495803321406668

25. Liz Szabo, "Forgotten Vials of Smallpox Found Near D.C.," *USA Today*, July 9, 2014, http://www.usatoday.com/story/news/nation/2014 /07/08/forgotten-vials-of-smallpox-found-in-storage-room/12363365/

26. Bui Hoia-Tra, and Alison Young, "Chilling New Details on Cold-Storage Smallpox," *USA Today*, July 17, 2014, http://www.usatoday.com /story/news/nation/2014/07/16/fda-update-on-vials-found-in-cold -storage-at-nih/12744543/

27. "What CDC Is Doing to Protect the Public From Smallpox," *Centers for Disease Control and Prevention*, March 13, 2009, http://www.bt.cdc .gov/agent/smallpox/prep/cdc-prep.asp

28. "Vaccine Overview," *Centers for Disease Control and Prevention*, December 7, 2007, http://www.bt.cdc.gov/agent/smallpox/vaccination/facts .asp

29. "Questions and Answers About Post-event Smallpox Vaccination,"

Centers for Disease Control and Prevention, March 13, 2009, http://
emergency.cdc.gov/agent/smallpox/faq/post_event.asp

30. Ibid.

31. "Shining Lights on 'Dark Winter,'" *Oxford Journals, Clinical Infectious Diseases*, January 25, 2002, http://cid.oxfordjournals.org/content/34/7/972.full

32. "Dark Winter," *UPMC Health Security*, http://www.upmchealthsecurity.org/our-work/events/2001_dark-winter/about.html

33. "Shining Lights on 'Dark Winter,'" *Oxford Journals, Clinical Infectious Diseases*.

34. Simons, "Weapons of Mass Destruction."

35. Ibid.

36. "Dark Winter," *UPMC Health Security*.

37. Thomas J. Ridge and Joseph Lieberman, "America Needs to Strengthen Biodefense Now," *Roll Call*, June 12, 2015, http://www.rollcall.com/news/america_needs_to_strengthen_biodefense_now_commentary-242314-1.html?zkPrintable=true

38. "WHO: Ebola 'an international emergency,'" *BBC News*, August 8, 2014, http://www.bbc.com/news/world-africa-28702356

39. "Ebola (Ebola Virus Disease)," *Centers for Disease Control and Prevention*, January 15, 2015, http://www.cdc.gov/vhf/ebola/outbreaks/index.html

40. Syndey Lupkin, "Ebola in America: Timeline of the Deadly Virus," *ABC News*, November 17, 2014, http://abcnews.go.com/Health/ebola-america-timeline/story?id=26159719

41. Ibid.

42. Roberta Rampton, "Obama Says Ebola Travel Ban Could Make Things Worse," *Reuters*, October 18, 2014, http://www.reuters.com/article/2014/10/18/us-health-ebola-obama-idUSKCN0I708L20141018

43. Barack Obama, "President Obama Names Ron Klain to Coordinate the U.S. Response to Ebola," *The White House*, October 17, 2004, https://www.whitehouse.gov/blog/2014/10/17/president-obama-names-ron-klain-coordinate-us-response-ebola

44. Michael McCaul, "McCaul: U.S. Must Be Leader in Ebola Fight, Strategy," *Chron*, October 28, 2014, http://www.chron.com/opinion/outlook/article/McCaul-U-S-must-be-leader-in-Ebola-fight-5853779.php

45. Ridge and Lieberman, "America Needs to Strengthen Biodefense Now."

46. Bob Graham and Jim Talent, *World at Risk, The Report of the Commission on the Prevention of Weapons of Mass Destruction Proliferation and Terrorism* (New York: Vintage Books, 2008), 88–91, http://www .pharmathene.com/World_at_Risk_Report.pdf

47. "Biosurveillance: Observations on the Cancellation of BioWatch Gen-3 and Future Considerations for the Program," *U.S. Government Accountability Office*, June 10, 2014, http://www.gao.gov/products/GAO-14 -267T

48. David Willman, "Homeland Security Cancels Plans for New Bio-Watch Technology," *Los Angeles Times*, April 25, 2014, http://www .latimes.com/nation/la-na-biowatch-20140426-story.html

49. Russell Berman, "Democrats vs. Obama on an Ebola Travel Ban," *The Atlantic*, October 21, 2014, http://www.theatlantic.com/politics /archive/2014/10/democrats-defy-obama-in-favor-of-ebola-travel-ban/ 381712/

Chapter 7: Final Approach

1. *The Encyclopedia Britannica*, s.v. "Khorasan," http://www.britannica .com/EBchecked/topic/316850/Khorasan

2. Lawrence Wright, *The Looming Tower: Al-Qaeda and the Road to 9/11* (New York: Alfred A. Knopf, 2006), 233.

3. Heather Saul, "MI5 Head Warns Al-Qaeda Is Planning 'Mass Casualty Attacks Against the West,'" *The Independent*, January 9, 2015, http:// www.independent.co.uk/news/uk/home-news/mi5-head-warns-alqaeda -is-planning-mass-casualty-attacks-against-the-west-9967239.html

4. Saul, "MI5 Head Warns Al-Qaeda Is Planning 'Mass Casualty Attacks Against the West.'"

5. Aron Lund, "What Is the 'Khorasan Group' and Why Is the U.S. Bombing It in Syria?" *Carnegie Endowment for International Peace*, September 23, 2014, http://carnegieendowment.org/syriaincrisis/?fa=56707

6. Lund, "What Is the 'Khorasan Group' and Why Is the U.S. Bombing It in Syria?"

7. Associated Press, "Senior al-Qaida figure, Muhsin al-Fadhli, Killed in US Air Strike in Syria, Officials Say," *The Guardian*, July 21, 2015, http:// www.theguardian.com/world/2015/jul/22/senior-al-qaida-figure-muhsin -al-fadhli-killed-in-us-airstrike-in-syria-officials-say

8. Jeremy Bender and Brett LoGiurato, "Meet the Khorasan, the

Terrorist Group That's Suddenly a Bigger Threat Than ISIS," September 23, 2014, http://www.businessinsider.com/what-is-the-khorasan-group-airstrikes-isis-islamic-state-2014-9

9. Lund, "What Is the 'Khorasan Group' and Why Is the U.S. Bombing It in Syria?"

10. James Phillips and Josh Siegel, "Q&A: Meet Khorasan, the Terrorist Group That Might Be Scarier Than ISIS," *The Daily Signal*, September 20, 2014, http://dailysignal.com/2014/09/20/qa-terrorist-group-really-scarier-isis/

11. Bender and LoGiurato, "Meet the Khorasan, the Terrorist Group That's Suddenly a Bigger Threat Than ISIS."

12. Phillips and Siegel, "Q&A: Meet the Khorasan, the Terrorist Group That Might Be Scarier Than ISIS."

13. Charles P. Wallace, "Weaving a Wide Web of Terror," *Los Angeles Times*, May 28, 1995, http://articles.latimes.com/1995-05-28/news/mn-7023_1_project-bojinka-airliner-plot-ramzi-ahmed-yousef; Raymond Bonner and Benjamin Weiser, "Echoes of Early Design to Use Chemicals to Blow Up Airliners," *New York Times*, August 11, 2006, http://www.nytimes.com/2006/08/11/world/europe/11manila.html?_r=0

14. Pam Belluck, "Unrepentant Shoe Bomber Sentenced to Life," *New York Times*, January 31, 2003, http://www.nytimes.com/2003/01/31/national/31SHOE.html

15. "Yemen-based al Qaeda Group Claims Responsibility for Parcel Bomb Plot," *CNN*, November 5, 2010, http://www.cnn.com/2010/WORLD/meast/11/05/yemen.security.concern/; Duncan Gardham, "Al-Qaeda Plane Bomb 17 Minutes from Going Off," *The Telegraph*, November 4, 2010, http://www.telegraph.co.uk/news/uknews/terrorism-in-the-uk/8110255/Cargo-plane-bomb-plot.html

16. "Chairman McCaul to Deliver Speech at Heritage Foundation on Terror Gone Viral," Committee on Homeland Security press release, July 22, 2015, http://homeland.house.gov/press-release/chairman-mccaul-deliver-speech-heritage-foundation-terror-gone-viral

17. Jesse Byrnes, "FBI Investigating ISIS Suspects in All 50 States," *The Hill*, February 25, 2015, http://thehill.com/blogs/blog-briefing-room/233832-fbi-investigating-isis-suspects-in-all-50-states

18. Byrnes, "FBI Investigating ISIS Suspects in All 50 States."

19. Associated Press, "US Increases Security at Foreign Airports, with Focus on Cellphone, Other Electronic Devices," *Fox News*, July 7, 2014, http://www.foxnews.com/politics/2014/07/07/us-increases-security-at-foreign-airports-focus-on-cellphone-other-electronic/

20. Amanda Holpuch, "How Much Authority Does the TSA Have Over Foreign Airports?" *The Guardian*, July 7, 2014, http://www.theguardian.com/world/2014/jul/07/airport-checks-us-bound-flights-authority-tsa

21. "The Rise of Radicalization: Is the U.S. Government Failing to Counter International and Domestic Terrorism?" Committee on Homeland Security press release, July 15, 2015, http://homeland.house.gov/sites/homeland.house.gov/files/documents/07-15-15-McCaul-Open.pdf

22. http://www.dailymail.co.uk/news/article-2312470/Tamerlan-Tsarnaev-Boston-bomber-thrown-mosque-raged-filled-rant-Martin-Luther-King.html

Chapter 8: North Atlantic Storm

1. Franz-Stefan Gady, "US Navy to Deploy Robot Ships to Track Chinese and Russian Subs," *The Diplomat*, June 30, 2015, http://thediplomat.com/2015/06/us-navy-to-deploy-robot-ships-to-track-chinese-and-russian-subs/

2. Ihar Karney and Daisy Sindelar, "For Victory Day, Post-Soviets Show Their Colors—Just Not Orange and Black," *Radio Free Europe Radio Liberty*, May 7, 2015, http://www.rferl.org/content/victory-day-st-george-ribbon-orange-and-black/26999911.html

3. Peter Baker, "3 Presidents and a Riddle Named Putin," *New York Times*, March 23, 2014, http://www.nytimes.com/2014/03/24/world/europe/3-presidents-and-a-riddle-named-putin.html?_r=0#/#time315_8525

4. "Vladimir Putin," *The Moscow Times*, accessed October 19, 2015, http://www.themoscowtimes.com/mt_profile/vladimir_putin/432538.html

5. Baker, "3 Presidents and a Riddle Named Putin."

6. Ibid.

7. Ibid.

8. Rob Watson, "Putin's Speech: Back to Cold War?" *BBC News*, February 10, 2007, http://news.bbc.co.uk/2/hi/europe/6350847.stm

9. Ibid.

10. Ibid.

11. Associated Press, "Five Years On, Georgia Makes Up with Russia," *BBC News*, June 25, 2013, http://www.bbc.com/news/world-europe-23010526

12. Jim Nichol, "Georgia's January 2008 Presidential Election: Outcome and Implications" (Report No. RS22794), Congressional Research Service, https://fas.org/sgp/crs/row/RS22794.pdf

13. Steven Erlanger and Steven Lee Myers, "NATO Allies Oppose Bush on Georgia and Ukraine," *New York Times*, April 3, 2008, http://www.nytimes.com/2008/04/03/world/europe/03nato.html?pagewanted=all

14. Erlanger and Myers, "NATO Allies Oppose Bush on Georgia and Ukraine."

15. Sebastian Alison and James G. Neuger, "Putin Says NATO Expansion Is Direct Threat to Russia," *Bloomberg*, April 4, 2008, http://www.bloomberg.com/apps/news?pid=newsarchive&sid=aq34xuTFCvx0

16. Vladimir Socor, "Russia Moves Toward Open Annexation of Abkhazia, South Ossetia," *The Jamestown Foundation*, 5 (2008): 74, http://www.jamestown.org/single/?no_cache=1&tx_ttnews[tt_news]=33560#.VZwdIKbN8nI

17. "Russia 'Invades' Georgia as South Ossetia Descends Towards War," *The Telegraph*, August 8, 2008, http://www.telegraph.co.uk/news/worldnews/europe/georgia/2524550/Russia-invades-Georgia-as-South-Ossetia-descends-towards-war.html

18. Michael Emerson, "Post-Mortem on Europe's First War of the 21st Century," *Centre for European Policy Studies*, August, 2008, http://aei.pitt.edu/9382/2/9382.pdf

19. "Five Years On, Georgia Makes Up with Russia," *BBC News*, June 25, 2013, http://www.bbc.com/news/world-europe-23010526

20. "Ukraine Crisis: Timeline," *BBC News*, November 13, 2014, http://www.bbc.com/news/world-middle-east-26248275

21. Agence France-Presse, "Putin Describes Secret Operation to Seize Crimea," *Yahoo! News*, March 8, 2015, http://news.yahoo.com/putin-describes-secret-operation-seize-crimea-212858356.html

22. "Ukraine Crisis: Timeline," *BBC News*.

23. Andrew Higgins and Steven Erlanger, "Gunmen Seize Government Buildings in Crimea," *New York Times*, February 27, 2015, http://www.nytimes.com/2014/02/28/world/europe/crimea-ukraine.html?_r=0

24. Sangwon Yoon, Daryna Krasnolutska, and Kateryna Choursina, "Russia Stays in Ukraine as Putin Channels Yanukovych Request," *Bloomberg Business*, March 4, 2014, http://www.bloomberg.com/news/articles/2014-03-04/russia-calls-ukraine-intervention-legal-citing-yanukovych-letter

25. Yoon, Krasnolutska, and Choursina, "Russia Stays in Ukraine as Putin Channels Yanukovych Request."

26. Katya Golubkova and Timothy Heritage, "Russia Reserves Right to Protect Compatriots in Ukraine," *Reuters*, March 14, 2014, http://www.reuters.com/article/2014/03/14/us-urkaine-crisis-russia-east-idUSBREA2D0M620140314

27. Ilya Soming, "Russian Government Agency Reveals Fraudulent Nature of the Crimean Referendum Results," *Washington Post*, May 6, 2014, https://www.washingtonpost.com/news/volokh-conspiracy/wp/2014/05/06/russian-government-agency-reveals-fraudulent-nature-of-the-crimean-referendum-results/

28. "Ukraine Crisis: Timeline," *BBC News*.

29. Shaun Walker, "Russian Takeover of Crimea Will Not Descend into War, Says Vladimir Putin," *The Guardian*, March 4, 2014, http://www.theguardian.com/world/2014/mar/04/ukraine-crisis-russian-troops-crimea-john-kerry-kiev

30. David Mdzinarishvili, "Putin Acknowledges Russian Military Serviceman Were in Crimea," *Russian Times*, April 17, 2014, http://rt.com/news/crimea-defense-russian-soldiers-108/

31. Mdzinarishvili, "Putin Acknowledges Russian Military Serviceman Were in Crimea."

32. Michael Birnbaum, "Putin Was Surprised at How Easily Russia Took Control of Crimea," *Washington Post*, March 15, 2015 http://www.washingtonpost.com/world/europe/putin-was-surprised-at-how-easily-russia-took-control-of-crimea/2015/03/15/94b7c82e-c9c1-11e4-bea5-b893e7ac3fb3_story.html

33. Sam LaGrone, "NATO Commander Breelove: Imported Russian Missiles Have Turned Crimea into a Black Sea 'Power Projection' Platform," *USNI News*, February 25, 2015, http://news.usni.org/2015/02/25/nato-commander-breedlove-imported-russian-missiles-have-turned-crimea-into-a-black-sea-power-projection-platform

34. "Ukraine Crisis: Timeline," *BBC News*.

35. Eli Lake and Josh Rogin, "Ukraine Says Russian Generals Lead Seperatists," *Bloomberg View*, July 2, 2015, http://www.bloombergview.com/articles/2015-07-02/ukraine-says-russian-generals-lead-separatists

36. John Sweeney, "MH17 Disaster: Russians 'Controlled BUK Missile System,'" *BBC News*, September 8, 2014, http://www.bbc.com/news/world-europe-29109398

37. Adam Taylor, "Novorossiya, 'the Latest Historical Concept to Work about in Ukraine,'" *Washington Post*, April 18, 2014, https://www.washingtonpost.com/news/worldviews/wp/2014/04/18/understanding-novorossiya-the-latest-historical-concept-to-get-worried-about-in-ukraine/

38. "Russia Reportedly Issues New Threat to NATO over Forces in Baltics," *Fox News*, April 2, 2015, http://www.foxnews.com/world/2015/04/02/russia-reportedly-issues-new-threat-to-nato-over-forces-in-baltics/

39. Pavel Felgenhauer, "Estonia, Latvia and Lithuania May Be Bargaining Chips for Moscow in a Quid Pro Quo Game," *The Jamestown Foundation* 12, no. 124 (2005), http://www.jamestown.org/single/?tx_ttnews[tt_news]=44113&tx_ttnews[backPid]=7&cHash=ca3c5f4ed665677eb7ed6eade2d1f431#.VZxoI6bN8nL

40. Ibid.

41. Ibid.

42. Associated Press, "Obama's Pick for Joint Chiefs Sides with Romney on Russia," *New York Post*, July 9, 2015, http://nypost.com/2015/07/09/russia-is-greatest-threat-to-america-joint-chiefs-nominee/

43. David Nakamura and Debbi Wilgoren, "Caught on Open Mike, Obama Tells Medvedev He Needs 'Space' on Missile Defense," *Washington Post*, March 26, 2012, http://www.washingtonpost.com/politics/obama-tells-medvedev-solution-on-missile-defense-is-unlikely-before-elections/2012/03/26/gIQASoblbS_story.html

44. Chairman McCaul, *Chairman McCaul on CNN Ukraine* [VIDEO], March 6, 2014, https://www.youtube.com/watch?v=sK1N4E0xcYQ&feature=youtu.be

45. Julian E. Barnes, "U.S., Ukraine Weigh Expansion of American Training Program," *Wall Street Jounral*, July 8, 2015, http://www.wsj.com/articles/u-s-ukraine-weigh-expansion-of-american-training-program-1436386108

46. Kristina Wong, "Lawmakers to Obama: Arm Ukraine Now," *The Hill*, February 2, 2015, http://thehill.com/policy/defense/231874-senators-to-obama-arm-ukraine-now

47. Michael Cochrane, "Is U.S. Draw-down in Europe Encouraging Russian Aggression?" *World Magazine*, May 11, 2015, http://www.worldmag.com/2015/05/is_u_s_draw_down_in_europe_encouraging_russian_aggression

48. Keiran Corcoran, "The Army Puts on a Heavy Metal Tour of Eastern Europe for Mr. Putin: US Armor Mobbed by Delighted Citizens Waving Stars and Stripes as It Rolls Across Former Warsaw Pact Countries," *The Daily Mail*, March 30, 2015, http://www.dailymail.co.uk/news/article-3018579/Supporters-waving-Stars-Stripes-cheer-armored-U-S-convoy-Prague-strength-Putin-rolls-Europe.html

49. Bradford Richardson, "Ex-NATO Supreme Commander Rips Obama over Military Cuts," *The Hill*, August 9, 2015, http://thehill.com/blogs/blog-briefing-room/news/250665-ex-nato-supreme-commander-rips-obama-over-military-cuts

50. "Shortchanging Missile Defense," *Wall Street Journal*, February 16, 2015, http://www.wsj.com/articles/obama-shortchanges-missile-defense-1424130302

51. Martin Russell, "EU-Russia Energy Relations—Stuck Together?" *European Parliamentary Research Service*, March 25, 2015, http://epthinktank.eu/2015/03/25/eu-russia-energy-relations-stuck-together/

52. Rakteem Katakey, "U.S. Ousts Russia as Top World Oil, Gas Producer in BP Data," *Bloomberg Business*, June 10, 2015, http://www.bloomberg.com/news/articles/2015-06-10/u-s-ousts-russia-as-world-s-top-oil-gas-producer-in-bp-report

53. "McCaul Introduces Bill to Lift Ban on Texas Energy Exports," Office of Congressman Michael McCaul press release, April 1, 2014, http://mccaul.house.gov/media-center/press-releases/mccaul-introduces-bill-to-lift-ban-on-texas-energy-exports

54. Catherine Herridge, "Exclusive: Classified Cable Warned Consulate Couldn't Withstand 'Coordinated Attack,'" *Fox News*, October 31, 2012, http://www.foxnews.com/politics/2012/10/31/exclusive-us-memo-warned-libya-consulate-couldnt-withstand-coordinated-attack/#ixzz2Q0roLM53

55. "Transcripts," CNN, January 23, 2013, http://transcripts.cnn.com/TRANSCRIPTS/1301/23/cnr.13.html

INDEX

Page numbers in *italics* refer to illustrations.